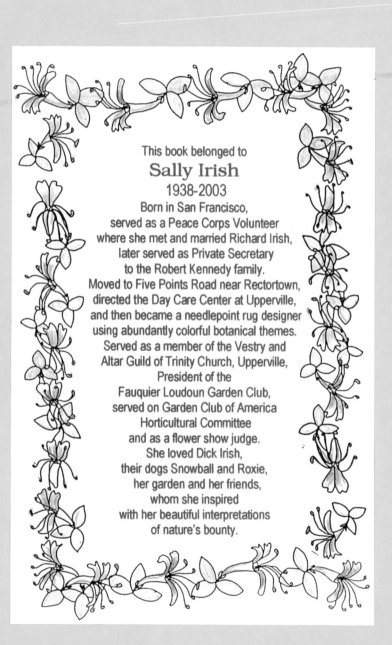

This book belonged to
Sally Irish
1938-2003
Born in San Francisco,
served as a Peace Corps Volunteer
where she met and married Richard Irish,
later served as Private Secretary
to the Robert Kennedy family.
Moved to Five Points Road near Rectortown,
directed the Day Care Center at Upperville,
and then became a needlepoint rug designer
using abundantly colorful botanical themes.
Served as a member of the Vestry and
Altar Guild of Trinity Church, Upperville,
President of the
Fauquier Loudoun Garden Club,
served on Garden Club of America
Horticultural Committee
and as a flower show judge.
She loved Dick Irish,
their dogs Snowball and Roxie,
her garden and her friends,
whom she inspired
with her beautiful interpretations
of nature's bounty.

A Rock Garden in the South

A Rock Garden in the South

Elizabeth Lawrence

Edited by Nancy Goodwin with Allen Lacy

Duke University Press Durham and London 1990

Portions of this manuscript were

published in slightly altered form

in the *Bulletin of the American*

Rock Garden Society, vols. 36,

37, and 38.

Library of Congress

Cataloging-in-Publication

Data appear on the last printed

page of this book

Contents ❋

Introduction ❧

The point has been made before that although Elizabeth Lawrence gardened in the South—first in Raleigh, and then in Charlotte, where for many years she was the garden columnist for the *Charlotte Observer*—her writings about gardening are not merely of regional interest. In one of her essays on horticulture originally published in the *New Yorker*, later collected in *Onward and Upward in the Garden*, Katharine S. White noted that even though she lived in Maine she had "learned more about horticulture, plants, and garden history and literature from Elizabeth Lawrence than from any other one person." She went on to say that Miss Lawrence's first book, *A Southern Garden*, originally published in 1942 and reissued in 1967, was "far more than a regional book; it is civilized literature by a writer with a pure and lively style and a deep sense of beauty." Lawrence herself had second thoughts about the aptness of the subtitle of her book, *A Handbook for the Middle South*, writing later that it actually was a handbook for Zone 8 on the hardiness map of the USDA— territory that embraces the Eastern Shore of Maryland, Tidewater Virginia, much of both the Carolinas, and parts of other southern states westward into Texas, as well as a thin band of the Pacific coast well into Canada. Elizabeth Lawrence was furthermore an assiduous letter writer, and the letters she received from gardening friends all over the country and used in all her writing assure that although she was solidly rooted in the South and its horticultural practices and traditions, her perspective was national and in no way merely local or parochial. Her breadth of vision, her close powers of observation, and her simple yet elegant prose style have in fact earned her a great many admirers in Great Britain, a nation more inclined to pay attention to native American plants than to native American horticultural literature. In *The Garden in Winter* (1988), Rosemary Verey, one of England's best contemporary garden writers, called Miss Lawrence "one of my favourite garden authors."

And now one more book, of special interest to all who live and garden in Zone 8—and to some extent its adjacent zones, particularly east of the Brazos River—takes its place in the Lawrence canon, alongside *A Southern Garden, The Little Bulbs, Gardens in Winter, Lob's Wood,* and *Gardening for Love*. In *A Rock Garden in the South* she considers the principles of gardening with alpine plants developed in Great Britain in the late nineteenth century, a style of gardening that spread to the northern tier of states in America in our own century, and weighs the possibilities of staying faithful to the style in regions where the climate is harshly unfriendly to the usual rock garden plants. Alpines, as a group of plants, are able to take the harshest blows that winter can bring only if they have an adequate snow cover. They flourish in thin and gravelly soil, to which many have adapted by developing deep root systems. But hardiness has a different meaning in the South, one which the USDA's system of zones leaves entirely untouched. It means winter-hardiness, yes, the ability to survive a given average minimal temperature in the winter. But there is also summer-hardiness, a plant's ability to survive a growing season that can stretch from early February almost into December, annual heat accumulation far exceeding that of New England, hot summer nights, and frequent and prolonged periods of still air conducive to the spread of fungus diseases. Southern soils, furthermore, are often heavy clay, poorly drained when wet, and baked hard when dry. Under these conditions, southerners who want a rock garden and expect to grow the eritrichiums, lewisias, and other orthodox alpine plants will get to know failure on very intimate terms.

Can southerners then have rock gardens? Elizabeth Lawrence's answer is resoundingly affirmative, provided only that the traditional alpines be set aside and the search begun for other plants, many but not all of them low or creeping, which combine harmoniously, bloom in great sweeps of color or else have interesting foliage, and comport themselves well among rocks—even if rocks turn out, in her view, to be permissible omissions in a rock garden.

Easily the best gardeners in the United States are those who are members of The American Rock Garden Society. I do not belong to this communion of saints, but I respect them from afar. As a group, they are as diverse and varied as the plants they grow and love with such ardent passion. A few, I suspect, may look askance at Elizabeth Lawrence's vision of rock gardens sans alpines, even sans rocks or scree. But the majority of rock gardeners are tolerant souls, asking of one another only that the love of plants be deep and wide and consuming. They will welcome, I believe, Elizabeth Lawrence's contribution to the great conversation that has been going on among them ever since The American Rock Garden Society was founded more than fifty years ago.

A word about the history of this book and the manuscript it is based on is in order. The existence of the manuscript was something of a mystery and a surprise when it surfaced among some unpublished papers Elizabeth Lawrence gave Duke University Press before she died in 1985. (These unpublished papers also contained the manuscript of another posthumous book, *Gardening for Love: The Market Bulletins*, which I edited for publication in 1987.) Hannah Withers and other of Lawrence's close friends in Charlotte knew nothing about a book on rock gardening, even though she often discussed with them her book on the southern market bulletins and on her correspondence with the farm women who advertised their seeds and plants there. What slender evidence there is about the rock garden book suggests that Lawrence began the book in the 1940s, before she moved from Raleigh to Charlotte. It was submitted to a publisher in Manhattan, who turned it down. Its rejection is not difficult to understand. The world was not as heavily populated with rock gardeners as it is today—and northeastern publishers sometimes fail to realize that books on gardening have a southern audience as well as a northern one. In essence, *A Rock Garden in the South* was ahead of its time, a book out of season. After the book was rejected, some portions were published in *The American Rock Garden Society Bulletin* and in *The Little Bulbs*, and the remainder quietly set aside during her work on *The Little Bulbs, Gardens in Winter*, and the manuscript about the market bulletins.

When the manuscript on rock gardening in the South came to light, it had two sections. First came Lawrence's meditations on the whole enterprise of rock gardening and of possible ways of adapting its spirit and its style to the conditions of climate and soil typical to Zone 8. Then came her encyclopedia, genus by genus and species by species, of plants she believed appropriate in a southern rock garden. The passage of time has treated the first part of the book very well indeed. It is sprightly and wise, and Lawrence's many admirers will hear her personal voice speaking clearly on every page. A few sections have been rearranged, but the editing has been very light indeed. Matters are somewhat different with the encyclopedic part of the book. Partly because of Elizabeth Lawrence's own precept and example, knowledge of and interest in gardening, including rock gardening, have burgeoned in the Middle South since she set aside this book to turn to other topics. When the American Rock Garden Society celebrated its fiftieth anniversary in 1984 at its annual meeting, the site chosen was Asheville—and many members trekked to the remarkable Arboretum of The State University of North Carolina at Raleigh to take a look at many a plant hardy to the South and fitting in a rock garden. Furthermore, in just the past decade a number of fine, specialized nurseries have sprung up in the Carolinas. We-Du Nurseries, Woodlanders, Montrose Nursery, Holbrook Farm and Nursery—these are just four of many excellent small nurseries offering rare and often wonderful plants that take in stride the insults of a summer in Zone 8. Considering all these things, Nancy Goodwin, Joanne Ferguson of Duke University Press, and I made the editorial decision to expand the encyclopedia to permit discussion of plants little grown or known when Elizabeth Lawrence wrote her manuscript. Much of the encyclopedia was written by Lawrence herself; where needed we have changed plant names to conform to *Hortus III*, the standard reference in questions of nomenclature. All added material has been enclosed in square brackets and flagged with the initials of the contributor, Nancy Goodwin in the vast majority of cases. Paul Jones, a horticulturist at The Sarah P. Duke Gardens in Durham, contributed substantially to the section on dwarf conifers and woody plants. We trust that Elizabeth Lawrence's many friends and admirers will not look on these additions as unwarranted trespass. And I, for one, suspect that

Miss Lawrence herself would be pleased with the result. All of her writing, as I have already mentioned, allowed her readers to eavesdrop on her conversations and correspondence with her gardening friends. In this final book, the conversation continues even after her death.

Allen Lacy

Preface ❋

This book records the work of many seasons and recounts a gardener's high hopes and disappointments. But the results are not final. As Liberty Hyde Bailey of *Hortus* points out, "There is no finality in the interpretation of nature." When a plant that has been described as blooming in a garden for many summers sickens and dies, a reader is sure to come along and say, "Where is that flower that you wrote about?" And when one dismissed as unsuited to the South blooms gaily for a neighbor, the reader is sure to come along to say, "There is that plant that you said would not grow here." Opinions are like seeds. Some are viable for hundreds of years, and some for a short time only. A gardener's opinions change with the seasons, and in my part of the world the seasons are extremely variable. In January of one year the children will be skating on the pond and the too-eager blossoms of the Japanese apricot will be seared; in January of another we will be having lunch in the sun and pansies and crocuses will be in bloom.

And yet, specific information is the only kind that is of use to the gardener. Generalizations are safe but not helpful. In order to collect the data that I need for my own garden I keep a card index of all of the plants that come into it. I put down where they come from, when they were planted, and when they bloom. All too often I put down when they die. I measure every petal and leaf, and sometimes even count the stamens. I sniff the flowers to see if they are fragrant, and if they are, I try to tell what their perfume reminds me of. Unfortunately there is no standard for odors, so I alone know what I mean when I say that a flower's scent is like that of my grand-mother's garden, or that it smells of spring, or even that it smells like almond blossoms. Who really knows what almond blossoms smell like?

There is a standard for color, and so when I hold the petal to the chart and note that it is carmine or heliotrope, I have a record that is as accurate as my eye. The chart I prefer is Ridgway's because it is so scholarly and so beautiful. My friend Isabelle Henderson says that it is so beautiful because the colors are washed on, not printed. But my poor old Ridgway is getting dim from being taken out in the dew and opened in the sun (which you are warned never to do), and so, since it is out of print, I have turned to the British Color Council's *Horticultural Color Chart*, available from the Royal Horticultural Society.

When it comes to plant names, it is hard to decide whether to use the familiar ones of gardeners and nurserymen or to follow the scientists in their search for accuracy. In order to be consistent one must choose the latter, and for this reason the nomenclature of this book will be as nearly as possible that of *Hortus Third*. There are those who sometimes find more value in the common name than in the scientific one, and they are not always laymen. Henry Totten, of the University of North Carolina at Chapel Hill, says he would never have been able to profit by the woodlore of the countryman if he called the blue haw *Viburnum rufidulum,* or the black haw *V. prunifolium.* But the blue haw is also called the southern black haw, and confusion begins.

You can get along best with the Latin names if you regard them as friends instead of enemies. *Saxatilis* tells you that a plant grows among rocks, *monticola* that it loves the mountains. *Caespitosus* lets you know that it is a tufted plant, and therefore low, and *pulvinatus* that it is cushionlike. *Fragrans* and *suaveolens* mean that it will be sweet smelling, and *foetidus* warns you that it will not. *Sylvestris* (of the woods) indicates a shade lover; *palustris* (of the swamps) suggests that the plant will need moisture; *pratensis* (of the meadow) usually describes a plant that likes sun. Even more helpful for choosing plants for a special part of the country are the geographical names. The plants most likely to be able to withstand our long, hot summers and open winters are those from parts of the world where the climate is similar to ours. A plant with a specific name of *nootka-tensis* (of Nootka; Nootka Sound, though in Canada, is in Zone 8) or *ludovicianus* (of Louisiana) or *formosana* (of the island of Formosa) is more apt to be a wise choice than one with a specific name of *mistassinicus* (of Lake Mistassini in Quebec) or *groenlandicus* (of Greenland). This does not always hold true, however, for *Galium borealis,* though its name indicates that it is from the North, blooms more persistently than most plants through the dry, hot summers of the South. And I would not have its name, "of the Alps," deprive us of *Alchemilla alpina,* which is flourishing in my garden in dry shade, in a spot where many a plant from low altitudes has perished.

We all want to know the names of flowers that can be counted on to bloom year after year in spite of the weather and in spite of neglect. This book is written to give gardeners in the southern half of this country some idea of the kinds of saxatile plants that can be expected to flourish and to be reasonably permanent in these parts.

The Rock Garden ❊

Such Are the Seasons

In our part of the country the year is evergreen, and against this green background bloom is almost continuous. There is no ending of one season, no beginning of the next. All melt together. Even when early and final frost puts a sudden end to summer, winter is not without its blossoms. Though the perennial borders are bare, there are drifts of color among the rocks and beneath the trees, where lowly saxatile plants bloom in the stern season when plants stay close to the ground for protection against the elements. At summer's end the toad lily and meadow saffron are in flower; and before these have bloomed themselves away, the autumn crocuses spread in small patches of delicate color, one species taking the place of another, linking summer to spring. And before the calendar year ends, another garden year has begun.

While branches are still bare, pale sunlight filters through to bring the early flowers into bloom, and this foretaste of spring "ere a leaf is on the bush" is more to the rock gardener than the season's lush fulfillment. When the trees are in leaf there is a cool green shadow beneath them, and bloom moves to the open parts of the garden where the tender bulbs flower from frost to frost.

"Such are the seasons," Theophrastus wrote from another land of continuous bloom. "To speak generally, there is no interval of time nor flowerless period; but even the winter produces flowers, for all that it seems to be unproductive by reason of the cold, since autumn flowers continue into winter, and to a much greater extent if the season be mild. For all things, one may say, or at least most of them, extend beyond their proper season, and all the more if the place be sunny; so that there is a continuous succession."

Many of the flowers Theophrastus mentions as blooming in succession bloom for us still, and among them are enough to fill a southern rock garden: the snowdrop, the "kind of anemone which is called the mountain anemone" (*Anemone blanda*), the squill, the lesser celandine, the wall flower, the iris, savory and thyme, the meadow saffron in autumn, "the crocus, both the scentless mountain form and the cultivated one; for these bloom directly the first rains come. . . . While the violet . . . blooms throughout the year if it receives tendance."

Concerning the Gardener

All rock gardeners are snobs. I say this without fear of offending, for no one will take it to himself. "How right you are," he will say. "I have often noticed it in one or another, and there are times when I think you are something of a snob yourself."

Some snobbery is to be expected, for all are agreed that the cultivation of rock plants is the highest form of the art of gardening, and rock gardeners are essentially individualists, each with his specialty, his own dear delight. That every gardener should be a specialist is very right and proper, and that the specialist should hold himself a little above the common flower grower is understandable, but the specialist is perilously near the expert, and the expert is apt to put skill above enjoyment. Gardening ceases to be an art when the gardener admits that the choicest subjects are generally the ones presenting the most difficulties, and are therefore the ones most sought for.

But gardening *is* an art, and the rock garden is its purest form. Here the plants are grown for themselves alone—not for exhibition, not for cutting, and not primarily for display. All gardeners become rock gardeners if they garden long enough. They may not mean to, or even desire it, but it is natural to one long familiar with plants to single out certain individuals too newly come from wood or waterside to accommodate themselves to the perennial border and to put them where stones can protect their flowers from the weather and keep their roots cool and moist. One by one, special corners are singled out for special treasures, until they become so numerous that they must be drawn together. In this way the rock garden is created, and for this reason it is the most personal of all forms of horticulture.

A delight in the individual plant, a desire for the rare and choice, and a love of the miniature are traits common to all lovers of rock plants. From long intimacy with the earth and all that springs from it they become aware of the way a stem curls or a leaf unfolds. To those whose thoughts are "one with wind and leaf and mist," beauty has an elusive quality that depends more upon the texture of the petal than the size of the bloom. They take pleasure in the frail, the perishable, and the uncertain flower. But above all else they love these plants because they are small.

A passion for the minute and perfect and a desire to possess the smallest thing of its kind are not traits confined to gardeners. Do you remember how the old king in the fairy tale promised his kingdom to the son who could bring him a dog small enough to lie in a walnut shell? None of the tiny creatures they produced was able to do so. Always a paw or a tail or at least an ear protruded. At last the youngest son handed his father a hazelnut, begging him to crack it very gently. When this was done, a beautiful little snow white dog jumped out, wagged his tail, and licked the king's hand, and barked at the other little beasts in the most graceful manner. The delight of the king and the whole court was indescribable, and the king told his people to throw all of the other little dogs into the sea.

The old king reminds me of the rock gardeners who search for years for a tiny form of a forest tree, who desire a rose small enough for a thimble vase, a primrose smaller than a buttercup, a four-inch thalictrum with flowers like fine mist, an iris an inch high, or a sedum that is less than an inch. The rock garden is a world of dwarfs and creepers and trailers, frequently with names that indicate their size. *Nanus, pumilus,* and *pygmaeus* mean dwarf; *minus* and *minimus* are smaller and smallest; *parvus, parvulus,* and *parvissimus* are small, very small, and smallest; *minutus* means minute, and *minutissimus* means most minute. Then there is the unflattering *pusilla* for the small and insignificant, and *exiguus,* small and poor, while *humilis* means low-growing, *demissus,* low and weak, *humifusus,* sprawling, and *procumbens,* lying on the ground. The creepers have names like *repens, reptans,* and *serpens.* When these terms denoting a low or small form of a plant are added to the generic and a specific name, and perhaps to another varietal name describing the color or form of the flower, it sometimes seems that the smaller the flower, the longer and more complicated the name. A tiny primrose is *Primula* × *polyantha lilacina plena;* an inch-high stonecrop is *Sedum dasyphyllum glanduli-ferum;* while a houseleek that does not grow above a quarter of an inch is *Sempervivum arachnoideum* 'Colletti.' My friend Elsie Hassan of Birmingham, Alabama, says they all remind her of the little boy in the limerick,

> Infinitesimal James
> Had nine unpronounceable names.
> He wrote them all down
> With a terrible frown,
> And then threw them all in the flames.

Regional Gardening

Years ago, when I first thought of making a rock garden in North Carolina, I felt as if I were left all alone to face the rocks. Everything that was written seemed to be written for the North. Nothing was written for me. For rock gardening, which had its origin in cooler climates, has been so long associated with the culture of alpines that it is hard to learn to think of it in terms of regional material. Southerners have been slow to resign themselves to the fact that alpines cannot be depended upon in a section where the winters are snowless or nearly so, summer nights are hot and humid, and the growing season is a long seven months instead of the bare three or four that plants from the mountaintops are accustomed to and require. Only after years of disappointment and failure are we now learning to grow material adapted to our region. "Time was," a Virginia gardener wrote, "when I felt that no plant that grew below the timber line held any interest, and that only seeds provided by the Swiss nurseryman Monsieur Correvon were worth planting; but now with my third rock garden in its fourth year, I have learned that it is futile to weep over a blighted edelweis, when so many lovelier plants rejoice in our summer heat and grow naturally close to our native stone."

The growing of alpines is suited neither to the habitat nor the temperament of the southerner, who is not given to fussing over flowers. One of the most endearing traits of the true alpine gardener is his tender solicitude for the comfort of his plants. "The alpine primrose," Anderson McCulley warns its lovers, "is better watered from beneath, but it will get along nicely if the hose or watering can is laid on the soil surface. A jar can be inverted over the crown of a plant to protect it when one is watering nearby neighbors. And when the temperature soars to the nineties, I usually stand a rock to the south of it for temporary shade." When the temperature soars to the nineties, few southerners will be thinking about the alpine primrose. They will be seeking shade for themselves.

This is not to say that alpines cannot be grown south of Washington, D.C. If I made any such statement, good gardeners would rise up on all sides to confound me. "I do not guarantee that you can grow a mossy saxifrage in full sun in Virginia or Missouri, or *Primula mistassinica* on pure sand in Ohio," Mr. Mitchell of Barre, Vermont, remarks in the introduction to his catalog of rock plants for New England, "but these difficult plants are being grown by skilful gardeners in all of these states." Which is all very true. I suppose that you can grow any plant anywhere if you have determination. But this book is not written for determined gardeners. It is for gardeners who would rather spend their energies on finding the plants suited to their region than in devising ways to grow those that are not suited to it.

If alpines will not grow in the milder sections of this country, what will? I asked myself this question long ago, and it is still only partly answered. It cannot be answered in a word; it cannot be answered by one gardener or even by one generation. It is the pleasure of each gardener to ask it anew, and always there will be a new answer. It is seeking that makes gardening, particularly rock gardening, an art that never grows old. Rock plants for the South must be sought in country gardens; they must be gathered from friends, imported from foreign countries, and culled from the lists of dealers in rare bulbs. They must be collected one by one, and they need not belong to the traditional types that we think of as saxatile. I would not even call them rock plants if there were any other term to cover the little bulbs, the perennials that creep and crawl, and the delightful low-growing shrubs that are, or should be, characteristic of the gardens of the South. "Rock gardening among southern gardeners must be an independent art, developed to meet peculiar climatic conditions," Violet Walker of Woodberry Forest, Virginia, once wrote. "This opens up an enormous field of rare, beautiful material which can give to the southern rock garden an individuality of its own."

Dear Violet. Her pioneering spirit found an outlet not only in her provocative articles but also in putting her theories to the test in piedmont Virginia. From her teeming rock garden in Woodberry Forest came flowers that now bloom in mine, and through her endless enthusiasm and generosity I learned to search out and grow the plants and bulbs that we once dismissed as unsuited to our gardens because they are not hardy in the North. She would sit on the hearth rug late into the night, telling me (while I made eager and illegible notes) of a nurseryman in Texas who could supply an exotic amaryllid or a collector on the West Coast who listed a rare allium. Through Violet I learned that regional gardening is not learned from books. It is built up little by little through the efforts of the gardeners of the region. When you become interested in working out a problem, you find that you are not alone.

All gardeners are great letter writers. Those with similar enthusiasms come together eventually, even though they may never meet in person, even though they live a continent apart. My correspondence has been cultivated as diligently as my garden, and its blossoming has brought me as much pleasure. One of the first fruits of letter writing was the realization that the region I garden in is much wider than I thought. When letters and plants came from farther and farther west, I realized that this area is not limited, as I had supposed, to the southeastern states. I found gardeners in Birmingham, Alabama; Jackson, Mississippi; Shreveport, Louisiana; Wichita Falls, Texas; and San Francisco, California, with problems much the same as mine.

I am writing for the South in general but primarily for gardens in Zone 8 of the Plant Hardiness Map of the Agricultural Research Service, USDA, where the average annual minimum temperatures range from 10° to 20°F. In Charlotte, North Carolina, we occasionally have temperatures nearer zero, and on very rare occasions a short period of subzero weather. Roughly speaking, Zone 8 begins in Virginia along the shores of the Chesapeake Bay and winds in a narrow strip along the coast through North and South Carolina, widening through Georgia and the Gulf States, then narrowing again to end in southwest Texas. It starts again in Arizona on the Mexican border and meanders in a thin stream up the West Coast all the way to British Columbia.

I would say in general that gardeners in USDA Zones 6, 7, and 9 have much the same problems and find the same type of plant material congenial. The main thing that these areas have in common is that the plants best suited to them are those that withstand heat better than cold. Temperature is not the only factor that determines where a plant will grow, but it is the one that you can do least about. Exposure, soil, and the amount of water a plant gets can be controlled to some extent, but not much can be done about the heat of the sun or the furious winter's rages.

Gardeners in these three southern zones also have in common their short and mild (or comparatively mild) winters and their long, hot summers, but they differ in the amount of moisture that comes to them. Claude Barr of Smithwick, South Dakota, once wrote to me,

A general statement which I believe is true is that all east of the eighteen-hundred-foot level where, roughly, the Great Plains begin, is moist and points west are dry. This notwithstanding that there is much talk of heat and drought all of the way to the East Coast. "Hot" on the Plains means not a humid or smothering heat but a dry, almost burning, dwarfing atmosphere. Sometimes a light shower doesn't create any humidity. Sometimes refreshing raindrops fall upon your hand while the air about your hand is hot and dry. In July, and rains mostly don't occur in July, the humidity following a good rain doesn't last thirty minutes.

The only relief is in the fairly cool nights. Most summers have no hot nights here in the corn belt. But these nights are sometimes so dry for weeks on end that there is no dew. Or the air can be heavy with moisture even when the ground is parched, and we may have heavy dews when there has been no rain for weeks on end.

In so vast a region as the southern half of the United States there are, of course, great differences in the plant material suited to various sections. A greater number of alpines can be grown in the mountains than at lower elevations, even though in midsummer the gardens at Nik-Nar, Asheville, North Carolina, look as parched as mine. When we came to Charlotte, which is definitely Piedmont, from Raleigh, which is at the edge of the Coastal Plain, I was amazed at the number of plants I could grow that had not been successful before. This is partly because the soil is better in the new garden and because things grow better under pines than under oaks, but the slight change in elevation does make some difference. There is even a difference in gardens in the same neighborhood, but in general the plants in my garden will grow wherever the winters are short and mild and the summers long and hot.

As Orland White of Charlottesville, Virginia, points out, "there are plenty of opportunities for rock gardening in this region. Andrew Jackson's country is naturally a superb sedumry. In late April and early May, *Sedum pulchellum* in pink perfection reminds one of Europe's heather. Efforts should be made to preserve the natural rock gardens, the Peaks of Otter, Crabtree Falls, Catesby's Mountain, and Stone Mountain." Even where there is no natural stone in the neighborhood, rocks can sometimes be salvaged from an old house or a chimney that is being torn down, or curbstones or cobbles from a street that is being paved. And these need not be used in the conventional way, for the affinity between rocks and plants applies to walls and steps and paved terraces as well as to ravines and mountainsides.

In the South we must be allowed some latitude in design as well as in choice of plants. Even where there is a shortage of stones, the gardener need not forgo the pleasure of growing tiny bulbs and dwarf shrubs and creepers and trailers and tufted perennials that luxuriate in the long, sweet nights of summer or come to life on winter days when the air is as soft as spring.

"We have not many hills about here," Wyndam Hayward wrote

from Winter Park, "so the Florida rock garden is pretty likely to be on the level and with no rocks, which is pretty unorthodox; although I believe at one of the meetings of the American Rock Garden Society they thrashed it all out and decided that it is all right to rock garden without rocks!"

In Ferriday, Louisiana, Mrs. U. B. Evans grew rock plants on a "shady slope of a cypress slough, miles from any rocks," and from northern Missouri Mrs. Fordyce wrote, "I have always wanted a rocky hillside for a garden, but here I sit on a level prairie farm, my garden as flat as a tabletop. Have to dig drain ditches, raise my beds, do all the work myself; yet I have hundreds of plants and get away with the raising of rock plants very nicely. Of course, I have to fix my soil to their liking and give them the advantage of sun or shade where possible."

When it comes to design, there are as many opinions as there are gardeners, but the majority are with the nineteenth-century English writer Reginald Farrer: "The rules of the garden itself are the rules of art; the rules of the rock-garden are the more awful rules of nature."

Orland White said it should "so fit the world in which it exists that any grocery boy will tear through it without thinking it other than a stony hillside," but unless it is part of a natural landscape, as his garden at Blandy was, it would be difficult—if not impossible—to take him literally. It seems to me that the awful rules of nature can be followed even in a small backyard. It is enough that each mossy stone, with the plants that cling to it, looks as if it were inevitable; that it is where it is and nowhere else. It is impossible to make a rock garden from a preconceived plan, or to do it all at one time. It must be created by fitting the rocks to the ground as a costume designer molds the cloth to the figure; and it is more natural for it to come into being as the plants mature than to emerge all at one time in its final form.

Making the Rock Garden

My rock garden in Raleigh, North Carolina, grew slowly, of necessity, for I had only Page, our houseboy, to help me, and he had a full-time job within. But he could always find time to work out-of-doors, and no mention was made of dust on the parlor table. The rock garden followed a curving path that led from the driveway at one end to the wall fountain at the other. From the garden proper it was entered through an ivy-covered arch in the hedge. Beneath the arch was a flight of concrete steps with steep risers and narrow treads. Page and I began by replacing these with wide and shallow stone steps. Page said he would rather lay stone than anything he had ever done, and he went about it with the same deftness and intuition that he put into making his perfect soufflés.

Garden steps can scarcely be too wide or too shallow. "The wider and shallower the steps," Gertrude Jekyll says, "the pleasanter they are to go up and down, the extreme of comfort being a step from four to five inches high and twenty-two to twenty-four inches from front to back; such steps as one may run up and down." Such steps are not only the extreme of comfort, they are also the extreme of beauty. Equally important to beauty, and also to comfort, if garden visitors are not to be herded single file, is the breadth of the flight. A wide flight is pleasant and inviting; a narrow flight is cramped and inhospitable. A common fault in garden steps, and a bad one, is a tendency to dip forward with the slope so that you feel as if you are going to fall forward on your nose as you descend them. In laying them myself, I found out how this happens. It is hard to avoid, unless you back away frequently and look at the steps in relation to the slope. Invariably the step that seemed level when you knelt close to it has a forward slant when you get a longer perspective.

We picked out the flattest and smoothest stones in our rock pile. None were very flat or very smooth, but this, up to a point, is all the better. Stones with straight front edges are preferable in parts of the garden that are laid out in a regular pattern, but rough ones are better where the lines follow the contours of the earth. The rocks at hand were a kind of modified granite that crumbles like sandstone and weathers a dark gray. They were already mossy and worn, and the edges rounded.

When the steps were finished, I sat at intervals on the top one, staring at the space in front of me until it opened up like a fan. I used to feel guilty about the time I spent merely sitting on that top step when I could have been weeding the borders or tying up the chrysanthemums, but I was much comforted when Elsie Hassan wrote,

"I sat on the terrace when weather permitted, and after staring for days at the woods, I began to have ideas. We cleared most of the saplings and underbrush out of the center, making a wide path and leaving room for bulbs, violets, and such along the sides."

With the outline of the fan in mind, I explained to Page that I wanted to extend the third step to curve into a line that would take a definite direction but not be perfectly straight. You cannot tell a person how to lay rocks. He has to see what is to be done as you see it. If you have ever been dependent upon someone with a stronger back than yours to lay a stone the way you want it laid, you will know what I mean. I told Page that the contours of the rocks were to determine the direction of the line, and I showed him the excellent pictures in Jekyll and Weaver's *Gardens for Small Country Houses*. Some of these, such as "bold stratified rockwork and small cascade," were beyond our scope, but "cypripediums thoroughly at home on the upper margin" had the quality of careful carelessness that I wanted to emulate. Page studied the pictures long and thoughtfully, absorbing the principles underlying them. Then he set out to get a similar effect with a very different kind of stone, carrying out a different kind of design. He had an unerring eye for line, and he was much quicker than I to pick the rock that seemed inevitably to be the fellow of the one before it.

I had read, and I have found it to be true, that more of the rock should be below the earth than above it. This, and laying it with the broad side downward, gives a look of stability. Using the same kind of rocks throughout and setting them so that they all tip the same way preserves unity. If the rocks are stratified, the strata should run in only one direction. Too many small rocks cause confusion, but a variety of sizes is pleasing. These principles, picked up from observation and reading, are helpful, but the creation of a garden that looks as if the rocks belong where they are is more a matter of emotion than of forethought. I do not believe that anyone can tell you how to accomplish it. And I do not think that many gardeners ever find out. But this does not matter, for each one of us will be satisfied with his own, because no other kind of a garden is so individual, so personal, or so much an expression of the gardener himself.

Page and I were well pleased with our efforts, and never thought —until Mr. Sturtevant, a landscape architect, came in the spring

—that our construction was open to criticism. Mr. Sturtevant said that we had created an effect of confusion by laying the stones too close together. We had not been aware of this until he pointed it out. Then we wondered how we could ever have failed to see it. Under Mr. Sturtevant's direction, a number of major and minor stones were removed. Those we left formed definite units that were tied together by a series of transitions like modulations in music.

Between the rock garden and the driveway, Page and I built a wall of stone cut from the quarry. It was a nice wall with a graceful curve, but we did not build well and it kept falling down. An instinct for beauty will not make a wall stand, and after this one had twice been knocked down by the coal truck, I was forced to let Day come and do it over. Day was an obstinate and surly old man, nearly always drunk. We invariably ended in a quarrel, but I was always forced to take him back—or rather, to allow him to come back—when he returned, for he always did. And he knew how to fit stones one to another in such perfect balance that they would stay forever.

In time, more rocks were fitted to the slopes above and below the path that led to the wall fountain. In front of the fountain was a flagged terrace with a south-facing retaining wall to the right. Between the flags and the rocks of the dry wall, and on top of the wall and at the foot of it were the rock plants that must be grown in the open and the little bulbs that need all of the sun that they can get.

A rock garden can be natural even though it is somewhat formal in character, for a garden that is functional is natural in the best sense. Dry walls that offer a solution for sharp slopes are also a happy place for growing rock plants. Low ones are not difficult to build. Elsie Hassan said that she built hers with stones that were not too large for her to handle. "We sit on a knob," she wrote, "and I have built walls and more walls to stop the wash. When Victor Reis, a friend from Ohio, came to visit us, he said, 'Why not more open spaces instead of so many flat terraces?' and I replied, 'I hope it rains while you are here.'"

Gertrude Jekyll says that "a terrace is always friendly to quiet thought." When the space for the garden is small and flat, and especially if it is near the house, a little paved terrace with creeping plants between the stones may be the best kind of rock garden. The English cottagers call this a crawl garden. I have in one of my scrapbooks a picture of a garden like this. It is a small rectangle with low brick retaining walls on three sides and the house on the fourth. Bricks are left out of the retaining wall at intervals, and rock plants are growing in the interstices. More plants are growing on top of the wall, and some of these hang over it. Down the center are two long, narrow beds filled with low perennials and edged with thrift or pinks. Between these beds there is a birdbath, a very charming one. It looks like an English garden, or one in New England, but I can imagine it as very delightfully planted for the South, with rosemary on top of the wall and the small beds edged with lily-turf (*Liriope muscari*) and filled with the little amaryllids.

Since rock plants are so varied in their needs, it is necessary to create a variety of situations. There must be places that are high and dry for bulbs that require a summer baking and low-lying pockets for those from meadow and marsh. There must be sun for flowers from the fields and shade for those from the woods. In the South, especially, there must be shade. Large trees protect garden and gardener from the sun in summer, break the winter winds that blow on half-hardy plants, and temper the air when treacherous late frosts follow a false spring. The idea that shade or even the proximity of trees is to be rigorously avoided applies only to gardens where plants from above the timberline are in the majority. "Caroline and I get so disgusted when people say that we cannot have rock gardens in the South," Ruth Dormon of Salina, Louisiana, once wrote. "Of course we can't when we try to grow alpines. We have both tried a number. I find that another reason some people fail is that they just put plants on top of rocks in the broiling sun. Caroline has a lovely rock garden in semi-shade, and I have mine in semi-shade."

"I wish that all doubters could see the beautiful garden that Inez [Conger] has created in the red clay hills of northwest Louisiana," Caroline Dormon wrote in *Natives Preferred*. "A good part of it is made up of brown stones which she had transported from nearby and skillfully embedded in the hillside. Here are *Iris cristata*, clumps of nemostylus, *Phlox divaricata* in every shade, silenes and masses of violets. Mostly this is in high shade."

Since the plants in the open part of my garden lay in the afternoon shadow, I have often wondered whether, even in the South, an ideal rock garden should not have a small space in full sun. I asked Claude

Barr, who used to send me plants from the "High Plains, Badlands, and Black Hills," whether he thought that my almost total failure with these lovely things was due entirely to the climate or partly to the background of trees. He answered wisely, "I will not make any suggestion for full sun in your garden. I know a man who cut down many large trees on an old residential street in the interest of his rock plants. Under certain conditions full sun may not be worth the price. Your lack of it may not be a detriment to most of the Plains plants, but it may explain why you can't get bloom on *Thermopsis rhombifolia*, and why you can't hold *Asclepias pumila*. Those which grow in open, exposed places must have sun. If you give them all you've got and the most suitable footing, and they don't prosper, they are hardly for you, I guess."

The "suitable footing" is the first problem of the rock garden. Most saxatile plants require good drainage along with a moisture-holding soil. As Claude Barr put it, "The great problem is to provide the right drainage for certain exacting plants, and not get a medium so porous that they cannot hold out between drinks." A good general mixture for the rock garden is loam, sand, and leaf mold in equal proportions, with more humus for the moisture-loving kinds and more sand for those that require sharp drainage.

The leaf pile is the heart of the rock garden. It seems to me that in my Raleigh garden most of my waking hours were spent dragging oak leaves in and out of the holes I kept them in, and in the few hours that were left for sleep I dreamt of leaves. I kept them in holes at the back of the surrounding shrubbery so that they would be out of sight but close at hand for mulching and planting. If they were piled very high in the fall, they would sink to ground level by spring. They were never turned over, for there was no one to turn them over, and nothing was ever mixed with them. They just rotted. In a year or less they would do for a mulch, and in a year or more some were so thoroughly decayed that they could be mixed with the soil at planting time. I used the holes in rotation, always keeping one with well-rotted compost in reserve. When they were mixed with the loam and sand, bone meal or lime rubble or old manure would be added to suit the individual plant. It is to be remembered that only the partly decayed leaves are acid in reaction; those that have become fine dark compost are circumneutral.

According to the British, who garden so sternly, the soil beneath the rock garden should be dug to two and a half feet and thoroughly mixed with compost. The rocks should be laid upon this with the special mixture for each type of plant in the spaces between. If I had waited to do all of this, I should never have had a rock garden. Mine was planted inch by inch, and I dug the stiff, rocky clay as deeply as I could (which in some cases, obviously, was not deep enough) and dug in sand and rotted leaves. Due to faithful mulching thereafter, the soil improved a little each year.

Planting the Garden ✻

In the spring all people are gardeners. Everyone wants to rush to the local nursery, dig up plants in full bloom, and bring them home to set out in the moist, receptive earth. In the South this will not do. Sometimes when new spring lists came from the North with long-sought rarities offered for the first time, I was weak-minded enough to sit down and order from them at once. Nearly always I was sorry. In the North plants cannot be dug until March, and by that time we are having summer days and drying winds. No matter how carefully spring-set plants are sheltered and watered, it is almost impossible to keep them alive until they can become established. With a few exceptions, such as bulbs of uncertain hardiness, all planting should be done before Christmas. But it is hard to get southerners to make up their minds to this. No one wants to garden in late fall. There is a portent in fading petals and falling leaves that chills the heart even while summer lingers, and it takes a Spartan gardener to set out newly arrived plants in a cold November drizzle.

Since our late, and often terribly dry, falls permit little planting of herbaceous material before the middle of October, I order first the little bulbs that should be in the ground in September. When these are planted, I order plants from nurseries where frost comes early, for if I wait too long they will have stopped shipping for that season. Then I order from dealers in the South and Southwest. I try to have everything in by the end of November so that the new plants can get settled before bad weather comes, but, because I am so greedy, this cannot always be managed.

Along with fall planting, I try to take up the leaves as they come down from the trees. "What!" visitors often say when they see the (comparative) tidiness of my garden at the end of winter, "Isn't it very early to be uncovering?" They are surprised to hear that it has never been covered at all. The purpose of a winter covering is to keep the ground frozen and the plants dormant. Where the ground freezes infrequently, and then only on the surface, and plants may start into new growth in midwinter, protection does more harm than good. When the garden is made tidy for the winter, after the leaves have fallen, I cover it with a mulch of leaf mold that is in the crumbly state, a mulch thick enough to protect, but not to smother, the plants that do not die down completely in winter. By spring this mulch has become a powder that can be stirred into the soil with the addition of bone meal or old manure for plants that need a richer diet, and then another mulch of semidecayed leaves is put on for the summer.

I once had an idea that by a consistent use of mulches I could forgo summer watering. But this will not do. There are plants that will survive and even bloom through the hottest, driest seasons, but an unwatered garden loses its summer freshness. If you are going to water, however, do not let the ground dry out before you start. It is fatal to put off getting out the hose because it looks like rain. Once the ground gets dry even a good rain fails to penetrate, and summer showers only make the air a little fresher. It is better to let the plants take the weather if you are not going to keep the ground always moist. The best method is with a porous hose, leaving it in one place for a long time and letting the water trickle very gently. Be sure that the ground is thoroughly soaked by digging down several inches to see how far the moisture has gone before the hose is moved on. You will be surprised to find out how long a thorough soaking takes. Apart from the plants that need summer moisture, there should be a place that the hose never approaches. Here little bulbs that require summer baking can be planted with drought-resistant plants to cover them.

Many rock garden failures are due to the size and age of the plants set out. Young, homegrown plants have much the best chance for survival in any climate. Moreover, a collection grows much more quickly if cuttings and seeds are acceptable than if—like me—you are willing to deal only in plants and bulbs. Being too trifling to undertake any sort of propagation myself, I begged permission to quote Elsie Hassan, as she was very good at it; she always had plants to give away.

Everything you read about raising plants begins with a cold frame. I asked Mrs. Hassan if a cold frame is necessary in this climate, and she answered, "No, it is less necessary here than farther north. Most of the things do not need that much protection, and unless they are carefully watched grow too soft in mild climates. You do have the advantage of sustained humidity in the air. I have used a frame more for seed sowing than for cuttings."

She said that her propagating bed was in the shade against the back of the brick garage and was raised above the ground to the height of four bricks. For use on a smaller scale she suggested a galvanized bucket with a drainage hole three inches from the top, filled with coarse, washed sand, and watered only through a lead pipe an inch in diameter set vertically in the sand. This should be kept in the shade under the eaves of the house and is especially recommended for rock plants that are finicky. As to the propagating mixture (every plant raiser has his own pet one), she said she had changed from her original combination of sand and sifted peat to one of half sand and half vermiculite about ten inches deep. "That is plenty for most small things. After the cuttings are well rooted, I move them to the other half of the same bed, which is filled with a potting mixture that is about one-fourth vermiculite. From that you can transplant to permanent positions without many casualties."

"I use large pots for seeds," she said, "and if they are not too thickly sown, like to have the pot about two-thirds filled with a good potting mixture, with an inch of vermiculite on top of that. Then, if you don't get around to transplanting right away, the roots go down and find food about the time they begin to need it. If you use all vermiculite and want to leave them for awhile, it is necessary to water with a nutrient solution. In my haphazard state I find it much simpler to have the layer of good soil for the roots to seek. I have very good results with this method. Of course, on the cuttings, watering is imperative. If they once dry out, they are done for. A period when the weather is scorching hot and the wind is hot and dry is particularly difficult. When I water in such weather, I try to get the wall back of the seedbed dripping wet and soak the bricks that outline the bed in order to create a little space of humid air."

Labels are always a problem, but especially among rock plants. They must be permanent, easily read, and inconspicuous. The best and cheapest of all the kinds that I have tried are strips of zinc or copper. I got a sheet metal dealer to cut his scraps into strips about an inch wide and eight inches long. I print the name with acid and a gold pen. It is a good idea to begin at the end of the label and print toward the center, because rock plants have long names. It is also a good idea to put the date and the source on the label, as they do in botanical gardens. The labels should be deep in the ground with only the name showing. This looks better, and they are not so likely to be raked up with leaves and trash. The only fault I find with these labels is that the sharp corners sometimes cut my hands when I am working around the plants. I always wanted to get the sheet metal people to round the corners, but I was afraid to ask them as they were not enthusiastic about fooling with the labels anyway and might have refused to bother with me at all if I had asked for further favors.

The Little Bulbs

I did not begin a rock garden with any intention of devoting so much space to bulbs, but as Theophrastus observed long ago, "all bulbous plants are tenacious of life. They thrive when others sicken; flourish where all else fails." They demand less and give more than any flowering plants I know. In particular they seem to be suited to this part of the country, and I find that a large proportion of the little bulbs from all over the world can be made at home in our climate. Gardens in this latitude are the meeting place of bulbs from both cold and hot countries. Our winters are mild enough for an astonishing number of the half-hardy and even of the tender ones, and our summers not too hot for most of the hardy kinds.

Although the little daffodils are mostly mountain species, they are native to the mountains of southern Europe and northern Africa. It is not unreasonable to suppose that most of them can be grown in the South if their individual needs are not neglected. Mountain plants require a soil that is gritty, well drained, and on the lean side.

This means that garden soil should be mixed with coarse sand and leaf mold. The most important point in the culture of the very small species is to plant them in a pocket to themselves where they will not be disturbed and where no weeds or heavy plants will grow over them in summer. The ground cover, if any, should be a very light one with shallow roots. I have an idea that few of the little bulbs that have disappeared from my garden were victims of the climate. I think they were dug up by me when something new was to be planted, or else pulled up in the roots of large weeds that got ahead of me or annuals that were where they should not have been.

The small daffodils are all charming, and among them there is infinite variety. For each of the garden forms there is a miniature, a perfect little replica of exquisite proportions. In mild climates the species may be had in bloom from before Christmas to after Easter, even when Easter is late. The little trumpets vary in size from those with stems a foot long with flowers in proportion to the tiniest of all with a crown smaller than a thimble.

There are many additional useful and delightful bulbs, among them the crocuses for spring and fall, the chionodoxas, snowdrops, and scillas.

Herbs in the Rock Garden

There is an affinity between herbs and rocks. Yielding contours and subdued colors soften harsh outlines and cold gray surfaces, while stone walls and rocky ledges provide the drainage that herbs require and the warmth that draws out their fragrance. Herbs are thought to be more fragrant in poor soil, and I believe that those not encouraged to lush growth best withstand our humid summers. Humidity is the enemy. It is best combatted by sharp drainage, porous soil, air, and sunlight. Several good gardeners have told me that herbs need light shade in this part of the country, but my experience is that full sun is better. In general, herbs like a sweet soil. Lime rubble and wood ashes are good for them. They need continual shearing and pinching to keep them shapely. Pinching requires patience, and it is a pleasant labor. Allowing bloom tends to deplete the plant of strength, but it takes a determined gardener to do away with bloom in midsummer. Herbs are southern plants, thriving on heat and drought. Though some of them come from mountainous regions and have a preference for cool nights, I find that my experiences in Raleigh and Charlotte, North Carolina, are very close to Mrs. Bruce Chalfin's in the Blue Ridge Mountains area of Lynchburg, Virginia.

It is for color in winter that herbs are most wanted in the rock garden. A number hold their leaves all winter, or most of the winter, especially in the South, and especially with protection. The shrubby herbs, being mostly low-growing and prostrate, are typical saxatile plants and seem to me to fit into the rock garden, but there is no reason to exclude any of the others if they are not too large and coarse for the plants around them.

Annuals

The rock garden is not really the place for annuals, but in the South we cannot be too choosy, for continuous bloom depends upon temporary fillers to cover the ground when permanent plants are dormant. As soon as their peak of bloom has past, the fillers can be discarded. In my garden the annuals begin to bloom at the end of February, and one or another continues until frost. The sweet alyssum, if the fall has been mild, blooms on into winter. My list is short, for I have considered only the easily grown and dependable sorts, but with a little trouble and patience there could be many others.

Broad-leaved Woody Plants

Among the woody plants, the farther south you go, the more important evergreens become—especially broad-leaved evergreens, for more of them can be grown in the South than in the North. In all gardens they are indispensable for winter-furnishing, but in the parts of the country where there is bloom throughout the year there is even more need for a leafy background at all seasons. Some of the dwarf evergreens are difficult, while others are easily grown when their needs are supplied. However, too many evergreens give a heavy effect in the garden, which can be relieved by the seasonal changes of the deciduous plants.

Dwarf Conifers

When I first became interested in dwarf conifers few southern nurseries were growing them, but interest in them has grown, and a great many are now available. When I wrote to Ernest Yelton of Rutherford, North Carolina, for a list of those he had found satisfactory, he wrote back with some advice: "I must tell you that my experience only goes back about fifteen years. Several of the so-called dwarfs have since become small trees and have been moved or chopped down because they do not fit in the rock landscape any more."

Plants called *nana* or *pygmaea* or even *minima* may in time outgrow their allotted space, for some make up for their small stature by growing in girth. Gardeners sometimes choose to enjoy the charms of a slow-growing dwarf that one day may have to be chopped down, but all gardeners should become informed about the long-term development of these alluring plants.

Plant Sources

A source list of saxatile plants appears in appendix 2. The most valuable information a garden book has to offer is the names of plantsmen who supply the material, for that is all the reader really needs to know. Once he has the plants, he can discover the rest for himself. When the subject is saxatile plants, a list of sources is all the more desirable, for the dealer in rarities seldom advertises his wares, and it is he rather than the customer who must be pursued. "I hide myself from the general public, and have no signs," Brent Heath once wrote from Virginia. "It takes a real enthusiast to find me. Only yesterday a couple from Pittsburgh spent three hours hunting my place."

When you write for a list, do not expect a handsomely illustrated catalog: they need not praise who purpose not to sell. The fewer the pages and the poorer the print, the rarer the plants will be. And if, after repeated requests, one of these austere sheets is surrendered, do not pass it on to a fellow gardener or drop it in the wastebasket upon the receipt of a more up-to-date issue. Preserve all such publications; they are extremely limited editions, and each one is likely to contain some bits of information not to be found elsewhere.

One of the best places to look for otherwise unobtainable saxatile plants is from the seed exchanges of various organizations, a list of which is included in appendix 2.

I once asked a gardening friend how to go about getting plants not in the nurseries, and he replied, "write to botanical gardens and get in touch with missionaries and army officers in all parts of the world." I have not done this on a very large scale, but everyone that I have asked about plants has been eager to help find them, and many rare things have come to me from gardeners who did not even know that I was looking for them. And so I no longer make it a point of honor, as I used to do, never to mention a plant without being able to name a source for it. I have learned the truth of the saying that to seek is to find. I have learned something further: that seeking is sometimes an end in itself; the thing sought already found.

If, after studying the methods of the experts, I could go and do likewise, I could undoubtedly grow more kinds of plants. Since I cannot do better (and also lack ambition), I enjoy the plants that I can grow. Most of the gardeners that I am friendly with cultivate the same philosophy. I know charming gardens where interesting collections of plants have been brought to bloom in the same lackadaisical way.

We all want to know the flowers that can be counted on to bloom in this climate year after year, and so the following plant list deals mainly with those that are reasonably reliable in all seasons. For every one mentioned, many others—as much or even more to be desired—have been left out because of their brief tenure in my garden. If enthusiasm has allowed a few to creep in that cold fact would have kept out, these will find grace in the eyes of like-minded gardeners. As Gertrude Jekyll says, "I write for those who are in sympathy with my views."

Nonwoody Plants

Achillea

The yarrows are aromatic herbs named for Achilles, who discovered their healing properties. In addition to his prowess in battle, this great hero was a pupil of Chiron, a centaur noted for his skill in medicine. The achilleas are distributed over the temperate parts of the earth, but most of the choice rock garden sorts come from the mountains of southern Europe. Since they are sun-loving plants and usually head the list of drought-resistant material, I thought they would be just the thing for southern summers and started to collect all that were available. I found that they would come through the periods of heat and drought all right, but that they quickly disappeared during the steaming days that follow excessive summer rains. And I learned that even in England, where rock plants get every attention, the gray-leaved sorts require either the protection of a cloche or frequent renewal. Nevertheless I enjoyed the experiment, for I found the dwarf yarrows an appealing lot. They grow so neatly, bloom so generously, and smell so clean. And they look as if they belong among rocks, which, after all, is the first requisite of a rock plant. In the end I found a few little yarrows that are reasonably durable in these parts. Probably more would survive with a more careful gardener or in a sunnier garden. Full sun, poor soil, frequent division, and perfect drainage are needed to keep them going, and most of them like an alkaline soil.

Annuals in this section are designated by the abbreviation *ann*. in parentheses following the botanical name. Additions are in square brackets and are initialed.

A. tomentosa, the species commonly grown, is the woolly yarrow. It is generally an easy doer, and in some gardens even a weed. It does not last with me, although Mrs. Chrismon has no trouble with it in Greensboro, and Elizabeth Rawlinson found it one of the most dependable of rock plants in the Shenandoah Valley. It will bloom for me for a few seasons and is very thrifty while it lasts, flowering at the end of April and lasting until the end of May. This is one of the less minute forms, producing thick, broad mats of fine gray foliage and myriad chrome-yellow flowers in flat corymbs on eight-inch stems. There are several cultivars, among them one called 'Moonlight,' with pale yellow flowers.

Elsie Hassan finds *A. nana* reliable and says that in Birmingham, Alabama, it comes through the summer better than *A. tomentosa.* She sent me a flourishing mat of it, but it promptly disappeared during a wet summer. Another trial was more successful, and the plants bloomed in May. The silvery flower heads, like miniatures of the common yarrow, stand only a few inches above the foliage, which has no stature at all. The fine, fernlike leaves, which are covered with silky hairs, are used in making Chartreuse. It is difficult to find the true species, as a much coarser and less desirable one is in the trade under this name.

A. umbellata, which comes from Greece, has been the longest lasting of my small yarrows. It started out as a low, compact plant, but with the years the five-inch flower stems stretched up to twice that height. Perhaps the soil was too rich for it. On top of a low wall it bloomed for six Aprils, and it would probably be there still if I had taken the trouble to divide and reset the clump. The flowers are white, and the feathery foliage makes a soft mat the year around.

Another yarrow that persists for some years is *A. sibirica.* I had some difficulty in finding the right plant. The first one ordered under that name was tall and yellow-flowered, though described as small and white flowered. The true species, with its rosette of delicately scalloped silver leaves and bunches of white-rayed, bisque-centered daisies, is perfectly charming. It is said to be late blooming, but with me it comes in April with the others. In the North the small yarrows bloom from June to August, but here their season is over by June.

Acorus

[The growth pattern of some of the smaller acorus species is charming. There is a swirl of leaves around a central core. *A. gramineus* 'Variegatus' has, as the name implies, grasslike foliage and white-and-green-striped leaves. *A. g.* 'Pusillus' is similar except that the leaves are solid green and it is six inches or shorter. There are other fine cultivars of this species, all of which prefer light shade and moist soil. NG]

Adonis

[*A. amurensis* is one of the most wonderful winter-flowering plants. I am growing the Japanese cultivar 'Fukuju-Kai' in a rock garden which has shade from an enormous white oak in summer but considerable sunlight in winter. By the turn of the year it is possible to find the fat green buds just at the surface of the soil. By February the large, bright yellow flowers, each one decorated with a collar of green, filigreed leaves, open when the sun hits them and close when they are shaded. NG]

Aethionema

The stone cresses (we always called them Persian candytuft) are crucifers closely related to iberis but not so easily established in my experience. In Raleigh the spicy pink flowers bloomed in Mr. Tong's nursery every spring, but I rather think he bought new plants each fall, and those in my garden seldom tarried through the summer, though they are said to delight in heat and drought. In my new garden I am starting another collection, hoping that the Piedmont will please them better. Here they are growing on an exposed wall in soil mixed with sand and humus and a little lime. If they do not send their roots permanently and deeply into this good soil, I shall cease to think of them as dependable rock plants but still want an occasional specimen, for there is nothing to take the place of this dainty pink crucifer.

In North Carolina the Persian candytuft begins to bloom after the middle of March, or at the latest in early April. *A. grandiflorum* is the largest species and usually considered the handsomest. The prostrate branches cover themselves with heads of deliciously scented flowers of pale amaranth pink.

A. × *warleyense,* a garden hybrid called 'Warley Rose,' is described as a bright clear rose, but with me the flowers had a violet cast and were rather a muddy color. I have had several others, but there seems to be little difference in them.

[Although the individual plants are short-lived, *A. cordifolium* has proven permanent in both the rock garden and perennial borders. The rounded, succulent blue-green leaves turn a splendid bronzy purple in the winter sun, and the tiny pink flowers are so prolific that in spring there are areas that look carpeted as if with heather. It self-sows liberally, and unwanted seedlings are easily removed. NG]

Ajuga

In the South we cannot afford to spurn easy-to-grow rock plants like the bugleweeds just because they are easy. *A. genevensis brockbankii* grows in clumps and does not throw out runners. The flowers are a clear blue violet.

A. pyramidalis 'Rubra Contorta,' the best of the bugleweeds, is a garden form that originated in Germany. It is very dwarf, with flowers in stocky spikes not over five inches high and leaves in flat metallic rosettes. The wine-red leaves are dark and burnished and crisped and curled. They keep their color and high polish all through the summer and winter. The blue of the flowers is a color as intense and metallic as that of the leaves. The flowers begin to bloom any time from the middle of March to the middle of April, according to the season. In flower and in leaf this is a most decorative rock plant. It is easy and permanent and a very rapid spreader, but its roots are shallow and it is easily removed if it spreads too fast and too far. The dark leaves are pleasant in combination with the red or rosy flowers of other plants. I particularly like them next to the magenta flowers of the maiden pinks.

A. reptans is a coarse and untidy plant with flowers that are typically a rather dull blue, but the cultivar 'Rosea' is one of the best low ground covers for partial shade, where it endures and increases slowly and steadily. With me it does not persist in full sun. The flowers are a soft and beautiful deep rose pink, coming at the end of April, later than the blue varieties, and repeating in summer and fall. The flower spikes are six or eight inches to a foot tall, and the plants are neat and compact. The foliage is a fresh light green. There is a form of *A. reptans* with white flowers, *A. r.* 'Alba,' and one with leaves that are variegated pink and cream.

[*A. reptans* has a few more excellent cultivars beyond those mentioned by Elizabeth Lawrence. 'Burgundy Glow' is reddish brown, green, and cream with overtones of beet red, and is lovely with colchicums coming up through it. 'Multicolor' has bits of yellow with red and green leaves. 'Silver Beauty' is one of the better-behaved cultivars. Its gray-green leaves variegated with streaks of cream are lovely, and its slow rate of increase makes it appropriate for growing near smaller rock plants. NG]

Alchemilla

[Alchemillas like cool, moist soil, a situation which is difficult to produce throughout the summer in the South. There are two species which are tolerant of our conditions but happiest with some shade. *A. alpina*, which may be *A. conjuncta*, is a wonderful foliage plant for the front of a border or a lightly shaded rock garden. Beautiful rosettes of green leaves edged with silver and with silvery, hairy undersides characterize this species, which increases slowly by stolons. *A. erythropoda* is another lovely one, with scalloped blue-green leaves. One of the most delightful features of the lady's mantles is the way raindrops rest on their leaves. NG]

Alyssum, Alyssoides, Aurinia

The alyssums and plants formerly considered alyssums are so much a part of spring that a rock garden without them would be unthinkable, but they are short-lived with me, and yearly bloom comes only from seedlings or replacements. This is not true in all southern gardens, for when I told Mrs. Chrismon that I could never keep *Aurinia saxatilis* (formerly *Alyssum saxatile*) for more than two years, and seldom for more than one, she pointed out a six-year-old plant that looked as if it would continue to bloom for six more years. It is easily grown in light soil that is on the alkaline side, in full sun and with thorough drainage, but, like most gray-leaved plants, it is sensitive to dampness.

Early bloom is always welcome, and my earliest date, the twenty-second of February, is for *Alyssum wulfenianum*, the most beautiful alyssum that has ever bloomed for me. The flowers are the soft color that is called strontian yellow. They are comparatively large and in domed heads like the flowers of sweet alyssum. The plant grows to about six inches in height and spreads to make a wide, compact, silver mat. It is amazingly floriferous over a long period, lasting until past the middle of May.

A species from southern Europe, *A. moellendorfianum*, was more name than plant, but I think from what I have read that I had a poor form. This too blooms early and long and perpetuates itself by volunteer seedlings. The pale lemon-yellow flowers are in umbel-like heads.

The best species for the South is *A. sinuatum* (now *Alyssoides sinuata*) for which, at present, I know of no source. I had it from Mr. Tong in Raleigh, and there is no telling where he got it. For several years it renewed itself by seedlings that bloomed the first year from the end of March to past the middle of May. The lemon chrome flowers are not in compact heads as in most species but in open racemes on thin, stiff stems that stand erect above the silver rosette of basal leaves. This one is from Macedonia. A similar Mediterranean species, *Alyssoides cretica*, blooms about the same time and seeds itself very freely. It is a sprawling plant with large lemon yellow flowers. I think this one crossed with *A. sinuata,* for there is great variety in the seedlings, some of them being much more compact than others. The silver rosettes are charming in the winter.

Yellow tuft, *Alyssum murale,* came to me as *A. rostratum*. It is the last to bloom and carries the pale yellow of the alyssums into June. Although it is not permanent, it is longer-lived than the others.

[*Alyssoides utriculata* is also very beautiful, but it has green leaves and clear yellow flowers. It has survived terribly hot summers easily, perhaps because it is growing in full sun in soil amended with stones.

Alyssum spinosum 'Roseum' (now *Ptilotrichum spinosum*) has been with me now for a year and is growing in the scree in a large iron pot. It looks like a tiny, spiny shrub with gray foliage throughout the year. In late spring there were many small pink flowers. This one is so small that it is best enjoyed at eye level on hands and knees or in a raised situation.

Aurinia saxatilis 'Sunnyborder Apricot' was also added to the garden last spring, and it too has been content with lean soil and full sun. It has apricot-colored flowers in spring. The large, floppy silver leaves look refreshingly cool even on the hottest days. NG]

Anemone

[The classification of anemones and pulsatillas is confused. Some authorities separate them into two separate genera; however, I will follow the examples of *Hortus* and *The New York Botanic Garden Illustrated Encyclopedia of Horticulture* and lump them together, dealing first with anemones.

Spring is the time for these lovely plants, for many of them go underground for the summer. One of the earliest to bloom is the delicate *A. apennina* with its finely cut leaves and pale blue flowers. At about the same time, *A. blanda* begins to open its flat, wide flowers to the sun. I have tried many named cultivars, but now that they are established I will settle for the thousands of self-sown seedlings which have appeared in the rock garden and underneath the pear tree. They come in white and all shades of blue and pink. There is supposed to be a red one, but the tubers I received were just a nice shade of pink. They require sun to open their flowers but will grow just about anywhere. *A. magellanica* is a wonderful species with creamy-white flowers appearing in late spring. The European wood anemones, *A. nemorosa,* have delighted me by establishing themselves and spreading slowly but surely in the shade of an enormous white oak. There are many cultivars and varieties of this species, but it has been difficult finding them all. I have yet to find a really dark blue one. Thus far I am growing *A. n.* 'Alba' with double white flowers. Actually, only the center is double, and is surrounded by a collar of flat petals. *A. n.* 'Allenii' is a very light blue and is not as vigorous as the white ones. The variety *A. n. robinsoniana* is also supposed to have powder-blue flowers, but it hasn't bloomed well enough for me to be certain. *A.* × *lesseri* is a charming native with bright pink flowers in both spring and fall. The largest of the anemones suitable for a rock garden is *A. sylvestris,* with its fragrant white flowers appearing in abundance in late spring and occasionally throughout the summer. This is a stoloniferous plant which will spread when happy.

The pulsatillas in general require more sun than their anemone cousins, and they demand better drainage. My favorite is *A. cernua,* with its hairy stems and nodding claret-colored flowers. I had a large clump for years on the west side of a building. *A. pulsatilla* is the European pasqueflower, so named, perhaps, because of the time of blooming. It comes in many colors from white through red to purple. The American pasqueflower, *P. patens,* is a lovely thing, especially early on cool mornings when the captured dew glistens among the many hairs of the stems and leaves. It too comes in the same variety of colors. *A. halleri* has been the most persistent species for me, and it can be counted on for an extended bloom period from late March through April. The form I have has lilac-purple flowers on twelve-inch stems. NG]

Anemonella

[*A. thalictroides,* the wood anemone, is one of the most charming woodland plants to appear in the spring. It is small enough for any rock garden and will succeed in almost any soil given high shade. The plants spring forth from tuberous roots early in the season and produce many delicate white or pink flowers among lovely thalictrumlike blue-green leaves. There are some named cultivars. The pink one which grows in the Midwest is *A. t.* 'Rosea,' and there is a beautiful, but difficult, double pink one offered in catalogs as *A. t.* 'Shoaf's Pink.' I have also a double creamy-white one with the name *A. t.* 'Cameo.' Although they are very beautiful, neither of the double forms has proved permanent for me. This is a plant to grow in masses, and happily it self-sows readily, making this possible within only a few years. NG]

Anthemis

[*A. cretica* subsp. *pontica* is a splendid plant for a sunny site and well-drained soil. It is native to Turkey, and I obtained my plants from seeds collected there by Jim Archibald, a Welsh seedsman. They are growing in a large pot containing mostly sand and gravel. The finely dissected silvery leaves grow close to the soil line, and for an extended time in early spring masses of small white daisylike flowers appear on stems up to five inches tall. NG]

Anthericum

A. liliago, Saint Bernard's lily, is not at its best in the South. Even so it is worth consideration, especially in the variety *major*. When it is in bloom, early in May, dainty white flowers widely spaced on almost invisible stems seem to float in the air. It is easy enough to grow, requiring only sun, moisture at the blooming season, and a rich, leafy soil. It goes dormant during the hottest part of summer, reappearing in early spring.

A. ramosum is at its best in the South and is one of the easiest and most enduring rock plants. It is drought resistant, likes poor soil, and does not seem to mind heat—except that it does not bloom here all summer, as it is said to do in cooler climates, but only from the end of May into July with a later display in early fall. The fugitive blossoms are smaller than those of Saint Bernard's lily, but there are many of them. Both species are tallish plants, to about two feet, showing short grassy foliage that fits in with the smaller plants and airy racemes that are delicate and graceful. They do not take up much room and can be fitted in among the early bulbs to make a later showing.

Aquilegia

With such a small chance of survival it seems a waste of energy for southerners to attempt to grow such mountain columbines as *Aquilegia alpina* of the European Alps, or *A. pyrenaica* and *A. discolor* of Spain, or the notoriously difficult species of our own western mountains; but always if we look long enough we will come upon species that will endure even our hard conditions.

At the Greensboro flower show on April 21, I found the fragile and arresting blossoms of *A. ecalcarata*. They had been brought by Mrs. Chrismon, who wrote later that both three-year-old plants and some from seed sown last spring were covered with blooms. Studying the flowers, I tried to discover the source of their charm, for they are neither brilliant nor spectacular. I think it is the lightness and delicacy of form, combined with the weight of the wine-dark color, that gives them such grace and individuality. The small spurless flowers hang like bells on their fine, thin stems above lacy leaves that are edged with red. The whole plant is less than a foot in height.

"This plant is a native not only of Japan but of the Asiatic mainland as well," Clara Regan wrote in the *Bulletin of the American Rock Garden Society* (vol. 6, no. 3, p. 41). "No treatment comes amiss in its cultivation, and it adds to its good qualities by producing true seed, something that columbines, as a race, are not too particular about."

The best-known dwarf columbine in the South is another Japanese species, a small form of the fan columbine offered as *A. flabellata* 'Nana Alba.' It is sturdy in both appearance and performance. The fat milk white flowers, which begin to bloom at the end of March or in April, are thick in texture—and so are the gray fan-shaped leaves. This form is only about six inches tall, less than half the height of the type.

A. akitensis (syn. *A. flabellata*) is a high alpine from the mountains of Japan. The soft, blue-violet flowers, plump and short-spurred, are edged with canary yellow. They stand just above the thick, low mound of gray-green leaves.

These columbines, like our natives, need some shade in this climate and require a soil that is light and porous but not too dry.

[Several of the smallest species of aquilegia can be grown in the South if special attention is given to their requirement for excellent drainage. By far the most permanent columbine I have ever grown came to me as *A. bertolonii*. Because it does not fit the description in *Hortus*, I have concluded that it is most likely *A. discolor*. The flowers, which appear in very early spring on short stems, have blue sepals and white cuplike petals. The blue-green leaves are not as attractive to leaf miners as those of most aquilegias, and so the plants never look as pockmarked as their North American relatives.

A. canadensis: If you can accommodate a much larger plant, success can be guaranteed with the acquisition of our native species. It blooms relatively early in spring with orange-red sepals and yellow petals and can stand full sun as well as part shade. There are several lovely forms: *A. c.* 'Nana,' which is more compact in every way; and *A. c.* 'Corbett,' which has medium yellow sepals as well as petals.

A. glandulosa is even shorter with more finely dissected leaves, and although I have had plants here through the past two hot, dry summers, I have yet to see it flower.

A. grata is a Yugoslavian species with black-purple flowers and short, straight spurs. Seeds are offered by Jim Archibald.

From the Colorado mountains have come seeds of *A. saximontana,* which germinated easily but grew with varying degrees of success. The best plants have been grown in very well-drained, screelike soil in very light shade. This is definitely one worth searching for, and if you are lucky you will have plants less than five inches high with blue-and-cream flowers.

A. vulgaris, the easiest species of all, blooms in mid-spring with deep blue or purple flowers on one-to-two-foot plants. It is somewhat susceptible to leaf miner. The simplest cure for this disfiguring of the leaves is to cut the plant down; the new leaves will be fresh and unblemished.

There are many columbines to try. Select them from seed lists but view the results skeptically; they are notorious for interbreeding, and very often the results, though interesting and attractive, are not what is expected. NG]

Arabis

The crucifers flower early. The perennial Candytuft and the Kew wallflower, *Cheiranthus kewensis,* bloom all through mild winters in protected places, and when the seeds are sown soon enough in the fall, the little annual violet cress, *Ionopsidium acaule,* blooms along with them. Aubrieta blooms early in the spring.

The wall rock-cress, *Arabis caucasica,* is not far behind. Though the last is one of the plants Elsie Hassan describes as "tough for the driest and sunniest spots," it is one that I never could keep in my garden in Raleigh. It is easy enough in spring, but it always melted away by the end of the summer, and in fall I would buy new plants. I never like to be without arabis, for it blooms both early and long. I have had it as early as January, and this year it bloomed from the middle of February until the first of May. It thrives in any soil, even a poor one, and is a good thing to plant on a dry wall, where the trailing mats of hoary leaves and white flowers show to advantage, but it should be sheared as soon as the bloom is over. The double form, *A. c.* 'Flore Pleno,' is even daintier than the type, and there is a pink-flowered sort too, *A. c.* 'Coccinea' but these are much less robust.

I have tried many of the other species of arabis that are available and have found only one that is satisfactory in this climate.

This is *A. procurrens,* also a very early bloomer and a good carpeter, spreading very quickly but not so much as to be a nuisance.

[Thus far I am succeeding with *A. ferdinandi-coburgii,* an early-flowering species from Bulgaria. The straight species has rosettes of green leaves that turn a dark bronze color with the winter sun; however, the real beauty is in the variegated form, which has vividly contrasting wide stripes of green and white on the leaves. It bloomed last winter in February and seems able to withstand any amount of cold.

A. sturii has been with me now for several years. It is growing just in front of a greenhouse and is similar to *A. procurrens* except that it spreads much more slowly. NG]

Arenaria

[This is a genus worth exploring. Many of the species have needle-like leaves, and most, but not all, have white flowers. The one that has done best for me is *A. montana,* which has dark green foliage and white flowers. It spreads nicely and makes a fine show in spring. I am growing it in light shade in well-drained soil and suspect that these are two essential requirements. NG]

Arisaema

[There are so many interesting and sometimes beautiful aroids that it is worth trying them all. One of the fascinating characteristics of arisaemas is their ability to change sex depending on their age or the previous year's growing conditions. Most are suited to the woodland garden with or without rocks. Our native *A. triphyllum* generally has two large leaves subdivided into three leaflets. The hooded flowers often have stripes of dark maroon or purple and red berries when the plants are mature.

There are several Asian species which grow successfully, and I am trying them all as I find them. *A. consanguineum* comes up each year but hasn't produced its green, white, and purple spathes yet. *A. candidissimum* will in time have white or palest pink spathes. I am expecting yellow from the small *A. flavum,* green and white from *A. japonicum,* and maroon-and-white stripes from *A. sikokianum.* NG]

Armeria

[Armerias are easy-to-please perennials for well-drained, sunny sites. Their narrow, needlelike leaves are arranged in a dense mat, above which rise stalks with heads of white or pink flowers to two and a half feet. The smallest of these are the best to look for. *A. maritima* comes in many colors and forms; there are cultivar names, but none are listed in *Hortus*. I am growing a lovely white one called 'Alba,' the straight pink species, and a delightful darker pink form, 'Merlin.' The darkest form I have now is *A. m.* 'Dusseldorf Pride' with nearly red flowers. The smallest member of this genus which has been with me for longer than a year is *A. setacea*. It has remained less than three inches high and has rose-pink flowers and a long bloom period. NG]

Arrhenatherum

I had from Elsie Hassan *A. elatius bulbosum,* a low form of the tall oat grass. She said that her mother had brought the tubers from California. There are few more decorative foliage plants of small size. Mrs. Hassan says it always makes her think of clean cotton-print dresses, crisp and cool. The short spears of the foliage, not more than eight inches long, are neatly striped in cream and bright green. She says that it does well in light shade, or in full sun with sufficient moisture, and that it needs water in very dry weather. So far it has done very well for me in a light soil that is poor and dry and with afternoon shade. We have had such rainy summers since it came to me that I have never had to water it. So many of the striped grasses are such rampers and so untidy in habit that I would hesitate to recommend them, but this is tidy and restrained and charmingly fresh in winter as well as in summer. It is increased by division, but left to itself it spreads very slowly.

Artemisia

A. schmidtiana 'Nana' is like a fine silver moss that is curly and soft to the touch. Unfortunately this Japanese species fares poorly in the South, and I have been trying some of our own natives of the western plains. *A. frigida* is as beautiful as the Japanese wormwood, though not so small and compact, and it is much more likely to prosper. It is readily increased by division, and it is a good plan to keep some new plants coming on. The plants can be pinched in early summer to keep them tidy, but if they are allowed to bloom, the stalks should be left to wither. I cut some back last summer when they became discolored in the late heat, and all of them died. Fortunately, one plant was neglected, and I have it for next year. The same thing happened to the sagebrush, *A. tridentata,* a delightful local form that gets to be only thirty inches tall and is therefore much more suited to the rock garden than the taller kind that is typical. The foliage of these two wormwoods was particularly good during a very trying winter. Two other small ones from Claude Barr have got off to a slow start: *A. filifolia,* the sand sage with leaves like gray threads, and *A. cana,* a stiff little shrub similar to sagebrush. These grow to two or three feet, but I should think it would take a long time for them to do so.

The beautiful southernwood, *A. abrotanum,* is rather bulky for the rock garden, even in its dwarf form. *A. camphorata* grows only to two feet and is prostrate in habit. Its foliage is finer and more persistent, and it has a wonderfully clean and refreshing scent. It is supposed to smell like camphor, but to me it has the delightful aroma associated with comfort for all childhood ills.

Southernwood is called old man, and *A. stellerana* is called old woman. Mrs. Chalfin introduced another hoary one, *A. borealis* (now *A. campestris* subsp. *borealis*), which she called old lady. It is an evergreen species with delicate foliage a little over a foot in height.

Rock gardeners should be warned against the Roman wormwood, *A. pontica:* "Here is your Roman wormwood," Mrs. Chalfin wrote, "but I don't know what you want with it." I did want it, however (though I had to begin digging it up as soon as I had set it out, as it is a rapid spreader), for it is the best behaved of the gray-leaved plants in summer. Sometimes it looks well until midwinter. When it gets to be unsightly it can be cut back to the ground. In the spring fresh, feathery new foliage appears and makes a thick mat about a foot high. It can be kept under control easily—for the roots are shallow—unless it is allowed to get into a rock wall. Then it can be eradicated only by tearing the wall apart.

Artemisias like a light, poor soil, full sun, and, above all, perfect drainage.

[Though there are not many of the beautiful gray-leaved artemisias that are happy in the hot, humid summers, *A. maritima* proved itself to be a drought-resistant shrublet during a bad summer. The finely dissected leaves retained there freshness all year. There are others we can grow, but they are all larger and better suited to a perennial border. NG]

Arum

[Many arums will grow well in the South in shaded rock gardens or woodland areas. The showiest by far is *A. italicum,* with bold leaves which appear in early fall and remain throughout the most severe winter. In spring the flowers are dramatic with broad, translucent spathes and yellow spadices. In early summer the leaves disappear, leaving only a stalk of berries which will be red by fall. *A. i.* 'Marmoratum' is similar but with yellow to greenish white variegation on the leaves. *A. i.* 'Albispathum' has white spathes, as the name suggests.

A. creticum has thus far surprised me by proving itself hardy during the past two years. It produces its leaves in the fall, and the flowers, which have not yet appeared for me, are fragrant and pale yellow.

I am growing *A. dioscoridis,* which is strangely beautiful with vile-smelling black-spotted spathes.

A. maculatum is better known in England as lords-and-ladies. It is even hardier than *A. italicum,* perhaps because it waits until spring to send up its leaves and inflorescences. The ones I am growing have unspotted leaves and, I suspect, are the cultivar 'Immaculatum.' The red fruits are poisonous.

A. pictum is an autumn-flowering species which produces its leaves in the spring. Thus far it hasn't bloomed for me, but I am expecting maroon spathes and a black-purple spadix. NG]

Aruncus

[*A. aethusifolius* is a Korean species which is perfect for a shaded location. It produces dark green, finely dissected leaves and short, white, upright panicles of flowers in early summer. NG]

Asarum

[All of the gingers are wonderful. There is something about having to search for the little brown juglike flowers at the base of the leaves that makes finding them exciting. There is some dispute over whether or not they should be classified into two genera: *Asarum* and *Hexastylis;* I will leave them all together as asarums. The deciduous native *A. canadense* has relatively large, medium green leaves and maroon flowers in late spring. It spreads rapidly when happy, and the welcome self-sown seedlings often appear in unexpected places. Other native North American species include *A. arifolium,* which has lightly variegated, somewhat elongated leaves. There is even a form with a stoloniferous habit. The many forms of *A. virginicum* have heart-shaped leaves often marbled with silver. One of the most beautiful is *A. shuttleworthii,* with striking patterns of variegation that look as if they are etched onto the leaves. The diminutive form with bright white variegated leaves and a stoloniferous habit is *A. s.* 'Callaway.' One of the best leaf forms is *A. minor,* which has large leaves overlaid with patterns of silver. The best-flowering form in my garden is *A. speciosum,* which has large flowers held three to four inches high. The European ginger, *A. europaeum,* has a pleasantly spreading character and shiny evergreen leaves. There are many Asian species, most of which have not yet become available but all of which are worth searching for. *A. nipponicum* has dark, somewhat oval-shaped, evergreen leaves. The first one to bloom is *A. faurei* with small flowers close to the ground; I had it for two years before it vanished. NG]

Astilbe
[I have just about given up on all of the astilbes as too difficult to please in drought conditions. There are two, however, which will survive. *A. chinensis pumila* blooms during the summer with pinkish mauve flowers above a mat of finely dissected leaves. This variety spreads in a pleasant way given some shade and sufficient moisture. I have succeeded with it in a very stony site with high shade provided by a white oak. It remains less than a foot high even at the peak of bloom. The Japanese species, *A. simplicifolia,* has deeply lobed leaves and white flowers less than one foot high. There is also a pink hybrid, *A. s.* 'Rosea.' NG]

Aubrieta
A. deltoidea, the purple rock cress, has bloomed for me as early as January. It looks like a smaller, daintier arabis in leaf and flower,

except that the colors are tints and shades between violet and a rosy red. This does well on a wall and is not choosy as to soil, but it must be well drained. Some shade is recommended for the South, but not the shade of trees, and I have read that it responds to lime. After flowering, some attention with the shears is advisable to encourage new growth in the center of the plant.

Begonia

B. grandis (formerly *B. evansiana*), the Chinese hardy begonia, can be grown outside with protection as far north as New York. It will grow anywhere, even in deep shade, though its preference is for part shade, humus, a rich soil, and moisture. In the South it may need restraint once it is established, but this is not difficult. It is not a conventional rock plant, but where bold foliage can be used to advantage it is invaluable for summer bloom in shady places. The translucent flowers, of the delicate color called hermosa pink, are produced in abundance from July on into the fall. Bulblets are supposed to bloom the first year from seed, but they have never done so for me, and even the divisions that I have planted take several years to establish themselves before flowering well. In the meantime there are the handsome leaves to enjoy—they are the usual begonia platter, green on top and wine red beneath, and some of them as much as nine inches long.

['Alba,' the rare and lovely white form of *B. grandis*, is another choice for a woodland planting. It is not as vigorous as the pink ones, nor is it pure white, but it is a fine plant for part to full shade and is just as hardy as the pink form. The underside of the leaves is pale olive with attractively contrasting veins of kidney red.

I recently added the Chinese species, *B. sinensis*. It appears to be a slighter plant and without the usual red under the leaves. It is too soon to declare that it will be as good as *B. grandis,* but I have hopes for it. NG]

Bellis

[Spring just wouldn't be right without a few patches of *B. perennis* (ann.). I have yet to get one through the summer, despite the perennial implication of the name; however, they bloom occasionally during warm spells in the winter and without fail in spring. It is best to sow seeds in August and transplant them into the garden in the fall. These daisies are considered pests in England, where they have naturalized into lawns; however, I believe that is impossible here. Grow them and expect to see white or rose flowers in spring on plants about three to six inches high. There is a cultivar known as 'Monstrosa' which lacks the delicacy of the true wild type. NG]

Bletilla

B. *striata* (sometimes offered as B. *hyacinthina*) is a terrestrial orchid brought to England from China in 1802 that seems never to have been appreciated in our gardens, although it has every good quality that a plant can have. It is said to be hardy under all conditions and came to me from California. There it blooms from March through June, but in Raleigh not until the middle of April—or in late seasons not until May. There are usually six or eight winged flowers in racemes on stiff, wiry stems about twelve inches tall. The segments are the translucent red violet that I think of as amethyst but is sometimes called phlox purple. The upper three stand over the lip like a hood. The lip is edged with a ruffle of true purple, and the lower lobe is pleated in the most intricate manner and marked with dots and dashes. The scapes reach nearly to the tips of the wide, pleated leaves, which are narrowed at both ends.

This hardy orchid needs half shade or full sun and is at its best in moist soil. I find that it endures drought extremely well but blooms better the next season if it is well watered when the summer is dry. Although a light loam is preferable, it has done very well in stiff clay. The soil should be one-half leaf mold or peat, and a topdressing of old manure is not amiss. The rhizomes should be planted in the late fall three inches deep. Bletilla is much easier to grow than any of our native orchids—in fact, it is one of the easiest rock plants and seems to present no problems. The clumps may not bloom freely until they become established, but they improve with the years. I have read that frequent division is advisable, but my advice is to leave them alone. If they must be divided, the time to do it is after they have bloomed.

The white form is one of the most snowy and delicate flowers in the rock garden. Sometimes the flowers are pure white, and sometimes they have a violet sheen.

[Bletillas are now available in the East; We-Du Nurseries offers several species and forms, and I have found them packaged at the old Farmers' Exchange in Durham, North Carolina, along with other "bulbs" imported from Holland. *B. ochracea* is a newly introduced Chinese species with yellow flowers and slender leaves. There is also a white cultivar, 'Alba,' of *B. striata,* and one with variegated leaves. I have acquired a new hybrid of *B. ochracea* × *B. striata* which will be exciting to watch. At a recent meeting of the Piedmont Chapter of the American Rock Garden Society the consensus was that bletillas grow best in full sun, so that is where the new ones will be grown. NG]

Brachycome

[*B. iberidifolia* (ann.), the Swan River daisy, is an attractive Australian plant which blooms all summer long in a sunny location. The flowers may be blue, rose, or white and are about an inch in diameter. *Hortus* says that the plants may grow to one and a half feet, but usually they are much shorter. NG]

Brimeura

The alpine hyacinth, *B. amethystinus* (formerly *Hyacinthus amethystinus*), blooms in early May. The color varies from bright blue through pale blue to white. They are sweet and dainty; mine were white with fine blue lines on the petals. They bring to a close the season of the small spring-flowering bulbs and come before the summer ones have well begun. This is an easy bulb to grow in the woodsy soil of a shady rock garden. I have had it for some years, and it is said to be long-lived.

Brodiaea

The brodiaeas are western American bulbs named for a Scotsman, James Brodie. Carl Purdy divides them into two classes: the harvest brodiaeas, a late-flowering group which requires full sun, and the earlier woodlanders, which do better with light shade. The first group is showier, and I have found them on the whole more tractable. Of these, *B. coronaria* (usually listed as *B. grandiflora*) is my favorite and the best species of all for the garden. It likes moisture and heavy clay but has bloomed for me for years in dry, sandy soil. The stems are short (not over twelve inches), and the wide umbel of

violet, campanulalike flowers has a metallic sheen. The season is May
—sometimes early in the month, and sometimes late—and lasts but
two weeks. *B. capitata* (now *Dichelostemma pulchellum*), flowering
in March in California and from late March to mid-April with me,
is the earliest species. Louise Beebe Wilder reports it for May, and
B. coronaria for late June, so this will give you some idea of how the
season varies in various parts of the country. *D. pulchellum* is one of
the woodland group. To me its half-open, dull violet umbels are not
attractive.

There seems to be some doubt as to the hardiness of brodiaeas in
the North, but there are reports of established plantings as far north
as Massachusetts, and I should think any gardener would be willing
to take a chance on a few, for they are cheap and easy and would
probably bloom for a season or so even if they did not persist. They
can also be grown in pots, but personally I should not think them
showy enough for house flowers. Most of them belong in the rock
garden or among the wildflowers.

Bulbocodium

[*B. vernum* is a fine rock garden plant. It produces pinkish-violet
flowers in early spring similar to a colchicum and is handy. NG]

Calanthe

I have made two attempts at *C. striata*, the golden orchid, which
is said to be as hardy as bletilla, and in California as easy to grow.
Evidently it is not as easily established in North Carolina, but a little
plant has come through the winter and still presents two rather pa-
thetic leaves. This is a Japanese species recommended for light shade
in well-drained, sandy soil enriched with leaf mold and cow manure.

[*C. sieboldii* bloomed beautifully the first year I had it but produced only leaves the following spring. *C. discolor*, a Japanese species,
is also hardy and produces brownish flowers with white or pale-pink
lips. Both of these orchids are growing in high shade in a woodland
garden. NG]

Callirhoe

[The native poppy mallow, *C. involucrata*, is one of the brightest
spots in the summer garden. Vivid wine-red, cuplike flowers are

produced for a long time from late spring on. They require full sun and good drainage but are remarkably drought tolerant, probably because of their large, tuberous taproots. NG]

Campanula

There is only one low-growing bellflower that I have ever been able to establish in my garden. I have tried countless others, but except for the Serbian harebell, *C. poscharskyana,* none remain for more than a season or two or three. This is a very pretty one and extremely useful for shade. With me it has never persisted in the open, but Robert Moncure describes it as growing in Alexandria, Virginia, in dry soil in the sun and in moist places in the shade, and as blooming all summer and fall when it is cut back. Here it blooms for about a month, beginning late in April or early in May, and once again after the shearing. The shearing is needed for form as well as for flowers, for this harebell is rather sprawling if left untended. The flowers are large—an inch and a half across—and shaped like stars. They are lavender violet with white at the center. The pretty leaves are rounded, sharply toothed, and evergreen. The plant spreads quickly and is a good one for a garden where there is space to be filled. Pamela Harper of Seaford, Virginia, recommends *C. p.* 'Elizabeth Frost,' a nice gray white form.

   C. elatines garganica is a form of *C. elatines* that takes its name from Mount Gargan in Italy. It is like the Serbian bellflower in the shape and color of the flower and the shape of the leaf, but it is smaller in every part and a much more charming rock plant. It blooms at the end of May. This I have never been able to keep, though I have planted it many times, both in sun and in shade and in various parts of the garden. *C. portenschlagiana* (sometimes listed by its old name, *C. muralis*) lasted longer when planted in the shade. It has flowers of the same lavender violet as *C. e. garganica,* but they are shaped like little bells. The impermanence of these two in my garden need not discourage other gardeners. Once in the middle of May I found both in bloom in Mrs. Godbey's garden in Greensboro, North Carolina, and from the way they wreathed the boulders that they were planted among I knew that they had been there a long time, for like most good things, they grow slowly. Mrs. Godbey's was one of the prettiest and most individual gardens that I have ever seen. I saw it only once, long ago, but often when some flower that grew there reminds me, I find my mind's eye entering the gap in the garden wall, admiring again the carved bench directly opposite, and turning across the wide grass panel to the carefully laid stone steps that led to the rock garden. In the wall, on either side of the steps, were the campanulas. They were glowing in the morning sun, and I expect that the size of the stones that they covered had something to do with their well-being, giving the stems a dry surface to trail over and the roots a long, cool run. I have also found *C. portenschlagiana* in bloom in Virginia in May and in the North Carolina mountains in August. These three bellflowers come from the mountains of the Adriatic region. They need sharp drainage and flourish in a light, gritty soil with some lime in it. All are deep rooted and should be left undisturbed once they have taken hold.

The harebell, *C. rotundifolia,* is so widespread in Europe, Asia, and North America that I am sure that there should be a form for every garden. It has not had a fair trial in my garden because it has only recently appeared, taken hold, and bloomed. I think it must have come as a stowaway from some of the western nurseries. It appeared this spring and bloomed at the end of June. I have seen it blooming in Raleigh as late as November. The little round leaves make a bright carpet beneath the high, swaying bells of methyl violet. One of the English names for the harebell is lady's thimble, and it would be only a real lady with tapered fingertips who could wear one. The stems are as fine as fine thread and so elastic that they rise again when trodden on—or so Jane Loudon says; I have never tried it. Scott bears her out in his description of Ellen in *The Lady of the Lake.*

> A foot more light, a step more true,
> Ne'er from the heath-flower dash'd the dew;
> E'en the slight hare-bell raised its head
> Elastic from her airy tread.

In most gardens the Carpathian harebell, *C. carpatica,* is the easiest of rock plants, and Elizabeth Rawlinson could never understand why it would not grow in mine. She gave me both the white and the blue forms, and they bloomed once in July but never again. I have tried plants from the nurseries, too, with no better success.

Carex

[Doug Ruhren of Durham, North Carolina, says that there are several members of this genus worthy of a place in any lightly shaded garden. *Carex conica* 'Variegata' is a lovely form only six to eight inches high with green leaves edged with white. *C. morrowii* 'Aurea-Variegata' is one of the most beautiful, graceful plants in the garden. The plants grow to about one foot, and the swirl of pale yellow and green leaves are splendid against a dark background. One of the most vigorous of the carices is *C. glauca,* a species with blue gray foliage. This one is stoloniferous and should be watched carefully lest it overwhelm smaller, slower-growing plants. *C. plantaginea* has a subtle beauty. It forms clumps up to twelve inches high of broad spring green leaves with a delightful seersucker texture. *C. siderosticta* 'Variegata' may not be the proper name for a beautiful green-and-white-striped sedge with wide leaves. It is at its most beautiful in the spring and summer. *C. stricta* 'Bowles Golden' is a lovely golden-yellow plant which will brighten a dark spot. NG]

Cerastium

[It is with some hesitation that I recommend *C. tomentosum,* for in some gardens it is considered too invasive to admit. But we have a problem finding gray-leaved plants where the summers are long and hot, and this one is lovely with its mats of silver foliage and masses of white flowers in spring. It is an excellent contrast to *Geranium sanguineum,* and they have intermingled in my rock garden, much to my delight. NG]

Chionodoxa

These are not bulbs to be cherished as individual flowers, but they rate a doxology when planted in quantity. The gentian blue of *C. sardensis* is a telling color, especially in contrast to the well-defined white star in the center. The spikes are comparatively small. In some places this species blooms early, and I have found it in flower on February 9.

C. luciliae, now more properly called *C. siehei,* has light blue-violet flowers which are large enough to cover a fifty-cent piece. They bloom in my garden with great regularity about the tenth of March. Every spring I look for the bits of blue that return so faithfully in shady corners and between the roots of trees, but I have never had room to plant them as they should be planted and as I saw them at Duke University in a solid bank of blue. There are also white and pink forms of this species, among them one called 'Pink Giant' with large, bright flowers on tall stems.

Chrysogonum

[*C. virginianum,* a constantly blooming native plant, is fine for southern rock gardens or for anyplace where bright, golden-yellow flowers can be appreciated. It is accommodating and will thrive in sun or shade and bloom from the first warmth of spring until the winter curbs its cheerful display. There are many sorts, two of which are *C. virginianum australe,* which is compact with shorter stems and a tighter growth habit, and *C. v. virginianum,* which spreads more rapidly. Their common names, pots-of-gold and green-and-gold, are delightfully descriptive. NG]

Claytonia

[Spring-beauty, *C. virginica,* gives a promise of spring just as winter begins, for often the first leaves are out by the end of November. The narrow, dark maroon foliage is easily missed, for it lies close to the ground throughout the winter. From the base arise stems with several white or pink flowers with pink stripes in early spring. They require only a bit of sunlight to open widely their delicate flowers, which close as the shadows fall. They grow from a cormlike root and are dormant for the summer and most of the fall, but they will spread readily when given moisture and part sun or light shade. *C. caroliniana* blooms earlier and has larger leaves. NG]

Collinsia

[*C. verna* (ann.) is a new plant for me, but it came from friends in Charlotte who assured me that it would be a permanently reseeding addition to the woodland spring garden. Better known as blue-eyed mary, I am expecting to see flowers that are bright blue with white or purple lips. I received plants with seeds last spring and watched them die, but I have been delighted to find lots of seedlings germinating now in November when the mean temperature is getting lower and the days are shortening. NG]

Cooperia

It seems strange that *C. pedunculata* and *C. drummondii*, the prairie lilies of Texas and Mexico, bear the name of an English gardener, Joseph Cooper. They are among the easiest and most satisfactory of garden bulbs, hardy to northern Virginia to my certain knowledge and said to be hardy except in the far North, where they can be stored over winter. They are planted at a depth of four inches in the South and six inches in the North. With me the red-tipped buds begin to appear about the end of April, and they continue at intervals throughout the summer, especially after showers. They open wide into pure white lilies late in the afternoon, perfume the night, and last for most of the next day, sometimes longer. The stems are six to eight inches, with a single flower to a stem. They are not choosy as to soil and do well in rather poor places, although those in the shade have never bloomed.

Corydalis

[Almost all of the species of this genus are worth trying. *C. lutea* is practically everblooming, beginning early in the spring and continuing until late fall. The racemes of golden-yellow flowers are beautiful against the blue-green foliage. There is also a white form which breeds true. Similar but with creamy white flowers and even bluer leaves is *C. ochroleuca*. *C. bulbosa* makes a brief but welcome appearance each spring, producing lovely lilac blue or purple flowers. It then retreats underground for the remainder of the year. The beautiful blue-foliaged *C. wilsonii* is not hardy, and *C. pallida* is something of a pest, although it can be attractive when grown against a tree trunk. *C. sempervirens* has proven itself to be a hardy annual for me, but it is worth growing for its beautiful blue-green foliage and pink-and-yellow flowers in the summer. *C. rutifolia* also appears faithfully each spring in the rock garden, producing attractive red-purple flowers and then disappearing until the next year. *C. cheilanthifolia* has finally come to my garden, and thus far the finely dissected leaves have added a delicacy similar to that of some ferns. They are all desirable plants for partly shaded sites with adequate moisture. NG]

Crocus

If all species of crocus were available and could be grown in one garden, there would be bloom from midsummer to late spring. On the whole, crocuses are easy to grow. They flourish in ordinary loam, demanding only that it be light and well drained. In general the corms should be planted three or four inches deep, but the depth will vary because the corms vary greatly in size. Most species are sun lovers, although I have found that a number do well under trees.

C. banaticus is an elusive late-flowering species, formerly known as *C. byzantinus* or *C. iridiflorus*. It is a distinct species because the sharply reflexed outer segments give the flower the appearance of a fleur-de-lis. The unusually broad leaves lack the center line of silver that is characteristic of the genus. It is easy to grow in moist, cool, woodland soil.

C. laevigatus ends the year in my garden, with bloom beginning in December and lingering through the first weeks of the new year. Once a single corm produced eight or ten flowers between mid-December and late January. The first flowers were a little marred by sleet, but on sunny days they came out with springlike freshness, even when there was a skim of ice on the pool. The flowers of this species vary from white to pale lilac. The blossoms of variety *fontenayi* are small cups of gray violet; the inner segments are pale mauve, the outer ones ageratum violet with precise feathering of a darker tone on the outside. They are lighted from within by the golden throat and style. Along with the flowers come the very fine, grassy leaves that mature in the spring. The corms of this lovely species should be planted in full sun with sandy loam and lime.

C. longiflorus, formerly known as *C. odorus* because of its delightful fragrance, usually blooms in November, but sometimes there are flowers in October.

C. medius needs a sunny but protected spot and light soil. It blooms well in November and December. The lovely mauve flowers have enough substance to withstand frost, but even if they are killed, more buds appear when the cold spell is over.

C. niveus, the snowy crocus, is one of the first to bloom, with flowers that are pure white except for the pale yellow throat, deep chrome anthers, and orange style.

C. pulchellus, a floriferous species, blooms early and long. Buds appear continually from the first days of October to well into November. Pale, translucent petals of a grayish tint that is on the blue side of violet, with delicate lines of dark blue, cup the cream-colored anthers and the orange style. The throat is deep yellow. Because the flowers are almost tubeless, the thick clusters seem to lie on the ground. The corms should be planted in full sun in a sheltered part of the garden.

C. speciosus flowers seem very tall because of their long perianth tubes. The color is described as lilac blue but is really a tint of pure violet. This year it was perfection, blooming the first two weeks of October, after weeks of rain, and during an interval of clear, cool weather. The buds are gray and slender, and the flowers never open out flat. The corms should be set six inches deep in good leafy loam in the shade; it even likes to be near water. The flowers of the cultivar 'Aitchisonii' are pale violet and appear early in October. The cultivar 'Cassiope' has even larger ones that are a pale, almost luminous, tint of violet lit by a pale yellow throat and scarlet style. The wisteria-violet flowers of the cultivar 'Globosus' are more egg-shaped than round.

C. kotschyanus is usually the first to blossom in my garden, putting in an appearance late in September and often blooming on into November. After six years, five corms had traveled from one end of my Raleigh rock garden to the other. The flowers vary from the rosy lilac of the type to a pure white, but all have the golden zone at the throat making them look as if they were lighted from within. The species is recommended for full sun, but it does well under the high branches of oak trees, or even under pines. I think it would grow almost anywhere.

The spring-flowering crocuses should begin as the fall-flowering ones depart, directly after Christmas. In favorable seasons they do, but there are years when we have continuous cold at this time, and then there may be an interval of several weeks between the autumnal and vernal species.

C. ancyrensis, a sun-loving crocus from Ankara, is advertised as the earliest of all. The flowers are charming and numerous. When open they look like small gold coins spilled on the bare ground.

C. biflorus subsp. *biflorus,* the Scotch crocus, is one of the oldest and best known of the species. There are many forms, but the type is white, the outer petals buff on the reverse with three distinct lines of dark purple. The flowers are fragrant. This species blooms about the middle of February and can be planted in light soil under trees.

C. chrysanthus appears in gardens in many forms, and among these are found some of the best of the early-flowering sorts. E. A. Bowles raised a group which he named for birds. 'Snow Bunting' is the first to bloom. I think if I could have only one spring-flowering crocus, it would be this. The first pearly bud often opens in the middle of January, and the flowering continues for about six weeks. The snowy flowers are tightly furled when the weather is dreary, but the sun brings them out as fresh as ever, even when the temperature drops to freezing at night. The fragrance is delightful, strong, and musk-like. The flowers of 'Canary Bird' are not canary colored but deep yellow with brown outside. I think 'Oriole' would be a better name. 'E. A. Bowles,' raised by Van Tubergen and considered the best of all, has flowers of a wonderful clear yellow. It usually blooms a little later than 'Snow Bunting.'

C. etruscus has large, scentless flowers that are lavender within with a yellow throat and gray outside with a satin sheen and a few delicate feathers of dark purple. They are characteristically globe shaped. A cultivar named 'Zwanenburg,' has lilac-blue flowers. This species prefers a rich, heavy soil and full sun.

C. flavus subsp. *flavus* has a flower that is all pure gold—petals, stamens, and style. When I saw the flowers for the first time, I thought that they glowed as if there was a light inside. The color is variable, ranging from primrose and pale apricot yellow to a golden tone. This is a fine species—fragrant, floriferous, and long blooming. The buds push ahead of the leaves, which make little growth until the flowers fade. The corms may be planted in a sunny place or in the shade of deciduous trees.

C. fleischeri is said to be preferred to all others by the bees, but I notice that the bees arrive with the first crocus of spring, for above each little patch there is the humming sound of summer. The flowers are small but numerous and look as if a breath would chill them, but they stand up sturdily to the frosts of early February. The fine scarlet style, the pale yellow throat, and some inconspicuous dark wine markings on the outside do not detract from the fragile whiteness of the narrow, pointed petals. Pale, threadlike leaves come up with the buds but make little progress until after the flowers fade. The netted corms are tiny, round, and golden. They should be planted in a sunny place.

C. korolkowii blooms cheerfully under the pine trees in January
—sometimes at the first of the month. The flowers are small, delicate, and very fragrant, cadmium yellow within, bronze without,
and burning with a metallic luster.

C. olivieri subsp. *balansae,* from Smyrna, sometimes blooms in
January. The flowers are small and numerous, deep orange within
and bronze without.

C. sieberi has bloomed each January, coming a little earlier each
season until it reached the first day of the new year. In Raleigh I have
found the small mauve flowers the day after Christmas, hugging the
ground for protection against the elements. Even after sleet storms
they return with the sun, looking as delicately fresh and perishable
as ever, the silvery tone of the petals lighted by the golden throat
and scarlet style. The comparatively wide, dark green leaves come up
with the buds.

C. susianus, a robust and free-seeding species, I have planted by
itself where the path takes a turn and where in February the deep yellow stars light the whole section when the flowers are open. When
they are closed, the brown-striped buds make a strong pattern of
their own. The yellow crocuses are so garish that to me it seems
better to plant them a little distance apart, leaving the softer yellow
of the aconite to accompany the lavender kinds.

C. tommasinianus is my favorite species and seems to be everyone
else's favorite, too. It thrives in all kinds of soil and in all climates.
It is very wayward in its blooming, which may take place at any
time between the middle of January and the first of March. The frail
blossoms are silver gray in the bud and variations of red-violet in
the open flower: from the palest tint of lilac to the deepest tone of
hyacinth violet, often darker at the tips of the petals, which are so
thin in texture as to be almost transparent. The flickering color is
delightful in the pale sunlight of late winter and early spring, and as
soon as the sun stops shining the petals are furled again into thin
silver spears. This must be the most prolific of all species. There
are some superb selected cultivars, including 'Ruby Giant,' 'Taplow
Ruby,' and 'Whitewell Purple,' all of which have dark flowers.

[*C. corsicus* in the garden gives two effects from one flower. When
the petals are tightly folded, you see a buff-colored petal beautifully
feathered with dark purple, and when the sun causes the flower to

open, the lilac purple interior gives no hint of the former view. It is excellent and easy to please under deciduous trees where it will have enough winter sun to bloom properly.

C. *minimus* has the same ability to transform itself and is similar in every way. The primary difference apparent to gardeners, rather than botanists, is that this is the smaller of the two species. This is an exquisite crocus for late-winter bloom. NG]

Cuthbertia

[For well-drained, sunny locations C. *rosea graminea* provides bright pink flowers throughout most of the summer. The grasslike foliage is a good foundation for the many three-petaled flowers. It is said to prefer sandy soil, and this may be its first choice; however, I have been pleased with its performance in my heavier clay loam. NG]

Cyclamen

[Although often grouped with bulbs, cyclamen grow from tubers rather than bulbs or corms. They are appropriate for partly shaded, stony sites and thrive in the dry summers that have become increasingly frequent. The flowers, which resemble shooting stars, have their petals flung back, revealing the stigma in a few species. It is this same characteristic which distinguishes the cyclamineus narcissus.

C. *balearicum* is hardy enough for North Carolina's winters, which was a splendid surprise. This is a spring-flowering species for shade. In February the pink-tinged white flowers appear with the exquisite gray leaves.

C. *cilicium* bridges the gap between the fall- and winter-blooming species. The dark red-violet, pink, or white flowers are smaller and more delicate than those of C. *hederifolium,* and in many ways this is a pleasant relief. The spoon-shaped leaves are as variable as those of most species, and the urge to collect the different patterns is hard to resist. I have found this to be a relatively short-lived plant but permanent in the garden because of the readily germinated seeds. It grows best among tree roots where summer moisture is scarce and where sunshine is abundant after the leaves have fallen.

C. *coum* will bloom during any mild spell throughout the winter. This is a difficult species to sort out, because of the variability as well as many patterns of similarities. Taxonomists generally agree that there are two subspecies. *C. coum* subsp. *coum* occurs in the western regions of Turkey and has smaller flowers and more rounded leaves. *C. coum* subsp. *caucasicum* occurs in the East, blooms earlier, and has larger flowers and larger, more heart-shaped, leaves. The flowers may be any shade from white through pink to dark magenta, and it is the last of these which shows up best in the winter landscape.

In spring the pure white or palest pink flowers of *C. creticum* may be found, preferably near a large rock where their roots will go deep in search of cool moisture. The ivy-shaped leaves are mottled green.

C. graecum prefers sun and often grows in exposed situations among rocks in Greece. In this country it blooms best in similar locations. Beginning in August, the magenta pink to nearly white flowers appear with the velvety heart-shaped leaves. The flowers are superficially similar to those of *C. hederifolium,* but the differences are streaks of darker red-violet from the mouth of the flower into the petals, purple anthers, and large fleshy roots.

C. hederifolium is among the easiest of the hardy species to grow. It produces its pink or white, sometimes fragrant, flowers in the fall. The appearance of the extraordinarily variable leaves signals an end of the blooming period. The different leaf forms are worth collecting. Some resemble the ivy which gave the species its name, while others are spear-shaped. Some are almost completely silvered, and occasionally a solid green leaf form can be found.

C. intaminatum is the miniature of the genus, with white or palest pink flowers with fine gray stripes. The round leaves may be green, green with an outline of silver dots, or brightly variegated. It blooms throughout the fall and is most easily viewed on a hillside.

C. mirabile, which is closely related to *C. cilicium,* is an elegant plant with medium mauve to near white flowers. The fimbriated petal tips and small vertical collar at the base of the corolla lobes are two differences between the species, but the most exciting one is the occasional bright pink cast to the young leaves. Unfortunately, this does not appear on all plants.

C. parviflorum, which is very rare, is like a miniature *C. coum* with short, fat flowers, but the violetlike fragrance is astonishing from such a tiny thing. This one wants cool, moist conditions in shade and is extremely hardy. It too blooms throughout the winter.

C. pseudibericum is considered by many to be the most spectacular member of the genus. The large, pink to dark red-violet flowers may appear at any time from Thanksgiving through March along with the brightly variegated leaves. Good drainage and shade are essential for success with this plant, and any effort is worth the result.

C. *purpurascens* blooms all summer, completing the year's cycle. It has a brief period of dormancy, producing new leaves and flowers just as the old ones fade. All of the pink-purple flowers are fragrant, and the leaves are as variable as those of any other species. Give it shade and a well-drained site that doesn't dry out. This is the hardiest of all of the cyclamen. There is a green-leaved form from Czechoslovakia which may sometimes be found listed erroneously as *C. fatrense*. I have read of individual plants of *C. purpurascens* blooming throughout the entire year in cool greenhouses.

C. *repandum* is the easiest of the spring species, with fragrant medium-pink flowers with elegant, twisted, elongated petals. This one must be planted about three inches deep. The leaves begin to appear in February and the flowers throughout March and April, after which the plants recede underground for the remainder of the year.

C. *trochopteranthum*, blooming throughout the winter, has leaves similar to those of *C. cilicium* and flowers most like *C. coum*. All of the ones I have seen have had fragrant pink to medium rose-pink flowers whose petals stand out like propellers. NG]

Delosperma
[This genus of succulent South African plants has proven surprisingly hardy. Two are growing successfully in my garden, and there are many more to be tried. *D. nubigenum* makes a fine ground cover with bright yellow daisylike flowers in late spring. The leaves turn a lovely soft red in the winter. For a longer blooming period, plant *D. cooperi*, with bright red-purple flowers which open with the sun throughout the summer. NG]

Delphinium
Although cold blue delphinium spires in the perennial border are not for the southern garden on the hot, humid days of midsummer, there is still the Chinese larkspur for low-lying rock gardens. The typical *D. grandiflorum*, sometimes listed as *D. chinense,* may grow

too tall for a small rock garden, but there are dwarf forms less than a foot tall. These are not reliably perennial, but they last several years and often reseed. Seed planted in January will produce blooming plants the first year. The colors range from the palest to the deepest blues.

[*D. tricorne,* the North American native, is superb for a woodland garden. Early in the spring the finely cut leaves unfold, and brilliant blue flowers are produced on stems to about one foot in my garden. There is also a white form. It goes dormant when the weather warms but has reappeared in the same place for ten years with a few seedlings nearby. NG]

Dentaria

[At least two species of this genus are happy in a shaded woodland garden, with or without rocks. *D. diphylla* produces its whitish flowers in early spring, goes dormant for the summer, and reappears in the fall with fresh new foliage. *D. laciniata* makes but a brief appearance in spring, with a good display of clusters of pale lilac or white flowers. The latter also spreads quickly through self-sown seedlings. NG]

Deschampsia

[The vivid chartreuse foliage of the tiny (five-inch-tall) grass *D. flexuosa* 'Aurea' makes it one of the most beautiful additions to any garden. I don't understand the common name of crinkled hair grass, but that doesn't lessen my opinion of it. The color intensifies from fall through midspring and is most effective when planted near something with dark foliage, such as the burgundy-leaved forms of *Ajuga reptans*. *A. pyramidalis* 'Metallica Crispa,' with its crimped purple leaves and extremely slow rate of increase, would be my preference over more vigorous ajuga cultivars. NG]

Dianthus

No pinks have ever taken up with me permanently, and few have survived for more than a season. Perhaps this is due to the shade of the trees, for even the sunniest places in my garden are soon reached by the long afternoon shadows. I have experimented with such a multitude of pinks in the past that a list of them would be depressing, and

I shall mention only a few of the easiest kinds. The majority of the species from the Alps of southern Europe are collectors' items that grow with difficulty even under favorable conditions, and it would be a waste of time to struggle with these in regions unfavorable to alpines. Since many pinks are counted as easy and permanent in the southern garden, however, with even less encouragement I would continue to try all species offered, for no garden is complete without their special scent. With a few exceptions they are easily satisfied, relishing lime though not requiring it and demanding only sun and a soil that is well drained and not too rich. Lime rubble, leaf mold, and a gritty medium will suit them perfectly, and I always add a little bonemeal for good measure.

The easiest of all, in most gardens only too easy, are the maiden pinks, *D. deltoides.* Even with me they persist for several seasons, spreading into wide mats and blooming lavishly from midspring to early summer. The earliest date in my records is the twenty-eighth of March. The flowers of the type are rhodamine purple, and there are several color forms in shades of carmine, cerise, and burgundy. All forms, even the white ones, are ringed at the center with a pattern of darker red, and the small scentless flowers are like bits of calico. They have a habit of closing on cloudy days and in the evening.

The frail stems of the maiden pinks rise eight inches or more above the coarse needlelike foliage. Belonging to the same group, but much smaller, daintier, and more compact, is *D. peristeri* (now *D. myrtinervius*). The tiny flowers are rosy purple with darker centers and paler rims. They stand two inches above the fine needles of the foliage. It blooms in April and is among the best for the South.

One of the species that adapts itself most readily to a variety of climates and situations is the sweet old-fashioned cheddar pink, long known as *D. caesius* but now called *D. gratianopolitanus,* which is very trying; but we might as well get used to it, if that is what it is to be called. The spicy, relatively large flowers are tourmaline pink. In the South the cheddar pinks bloom in April.

An especially choice and low-growing pink is *D.* × *arvernensis,* with dense silvery foliage and smaller bright rose flowers. It outlasts the alpine pinks and eventually makes wide mats in the rock garden.

The sand pink, *D. arenarius,* comes from Sweden, and so it is not strange that it does not endure long in the South. However, it is one of my favorites, and from time to time I renew my stock in order to have the pure white, deeply fringed, cinnamon-scented flowers along with the other sorts in April. The foliage is darker than that of most pinks, and this makes the flowers look whiter.

Out of curiosity I had once the yellow pink, *D. knappii,* from western Yugoslavia. Its flowers were rather like skinny sweet william but of a pale, cool, greenish yellow—a lovely and most unusual color. This pink is unusual also because it blooms at the end of May after all of the others. I cannot say that I find it attractive, but it is good to know about in case you need that particular color at that particular time.

In Mrs. Chrismon's garden in Greensboro, North Carolina, I found pinks growing much more thriftily than they grow in mine and heard no complaint of the length of their stay. Her garden is much more open than mine, but the success that she has with these and other rock plants may be due to the difference between Greensboro and Raleigh. One of the other pinks that I particularly like is called *D. petraeus* subsp. *noeanus,* a robust species from the southern parts of Europe and Asia. The large, fringed, sweet-scented, pure white flowers grow ten inches above the densely tufted, bright green mats. They were in full bloom in the middle of May.

[A few excellent plants in this genus can be grown in the South provided the drainage is adequate. Just to have those tufts of silvery blue foliage throughout the winter makes it worth the effort. I have had the best luck growing them in full sun in large iron pots filled with sand and small stones. The narrow, linear leaves and low stature of *D. alpinus* are intensified by the relatively large flowers in many shades from white through pink to crimson. Unfortunately this species is scentless. Similar but smaller in every way is *D. haematocalyx* subsp. *pindicola. D. nitidus* has tufts of narrow, dark green leaves, above which rise stems to one to two feet bearing clusters of bright pink flowers. Many cultivars of *D. plumarius* will persist in spite of our summers, and these are worth collecting. Often the best ones are found in old gardens. There are at least two mule pinks available. These acquired their common name because, in addition to being sterile, they are interspecific hybrids of sweet william (*D. barbatus*) and the clove pink (*D. caryophyllus*). The ones I have grown are *D.* × 'Napoleon III' and *D.* × 'Emile Paré,' both of which are long-blooming plants that aren't as fussy about drainage as the alpines and can tolerate some shade. NG]

Diascia

I first fell in love with *D. barberiae* (ann.), the twinspur, in the garden at Nik-Nar Nursery in Asheville, North Carolina, where it probably grows better than at lower elevations, though I did at last get it to bloom in Raleigh. South African plants do not grow well for me as a rule, but this exquisite annual is worth taking any amount of pains. The small pink flowers are that pure tint of spectrum red which is so desirable and so rare, and the low, spreading plant is of neat habit. I had the best luck with seeds sown in mid-April. The seedlings bloomed by the end of June, and I thought that they lived over a second season, though I could not be sure that the same plants bloomed the next April.

Dicentra

[The dicentras provide lightness to any area with their lacy, often fernlike, leaves, but I find them difficult to please. I have succeeded best with the summer-dormant ones. *D. canadensis,* squirrel corn, is primarily a northeastern species which is moderately happy in rocky woodland soil. Even happier is *D. cucullaria,* Dutchman's-breeches. Both have pendulous white flowers sometimes tinged with pink or yellow. *D. formosa,* from the West Coast, has flowers from white through rose purple. For several years I was able to maintain a good display of the exquisite white form, *D. f.* subsp. *oregana.* The eastern counterpart to this is *D. eximia,* which blooms throughout most of the summer when given adequate moisture. English nurserymen have produced some fine interspecific hybrids that are readily available in this country. They are all worth trying. NG]

Disporum

[The fairy bells are delightful plants for woodland settings. *D. sessile* 'Variegatum' is a spreading form with nicely variegated leaves but also with the ability to move great distances in a single year. *D. flavens* is a showy plant with clear yellow, pendulous flowers up to two feet or more. This plant, recently introduced from Korea, increases with greater restraint. *D. smithii* from the West Coast has lived in my rock garden for about seven years with no sign of a flower. I haven't given up hope yet. NG]

Draba

[Drabas are some of the most delightful tiny plants for experts and beginners alike. Many of them grow in tight mounds and in late winter cover themselves with carpets of bright yellow flowers. Many are true alpines, spending the winters blanketed under snow and the summers in cool, moist, well-drained conditions. There are about three hundred species, so it is worth experimenting to find ones that can tolerate our climate. Scree conditions seem to be essential for their survival. I have been most successful with the eastern native, *D. arabisans,* which produces rosettes of dark green leaves and racemes of white four-petaled flowers in midspring. NG]

Dracocephalum

[*D. rupestre* is a good blue-flowered, low-growing plant with flowers larger than most species in this genus. I planted several clumps at the edge of the aster border in full sun, and then read that it prefers part shade and moist conditions. It bloomed beautifully in the sunny site and came through an intensely hot and dry summer, so I am not tempted to move it. I planted its seeds and will try the seedlings where they can drape themselves over stones. NG]

Dyssodia

[*D. tenuiloba* (ann.), Dahlberg daisies, are delightful, easy-to-grow annuals which aren't slowed by continuous heat or high humidity. They are golden yellow and prefer sandy, well-drained soil in full sun. They bloom all summer long and even into fall and remain less than one foot high. NG]

Epimedium

The barrenworts are entirely satisfactory rock plants for shade, not only growing but thriving in poor soil and enduring the wet summers as well as the dry ones. The delicate little spurred flowers are like tiny columbines, and the pinnate leaves, with pointed oval leaflets of thin but durable texture, keep their spring freshness all through the summer.

E. pinnatum, the Persian species, is a coarse ground cover growing a foot tall and spreading rapidly by stolons. It cannot be allowed
among choice plants, but where there is space to be filled, it makes
a cool sea of green in summer and in spring produces quantities of
delicate floral sprays. *E. × versicolor* 'Sulphureum' has flowers which
are translucent with spurred sepals of a light greenish yellow and
sulfur-colored petals. The sulfur is repeated in the slender, dangling
flowers of the perfoliate bellwort, *Uvularia perfoliata,* which seeds
itself freely in the undisturbed parts of the rock garden. In the fall
the green leaves of the epimedium take on copper tones and are
decorative until they are burned by the severe weather of midwinter.
Then they must be clipped, for otherwise they would hang on until
the new leaves cover them, not only spoiling the effect of the spring
garden but also hiding the fragile flowers and the uncurling leaflets. This clipping must be done before the end of February, for
the flowers come sometime in March, and in early seasons begin to
make their way through the earth the first of the month.

In the hybrid *E. × rubrum* the flowers are of ruby glass and am-
ber. The pale new leaves are shaped like angel wings and piped with
narrow margins of bright red. The plants are the size of the Persian
barrenwort but not so aggressive.

The long-spur barrenwort, *E. grandiflorum,* is a dainty Japanese
species that forms small, compact clumps that spread little, if at all,
and never encroach upon neighbors. In spite of being called *grandiflorum,* the flowers of all forms that I have grown have been smaller
than those of the other species. They are distinguished by tapered
and unusually long spurs, and they vary in color. Those of *E. g.* 'Vio-
laceum' are tinged with lavender gray, and those of *E. × youngianum*
'Roseum' are pink. The cultivar *E. × y.* 'Niveum' is the most beautiful of all, with blossoms of fine white lawn. The leaflets are small,
thin, and pale, and as dainty as the flowers. Many of the epimediums
bloom in April. They will persist in soil that is poor and dry, but
they are at their best only with moisture and humus.

[*E. diphyllum* is one of the smallest of the epimediums, growing
to about six inches. It should be placed near a path so that its dainty
white flowers may be seen peeping from beneath the leaves. It is
one of the later-blooming species and is valuable for prolonging the

season. There is a fine pink form, *E. d.* 'Roseum,' with larger flowers held above the foliage.

E. perralderanum is similar to *E. pinnatum* except that the former has spiny leaf margins and red overtones on the young foliage. It is one of those plants to acquire when you are at the stage where the subtleties of the individual species begin to be noticed. Learning the epimediums is rather like learning the sparrows; they are all remarkably different when you know how to look.

The clump-forming *E. pubigerum* is another good evergreen species. This one has white flowers with purple spots and tiny spurs.

The flowers of the evergreen species *E. sempervirens* are similar in size to those of *E. grandiflorum*; however, in the former they are pure white. The leaves of this species are the best of the genus during the winter.

My favorite epimedium is *E.* × *warleyense*, with coppery orange sepals and yellow spurs. This is a vigorous, rhizomatous plant that has never overwhelmed its neighbors.

We-Du Nurseries offers many species and forms, and Richard Weaver gives excellent descriptions and cultural advice in the catalog. NG]

Eranthis

[*E. hyemalis* and *E. cilicica* are both highly recommended for their early bloom. The latter is a little later and has larger flowers. They are wonderful with their frilly green collars of leaves and bright yellow flowers that open when the sun shines on them. There are many references to sheets of winter aconites in gardens in this country and abroad. The best way to achieve this effect is to collect the seeds as soon as they are ripe and sow them immediately, being careful not to allow them to dry out. They will germinate the following spring and most likely bloom three years later. NG]

Erigeron

I have tried without success a number of fleabanes from the Rocky Mountains and the West Coast. Even the whiplash daisy, *E. flagellaris*, described by Louise Beebe Wilder as a "troublesome spreader," refused to take hold under the most favorable circumstances. But a small plant offered as *E. mucronatus* (now *E. karvinskianus*) spreads at will, without becoming a pest, and blooms throughout the growing season. It is a rather shabby little plant, and certainly not spectacular, but there is something comforting as well as charming in the succession of fragile pink-tinged daisies from early spring until late fall. When the garden is in full bloom it will not be noticed, but in the barren intervals of spring, summer, and fall the finely drawn flowers are like a delicate frosting on the dry stones of the garden steps or the damp flagging in front of the wall fountain. It seems to spread into all corners, whether wet or dry or sunny or dark.

Erinus

[*E. alpinus:* For years I had masses of these tiny plants, which produced pink flowers in such profusion that they completely covered an area about three feet square. They bloomed in early spring and seeded about freely. I found them completely self-sufficient in light shade and stony soil. And then they all disappeared. I have grown them again from seed in hopes of repeating that scene, for I believe their loss was due to being crowded out, and not from climate. NG]

Euphorbia

[*E. myrsinites:* The euphorbias are not happy in my heavy clay soil; however, this evergreen species is the exception. It has beautiful glaucous leaves in whorls along the decumbent stems, which produce masses of yellow flowers at their tips in midspring. It requires a sunny site with good drainage and is best suited if left to seed around and find its own place. NG]

Festuca

Years ago Nannie Holding brought me a clump of blue fescue (known in the trade as *F. ovina glauca*) from her rock garden in Wake Forest, North Carolina. I planted it in the flagged terrace in a cranny where nothing but weeds had ever grown, and it became one of the most favorably commented upon plants in the garden. It is very drought resistant and seems to thrive in poor soil. And besides, the steely eight-inch needles are extremely decorative.

Filipendula

[*F. palmata* 'Nana' is a charming low form of *F. palmata* that wants a moist, shaded site in the rock garden. It is never spectacular but is a fine reliable perennial with short stalks of pink flowers. NG]

Galanthus

I would like to grow every snowdrop I ever heard of. Although I started many years ago to make as complete a collection as possible, I still have only the common sorts, for many are rare and very hard to come by—and difficult to establish as well.

G. *elwesii* is a variable species; the size and earliness of the flowers depend upon the variety. With me it blooms in January in an average winter, and I have even found flowers before the new year. Since there is such a difference of opinion as to its culture, it must matter little whether the bulbs are planted in full sun or part shade, but they do require a rich soil that is well drained and not too dry.

G. *nivalis* has such a wide range, from the Pyrenees to the Caucasus, that the winged flower with its heart-shaped seal of green varies greatly in its season of bloom and in its size and shape. One of the best is the noble subspecies *imperati*, the large-flowered and broad-leaved Neapolitan snowdrop, which has been prized by gardeners since the time of Clusius. Although a southerner itself, it bloomed in my garden only one season before disappearing for good, and I am still seeking to replace it. The form 'Scharlockii' is the one that I have found most dependable. It prospered for more than a decade in a low, damp part of my rock garden in Raleigh. It is not the most spectacular form, but the small, drooping, green-tipped flowers come very early, often in late January. 'Lutescens' and 'Flavescens' are forms with yellow marks on the inner segments, and there is even a double form, 'Flore Pleno.'

The European snowdrop is a woodlander that likes cool soil in damp, shady parts of the garden, but it has lots of Mediterranean relatives that require full sun and sharp drainage, although they like moisture at the roots. G. *reginae-olgae* blooms in the fall with dull green leaves having a pale, nearly white, stripe down the center.

[Most of the bulbs found in catalogs and garden centers are collected from the wild, which is putting this genus into the list of plants in peril. Inquire about the provenance of such plants before purchasing bulbs and thereby encouraging this plunder. Or better yet, try to get a few bulbs from another gardener. NG]

Gentiana

[I believe every rock gardener aspires to heights attainable only by growing the deep blue gentians. Each year I try a few more, and to my surprise have found several that are content to settle down and live in the humid heat of the South. Perhaps the easiest and thus the first one to try is *G. septemfida*. It has compact growth and in its finest form produces intense blue flowers in summer. A similar but later-blooming species is *G. lagodechiana*. The low-growing form, *G. scabra saxatilis*, produces deep blue flowers in early fall and is persisting thus far with me. Some of the decumbent ones are somewhat messy but nevertheless have enough charm to be worth trying. I have succeeded with *G. gracilipes* and consider it a permanent resident after eight years here. They all seem to do best in light shade; some are growing in a woodland setting, while others are in the rock garden. *G. andrewsii* is a fairly easy taller species for the wild garden. NG]

Geranium

In Raleigh I tried a number of geraniums, even making an attempt to establish *G. pylzowianum*, a small lilac-flowered alpine that Reginald Farrer brought back from Tibet, but our native *G. maculatum*, the bloody cranesbill, is the only one that has proved to be satisfactory. The desirable forms of *G. sanguineum* are the cultivar 'Album,' with its succession of pure white flowers in summer and leaves that are an ornament even in winter, and the variety *lancastriense* (now known as *G. s. striatum*). The latter is a prostrate form that grows in ordinary soil in full sun or a little shade and blooms from March onward, even into the fall. The pretty pale pink flowers are veined in red violet.

Just before we left Raleigh I had the Himalayan cranesbill, *G. wallichianum*, in the variety 'Buxton's Blue.' Though described as late flowering, it bloomed in the middle of April, and the flowers were violet, not blue. They bloomed for two springs before we left, and —like the old lady under the hill—if they're not gone, they bloom there still.

[*G. argenteum* with its beautiful silver leaves is in its third season with me. It was grown outside in very gritty soil in full sun. *G.* × *lindavicum* is the name for all hybrids of *G. argenteum* and *G. cinereum*. *G.* × *l.* 'Apple Blossom' is a beautiful pale pink one which seems happy in full sun and is short enough for any rock garden. *G. cinereum* is another low-growing species worth trying with the addition of grit to the soil.

For years I have had both the pink and the white forms of *G. dalmaticum* growing and blooming well in the shady part of my rock garden. The dainty flowers and low height of the plants make them extremely desirable. The white form is not as vigorous as the pink one, but it is certainly worth growing. Another species requiring light shade is *G. macrorrhizum,* and it is splendid and vigorous with deep pink flowers. The pale pink–flowering cultivar *G. m.* 'Ingwersen's Variety' is extremely desirable with its pink flowers and somewhat glossy leaves. There are some fine hybrids of *G. macrorrhizum* and *G. dalmaticum* known as *G.* × *cantabrigiense.* These are a good size for the rock garden, for they are shorter than *G. macrorrhizum* and have fragrant pink flowers. The fine form *G.* × *c.* 'Biokovo' is white with just a tinge of pink. In the South this group is happiest in light shade.

G. endressii has lovely pink flowers, and it too can take considerable shade as well as full sun. The cultivar 'Wargrave Pink' has been with me for many years and produces flowers of an unusual shade of salmon pink.

The African species, *G. incanum,* is new to me, but the finely dissected, fragrant leaves and small size make it appropriate for any rock garden. I am trying it in very gritty soil in sun and hope to see magenta pink flowers this summer. I have *G. orientalitibeticum* in just such a site, and I delighted in its blotched leaves and pinkish-purple flowers last year.

G. renardii has violet-striped white flowers and is happy in either sun or light shade. The rounded leaves are silver underneath. I added two cultivars of *G.* × *riversleaianum* to the garden last year, and both did extremely well in the intense heat and humidity. 'Mavis Simpson' has light pink flowers, and 'Russell Prichard,' with its deep magenta ones, bloomed practically all summer long.

Any form of *G. sanguineum* is worth trying. The compact cultivar

'Shepherd's Warning' and the dwarf 'Nanum' are especially desirable for the smaller rock garden. 'Cedric Morris' has some of the largest flowers of the species, while 'Glenluce' has mauve-pink ones. Although this species is usually recommended for full sun, I have been amazed by how well it has grown in my shaded garden.

I was delighted to discover last winter that *G. sessiliflorum novaezelandiae nigricans* was hardy to 0°F. It bloomed prolifically throughout the early summer, with small white flowers on very short stems and beautiful dark bronze leaves. It perished in midsummer, but in its place have appeared many seedlings, so it is probably best regarded as a perennial annual.

For years I grew *G. stapfianum* with its blotchy leaves and deep magenta flowers. It had a gently stoloniferous habit but never made a good show because I had it in too much shade. I will try again. NG]

Geum

[A number of geums are fine for the larger rock garden. They grow best in full sun and seem to require a year to settle down and bloom well, and they need to be divided every three years or so. In the South they begin to bloom in early spring. The hybrid *G.* × 'Coppertone,' a seedling which appeared in Beth Chatto's garden, began to produce its lovely pale apricot flowers in March this year. *G.* × 'Borisii' does not bloom as long but is nevertheless worth growing for its bright orange flowers. One of the easiest forms to acquire is *G. quellyon* (formerly *G. chiloense*) 'Mrs. Bradshaw,' for it comes true from seed and has beautiful double brick red flowers. *G. q.* 'Lady Stratheden' is supposed to be just as easy, but I have never been able to produce this yellow double-flowered form. This year I added to my garden a plant of *G. q.* 'Starkers Magnificent,' which has produced flowering stalks up to eighteen inches and wonderfully vivid double orange flowers. This one may be too tall for most rock gardens, but it is worth finding a spot for. It has a long season of bloom. One other cultivar of *G. quellyon* is worth acquiring. 'Princess Juliana' is a vigorous plant with golden-orange flowers, and it requires only division every three years or so to stay happy. I have not tried *G. reptans* yet, but I will, for it is one of the parents of *G.* × 'Borisii' that can take the heat. NG]

Goodyera

[*G. pubescens:* If you are lucky, you will find this charming orchid already growing in shady areas in your garden. I have never transplanted it but always delight in its beautiful white-veined evergreen foliage and racemes of whitish flowers. I believe it a plant to be left in place; however, I have read that careful division in early spring is possible. NG]

Gypsophila

[One of the best perennial gypsophilas makes a fine rock garden plant. *G. repens* persisted for me in the front of a perennial border for many years. It remained less than six inches high and produced flowers larger than many others of the genus. It requires well-drained soil and appreciates the addition of some lime. It grew easily from seed, and I intend to plant it again. There is also a very desirable pink form. I have not yet tried any of the other rock garden species. NG]

Habranthus

H. tubispathus (formerly *H. robustus*) is a beautiful pink-flowering bulb which brightens one's spirits in those very hot days in August. It is practically evergreen and seems to be stimulated to produce flowers only after the August rains begin. It will grow well in full sun or partial shade and is easily increased by seed.

Hakonechloa

[*H. macra:* This Japanese grass is a wonderful plant for a partly shaded site. It is most readily available in one of its variegated forms, which may be anything from white to yellow-striped. There are often touches of pink in the new growth and red in the fall. All of these variegated forms are brilliantly colored. If something more subtle is desired, then the solid green type is worth growing, if just for its graceful habit. Hakonechloa will succeed and attain a height of eight to twelve inches in a well-drained soil with average moisture, but it increases slowly. NG]

Hedyotis

[If you are lucky, you will find bluets already growing in your rock garden. If not, it is worth the effort to try to establish them. *H. cae-*

rulea is native to much of the East Coast of North America and requires an acid soil in light shade. It is easily propagated by seeds. NG]

Helleborus

[The hellebores will always be welcome throughout my garden. *H. niger* is an extremely variable species, both in the shape of its flowers and leaves and in the time of bloom. I have several which can be counted on to bloom at Christmas, but most of mine wait until late February or March. Although they are primarily white, there are beautiful ones tinged with pink. Usually in February *H. foetidus* begins to open its curiously attractive purple-tinged green flowers. There are shorter forms of this species which are better suited to rock gardens than the typical two-and-a-half-foot plants. *H. orientalis,* the lenten rose, usually overlaps the blooming periods of *H. niger* and *H. foetidus*. Its evergreen foliage remains attractive until the bloom stalks appear, at which time it is best to cut off the remains and enjoy the fresh new growth which appears with the white to pink to deep purple flowers. *H. atrorubens* is similar to *H. orientalis,* with the difference being that the former is deciduous in all except the mildest winters and is virtually sterile. We are fortunate in the South to be able to grow the very beautiful *H. argutifolius,* a superb foliage plant. Its leaves have three leaflets and bright chartreuse veins against the dull green leaf surface. In mild winters there are small, pendulous clusters of green flowers. NG]

Hemerocallis

[I allow only one daylily in my rock garden, and this is an old cultivar, 'Little Minor.' It remains about a foot or less in height and blooms in April and again in the fall with fragrant golden-yellow flowers. There are many other small-flowered, low-growing cultivars available now. NG]

Hepatica

[One of the treasures in my rock garden is the collection of hepaticas. I like everything about them but most of all the sight of their furry stems coming up from the cold soil in late winter. *H. americana* grows best for me and has self-sown seedlings throughout the shady areas in the garden. Very often the leaves have beautiful dark patches, and the flowers vary from light blue to a medium dark blue. I have tried to grow the pink ones, *H. acutiloba,* but I fear that their preference for a limy soil has made them unhappy. I also have a clump of the Japanese species, *H. nobilis japonica;* however, it is merely existing for me. NG]

Hermodactylus

[It has taken me many years to get the real *H. tuberosus,* and the tubers were brought to me by friends of Elizabeth Lawrence this past spring. I have set them in a sunny site and look forward to their green foliage throughout the winter and flowers in early spring. NG]

Heuchera

[Several heucheras are suitable for rock gardens. The native alum-root, *H. americana,* is a beautiful plant throughout most of the year; the only time that it looks a bit untidy is when it blooms. The foliage is superb throughout the winter, often taking on beautiful red or bronze hues. It wants a shady site. I am also growing the small *H. cylindrica,* which produces spikes of yellowish green flowers in early spring. *H. villosa* is another species grown primarily for its foliage, although the flowering stalks in summer give it an airy quality. There is also a fine dark red form, often referred to as *H. v.* 'Purpurea.' For sunny locations, *H. sanguinea* and many of its cultivars are excellent plants, giving wonderful foliage throughout the year and good flowers in early summer. I have not succeeded with most of the newer hybrids produced in England, but I have had good luck with *H. s.* 'Shere Variety,' a fine form with red flowers, and *H. s.* 'Rosamund' with pink ones. I recommend trying any of the heuchera species which appear in catalogs or seed lists. NG]

× *Heucherella*

[This is one of the most beautiful plants for a shaded part of the garden. It is a hybrid produced in England of a heuchera species and tiarella. It grows best for me in good humusy soil and is beautiful at all seasons. The evergreen foliage is lovely through the winter, and the sprays of pink flowers are elegant in spring and early summer. It is a sterile hybrid and can be reproduced only through division. NG]

Hippeastrum

The genus *Hippeastrum* is named from the Greek words for knight and star and is called the knight's star lily. It is confined to tropical America.

H. advenum, the oxblood lily, is now sometimes referred to the genus *Amaryllis* or may be listed as a habranthus. It is a small fall-flowering amaryllid from Chile, with drooping dark red flowers, five to seven to an umbel. The scapes are short and thick, and the shiny, grassy leaves have a tendency to lie flat on the ground. It blooms along from August to October, the clumps increasing very fast and producing an unbelievable number of scapes. Hamilton Traub reports that this species is hardy to Beltsville, Maryland, and Cecil Houdyshel, a nurseryman in California, recommends it for trial to New Jersey, Missouri, and Kansas, but not for pots. It should be planted in full sun in a medium or heavy soil and moved only when dormant (but mine get moved at any time), which is in midsummer. The long-necked bulbs need deep planting; six or eight inches is not too deep in cold climates. Mine get a yearly mulch of cow manure. The leaves come up in the fall with the buds, remain all winter unhurt by cold, then die down in summer.

The hybrid hippeastrums popularly known as amaryllis (and some botanists now refer all of the hippeastrums to that genus) is grown out-of-doors in the warmer parts of Zone 7, but it is the most popular bulb for pots in all parts of the country. The pot should be twice the size of the bulb, and the bulb should be planted with the neck and top above the soil. Water it after planting, but not again until the buds appear. Then bring it into the light and increase the water gradually. Give water and liquid manure after flowering, but allow the bulbs to rest when the leaves begin to yellow. Hippeastrum hybrids and most species can be potted until the end of March, but it is better to start them early. They need a cool room when growing.

Hosta

Two plantain lilies are of rock garden proportions if these are not too strictly defined, their slender flower stalks rising from one to two feet above low clumps of narrow oval leaves. I first saw *H. minor alba* in the gardens at Cronamere, where it was used in the most delightfully lavish manner, the spikes of pure white bells appearing at every corner, in the margin of the path, and at the foot of the rock wall. I thought it so lovely that I redoubled my efforts to establish it in my own garden, but I never could. However, this does not mean that it will not grow in the South, for it flourished in Elsie Hassan's garden in Birmingham, Alabama, and bloomed there—as in Connecticut— in August.

Plants known in the trade as *H. lancifolia* sometimes turn out to be the variety *tardiflora*. I have also had this valuable late-flowering variety as *H. fortis*. In North Carolina it comes into bloom in August, and I have seen it still in full bloom at the end of October. The light mauve flowers are tinged with white, and the smooth, pale leaves are yellow-green. It is a robust form that flowers freely and increases rapidly.

Hostas like shade and moisture but will grow in any soil. They have no faults and increase in beauty every year.

[In the last two decades a great many small hostas have come onto the market. Their detractors dismiss them as "slug bait," and with good reason, since they may disappear almost overnight when under heavy assault from slugs. One of the best hostas for rock garden use is the species *H. venusta,* which forms a graceful mound of small lance-shaped leaves only four inches high; the blooms in midsummer are delicate and a rich shade of violet. AL]

Hyacinthella

Last fall I found *H. dalmaticus* offered for the first time, and this spring it bloomed in the middle of March. It is one of the tiniest and most enchanting of all the little bulbs. The little spikes are as thin as a thin pencil and daintily tinted and delicately scented. For those who like the very tiny rock plants, this is a treasure.

Hypoxis

[Yellow star grass, *H. hirsuta,* is a modest but delightful plant for dry, shaded areas. It is native to the eastern half of the country and bears many yellow flowers during late spring and early summer. Although I have read that they can have leaves up to a foot tall, all of mine have been less than eight inches. NG]

Iberis

I. sempervirens is common enough in southern gardens but too bulky to be allowed among proper rock plants unless in some of the small, compact forms such as 'Little Cushion.'

Early experience discouraged me from planting the miniature species, but recently I remembered how well *I. saxatilis,* a tiny alpine from the Pyrenees, grew in Elizabeth Rawlinson's garden in the Shenandoah valley—where it bloomed from late March to the middle of May—and I decided to try it once more in Charlotte. It bloomed about the middle of March and has come through the summer very well in spite of drought. Carl Starker says it blooms early and persistently in Oregon, and it might bloom longer here with a little more moisture, but I have it in a very dry place on top of a wall. It needs lime and a gritty soil, and I thought a little shade from a pine tree would not be amiss in this climate. It is a pretty plant and looks rather like a fine-leaved sedum.

Imperata

[*I. cylindrica* 'Rubra,' the Japanese blood grass, is one of the glories of fall. There are red highlights in its foliage all through the growing season, but in the fall this pigment seems to bleed throughout the entire leaf blade, coloring it a glowing red. The placement of this grass is important, for it is best with the sun lighting it from behind. It is a deciduous, stoloniferous plant which may grow to eighteen inches; however, its spread has never been rapid enough for me. This lovely grass is easily pleased in almost any sunny place in average soil. NG]

Ionopsidium

I. acaule (ann.), violet cress, is a minute and charming crucifer that flowers in English gardens all through mild winters. I first read about it in the sixth series of Sir Herbert Maxwell's *Memories of the Months.* It grew in his garden at Monreith, on the southwest coast of Scotland within a mile of the sea, and he wrote of it lovingly: "It might be deemed insignificant from its diminutive stature, which attains at most to a couple of inches; but once [you] get this little chap established by dropping seed into the chinks of a mossy wall, and you will be loath to lose it. Nor are you likely to do so, for this native of sunny Mediterranean shores sows itself as pertinaciously under our cloudy skies as its less desirable relative, the charlock or wild mustard." With me the violet cress did not renew itself, but this is not strange as I had only a few plants from one of Park's seed packages. Plants from seeds sown September 27 came into bloom on November 10, and those from October-sown seed bloomed early in March. They were planted between the stones of a sunny path, which is all very well for winter bloom, but Dr. Free thinks they need shade in summer. He said in *The Home Garden* in May 1953 that seeds sown in a sunny spot in the Brooklyn Botanic Garden were not a success, while those sown in his own garden on the north side of the house bloomed from June to Thanksgiving.

Iris

The beardless iris species are grouped together in a subgenus known as *Limniris,* and these are most important to the rock gardener. Among the European and Asiatic species are some small ones that will grow in the South as well as the North, and some others that will grow in the South only. From Asia come *I. lactea* (formerly known as *I. ensata*), *I. minutoaurea,* and *I. ruthenica.* The first is the least interesting and the easiest to grow. It is a widely distributed species, ranging from Kashmir to Korea, and it may be that among the many forms there are more desirable ones than the one in my possession. And yet there is a certain grace and distinction in the slender slate-blue flowers, and a nice relationship between the very narrow petals and the very narrow foliage. In early April when the flowers are in bloom the leaves are scarcely taller than the stems, but they shoot up in summer into a cool fountain of pale green. This species is among the most drought resistant, but it will also grow in moist places. It will grow in sun or shade but blooms best in the open.

I. minutoaurea is a very tiny Japanese species that I have had some difficulty with. It seems to be established now, but it has not yet bloomed. "*Iris minuta* should have done better," Mr. van Melle complained in an old issue of *Horticulture.* "It was well established and it is only a natural stinginess that keeps it from flowering regularly.

There was not a flower on it. Rare as it may be and much sought after, I never could admire its cold yellow or the cramped huddle of its flower stems."

I. ruthenica, the pilgrim iris, has thus far resisted all of my efforts to make it live. Nevertheless I shall keep trying, for Robert Moncure does not mention any difficulty with it in Alexandria, where it blooms in early May along with *I. graminea,* and Louise Beebe Wilder describes it as a Russian but not a temperamental one, "a perfect rock garden iris, easy, floriferous, and dwarf." The fragrant violet flowers are on stems shorter than the leaves. Mrs. Wilder grew it in full sun, but Mr. Moncure advises some shade for these parts. The soil should be mixed with humus and sand.

With me the most reliable of the small crested species that come from abroad is the plum-scented iris, *I. graminea.* It has a wide range from central Europe to the Caucasus and seems to adapt itself to most climates and soils. The flowers are described as smelling of all sorts of delightful things from cloves to various ripe fruits, but to me this fragrance is like Georgia peaches in the sun. They are as charming as the delicately drawn flowers in Japanese prints. This species comes into bloom any time between the middle of April and the first of May, with flowers on ten-inch stems among narrow leaves that are twice as long.

I. sintenisii is very like the plum-scented iris, except that it comes into bloom about a week later and is odorless. Botanically, the main difference seems to be that the stems of the one are round and those of the other are flattened. Both have the merit of not only blooming in shade, but preferring it.

"Just think," Elsie Hassan wrote one spring, "a clump of *I. unguicularis* established less than four years, and only fifteen inches across, has had one hundred and two flowers since the first day of December." Much has been written as to why this Algerian iris does or does not bloom. Some gardeners find it more floriferous in poor, dry, sandy soil in full sun, and others think that it flowers better in a rich, moist soil with part shade. In *The Garden in Winter* Patrick Synge observes very sensibly that a light soil with manure and water in spring, and after June no more water than the heavens deliver, gives the plants a chance to make good growth before their summer baking. It is generally agreed that lime in some form is needed if the soil is acid. I have come to the conclusion that the number of flowers depends more upon the form than the treatment. The species is nicely distributed in the eastern Mediterranean region, and there are a number of geographic forms as well as some garden varieties. I have had two kinds with violet flowers and three with white flowers. Of these the most prolific bloomer is a very vigorous one that I have seen in a number of Charlotte gardens and which came originally from Mrs. Garibaldi. This blooms very early, and continuously if the winter is mild. One year the first bud unfurled on October 24, and from then until spring a clump under a southern window was scarcely ever without bloom. The comparatively small flowers are of the clear bright color called violet. They seem extra tall because of the elongated tubes. I think that this is probably *I. u.* 'Cretensis.' The other violet flower is larger and more beautiful, with a shorter tube. It blooms late—not until the end of November, and sometimes not until after Christmas—and the flowers are not plentiful. I have been unable to get any of the white forms permanently established. The best and most vigorous is the cultivar 'Alba.' Long creamy buds open into large, pure white gold-crested flowers among stiff, bright green leaves. This seems to thrive for a few years, and then, piece by piece, it slowly rots away. The first time I thought poor drainage was the cause, but later it did the same on top of a wall. An iris that came to me as the cultivar 'Marginata Alba' was smaller and more delicate and no more dependable. The most exquisite of all is the tiny white flower of the cultivar 'Queen Elizabeth.' I had this years ago from Gordon Ainsley, and it produced a single and unforgettable blossom before it disappeared. I have seen it listed only once since Mr. Ainsley died, and when I got it, it perished without blooming at all. Two other cultivars, one described as pink and one as having very dark honey-scented flowers, never bloomed. All forms of the Algerian iris are delicately and delightfully fragrant when the flowers are warmed in the hand or brought indoors. It is best to pick them in bud. This is a mountain species and surprisingly hardy. Robert Moncure reports that it withstood fourteen degrees below zero in Alexandria, where it blooms from January to mid-April.

Some of the crested irises belong to the section Lophiris and are known as the evansia irises, named for Thomas Evans, who introduced the type species, *I. japonica,* into England. They are distinguished by having a crest like a cock's comb at the base of the fall. Since it is a very small group, I once thought it not too ambitious to try to collect them all, but I doubt if I shall ever get *I. wattii* and *I. milesii* to grow in North Carolina.

One of the real miniatures of this group is *I. gracilipes* from Japan. I first saw it in Harlowe's wonderful rock garden in the Poconos, where it blooms at the end of May, a month later than in mine. It seems to grow well throughout the eastern states, and Ruth Dormon has it in her shady rock garden in Louisiana. The only complaint I have heard is from Mr. Berry in southern California. However, it requires good drainage and a moist soil rich in humus. Though it needs some shade, it will not grow in poor soil under trees.

Another species of this group is also Asiatic. *I. tectorum,* the Japanese roof iris, is perhaps a little large to grow among choice rock plants, but it never gets above a foot high, and I like to see it blooming in April with the bletillas and rejoice in the knowledge that both will go on blooming for many Aprils after without making any demands on me. The roof iris will grow in the Gulf states or California and is hardy at least as far north as Massachusetts. It is equally indifferent to soils and situations as long as it is well drained. Here it blooms best in dry shade. The lovely blue-violet flowers of the type are splashed with violet, and the white form is even more beautiful.

The dwarf irises of the bearded group are choice and utterly charming. A number have bloomed cheerfully among my rocks, but not for long. I am so sure that the fault is with me and not the climate that I mean to continue my efforts indefinitely. *I. humilis* (formerly *I. flavissima*), a tiny species from southeastern Europe, is often listed as *I. arenaria,* the sand iris. I have one note to the effect that it likes sand, lime, and sun, and another to the effect that it likes leaf mold, acidity, and shade. I tried both ways and it liked neither, although it bloomed charmingly and fleetingly each time. The strontian yellow vanilla-scented flowers come in pairs and last but a day. They bloomed once in mid-March and once early in April.

The various forms of *I. pumila* bloom in March; some have lingered in my garden for several years, some for less. The earliest is the dark purple cultivar 'Atroviolacea,' the most permanent is a small pale yellow one, and the loveliest is the cultivar 'Caerulea.' The true variety is hard to find, and when you find it, it is hard to bring to bloom, but when it blooms at last it is a delightful flower, elusive in color and fragrance. The color is gull gray, a gray blue that reminds you of the sea.

My favorite is the tiny *I. suaveolens,* sometimes listed as *I. rubro-marginate* or *I. mellita.* Mellitus, if my latin is to be trusted, means honey sweet: "this flower smells of honey and the sea." Rubromarginata refers, I suppose, to the narrow margin of red on the minute sickle-shaped leaves. The flowers are tints of yellow, tinged olive or brown or smoky purple, with darker veins of bronze or violet. They bloom here early in April, and I have read that they repeat later on, but of course they do not do so for me. This species requires full sun, but it needs an acid soil.

The vesper iris, formerly *I. dichotoma,* now *Pardanthopsis dichotoma,* stands alone in a division of its own. Pardanthopsis means pardanthuslike and refers to the resemblance (in form only) between the iris and the blackberry lily, which used to be called pardanthus. This is another tall and slender species, but it has a wayward grace that recommends it to the rock gardener and a late flowering season that completes the cycle of bloom, making it possible to have irises in bloom in a southern garden almost every month in the year. For it is only a short time between the last of the dwarf Delta species in June to the first vesper iris in July, and from the last of these to the first flower of *I. unguicularis.* The fugitive flowers open only in the afternoon and last only a few hours, but there are many of them. The colors are various tints of red-violet. This species is more biennial than perennial, but it is grown very easily from seed and blooms the first year.

[There are a few more beardless irises that are appropriate for the rock garden. The reticulata irises are contained in the subgenus *Hermodactyloides* and are superb for rock gardens. Among the first to bloom in the winter are *I. histrio* and *I. histrioides.* They are somewhat larger than the later-blooming *I. reticulata,* and *I. histrio* is considered less hardy. Another member of the reticulata group came to me by accident. I have identified it as *I. pamphylica* and can count on one or two flowers in midwinter. The falls are brownish purple with a bright yellow blotch, and the standards are light blue. Its frail and delicate looks belie its toughness. I am growing it on the south side of the house where it gets winter sun. The many forms of *I. reticulata* are superb rock garden plants. They delight any gardener by appearing in winter and by managing to bloom regardless of temperature. There are many cultivated forms with names such as 'Cantab,' pale blue with orange blotches; 'Harmony,' sky blue with yellow ridges; 'Natasha,' ivory white; and 'Violet Beauty,' violet or purple. I buy a few each year and have found them reliable and permanent. Very often these can be had for very little at garden centers after Thanksgiving. Their bloom will be a little late the first year, but they will grow and bloom on time in succeeding years.

Much to my surprise I have found the Juno irises, more correctly known as subgenus *Scorpiris,* easy to grow in my rock garden. *I. aucheri,* with blue flowers, and *I. bucharica,* with yellow ones, have grown best for me. The foliage appears in early winter, and the flowers usually come in March. I am also growing *I. magnifica,* which is similar to *I. bucharica.* The foliage disappears by June, so it is important to mark the site in order to avoid injuring the bulbs and their fleshy roots when weeding in the summer.

Several other excellent rhizomatous irises grow well here. From the subgenus *Liminiris* come the low-growing forms of *I. setosa,* which are wonderful rock garden material. *I. s.* 'Nana' with its blue-purple flowers, one to a stalk, are always welcome in May. Grow this one in full sun for a better display of flowers and more vigorous growth. *I. tridentata* has a delicate blue-purple flower with widely spreading rhizomes. It never makes a mass but is valuable for its extremely late blooming period. Our native *I. verna* is a beardless dwarf species which has lilac blue flowers and an orange blotch in the center of the falls. I am growing it in both sun and light shade and find the latter a more satisfactory situation.

One other important member of the *Lophiris* section, or evansia irises, is the exquisite *I. cristata,* with small crested flowers and a spreading habit. This one prefers good drainage, a moist soil and shade, and some sun during winter and early spring. The rhizomes spread over one another and are best separated after several years lest they die out in the center. The many color forms available range from white to white with a pale blue edge to blue to a deep purple.

From the *Sibiricae* series come several more fine rock garden subjects. *I. clarkei* has been with me for only one year, growing happily in part shade. There are a number of short, small-flowered *I. sibirica* hybrids which are worth acquiring. *I. sanguinea* 'Nana' and its white form, *I. s.* 'Nana Alba,' are fine low-growing irises which can take the heat. I have grown some of the 'Pacific Coast' irises from seed and have found them fully hardy. These hybrids of the Pacific Coast natives are extremely variable. They are worth trying in sun or part shade. NG]

Kniphofia

The torch lily, named kniphofia for Professor Kniphof, is native to Africa. It is perfectly hardy with me, and generally south of Phila-delphia. It may overwinter farther north, but it is considered safer in severe climates to lift them in the fall and store the roots in dry sand in a warm place. In the South they should be left undisturbed in rich, deep, moist soil in full sun. There are a number of colorful and floriferous hybrids that are a great improvement on the old-fashioned red-hot poker, *K. pfitzeri*. One of the best is 'Towers of Gold,' which blooms for me in July or early August. Sometimes it throws up as many as ten stalks in the summer and then repeats in October. Others come in pure white, pale yellow, coral, orange, and red. These are from three to four feet tall. I am especially partial to the dwarf hybrids of *K. rufa*, which are small enough for the rock garden or the front of the border.

Sometimes the torch lilies are listed by the old name, Tritoma.

Koeleria

[*K. glauca* has the beautiful blue gray foliage of some of the better forms of *Festuca glauca* without any of the latter's problems. This low grass retains its steely blue color throughout the year. It is not stoloniferous but rather clump forming and very well behaved. It wants a good site in full sun. NG]

Lamiastrum

[There is only one form of this genus with a habit suitable to the rock garden: *L. galeobdolen* 'Herman's Pride.' This is an attractive plant with variegated leaves and yellow flowers in late spring. It grows well in shade and remains a compact clump. NG]

Lamium

[Several forms of *L. maculatum* are appropriate for the larger rock garden. *L. m.* 'Beacon Silver' is a beautiful foliage plant with nearly silver leaves and pink flowers. *L. m.* 'White Nancy' has the same wonderful leaves but pure white flowers. *L. m.* 'Aureum' has bright yellow or chartreuse foliage and pinkish mauve flowers. These plants will grow in light shade or sun, but I have been surprised at how much better they do for me in sun. NG]

Lapeirousia

[*L. laxa* is one of the charming summer-flowering bulbs which come from South Africa. The brick red flowers are produced on stems about one foot high. The foliage disappears for most of the summer and reappears in the fall, and the flowers come in early summer or late spring. There is a white-flowered form, but I have not been able to get it. NG]

Lavandula

Carl Krippendorf in Ohio refuses to believe that lavender will not persist in my garden. He says it is all my fault and due to my not shearing it properly. "I hope you will write about the importance of shearing rock plants after blooming," he repeats at intervals. "That is the only way you can get compact plants smothered with flowers. When I took pride in my wall garden I used to shear off about a hundred bushels during the summer. My candytuft looked like hummocks of snow, and I used to keep one or two unclipped as a horrible example. And that is why I can keep lavenders for twenty years."

Nevertheless, I have had difficulty with it in both Raleigh and Charlotte, though I renew it from time to time, for I cannot imagine any sort of a garden without lavender. Mrs. Bruce Chalfin had more success at the Plantation Garden in Lynchburg, Virginia. "The lavenders, even the more delicate *Lavandula latifolia,* proved to have great stamina," she wrote in the *Herb Grower* (Winter 1952). "Plants were pruned drastically after their final flowering in October but wintered well without protection. Where lavender is not quite dormant in winter, thinning out the old wood in the fall helps to improve the spring growth and keeps the clumps attractive the year around. A hot dry summer has its compensations as far as lavender is concerned because there was continuous bloom with no spoilage of flowers by rains, and the aroma of the blossoms and leaves was particularly concentrated."

There are many forms of *L. angustifolia,* but all bloom in May in these parts. The best that I have had came without names, and so I cannot recommend them. They came from the local nursery, which is a good place to get plants acclimated to the region but not a good place to learn their names. The labels, if any, have always been lost, and usually the plants have been grown in gardens for so long that no one knows their origin.

There are three dwarf forms that are particularly suited to rock gardens and to the South. My favorite is *L. a.* 'Twickel Purple,' a small, round, and compact plant with silvery leaves that I imagine to be particularly fragrant and flowers of a beautiful deep violet that is not at all purple. The cultivar *L. a.* 'Alba' is white flowered, and I have no use for a lavender with white flowers ("Lavender's blue, dilly, dilly"). The cultivar 'Nana' is low, compact, and early in bloom.

[*L. stoechas* has proven hardy here, and after several years is a lovely gray shrubby mound about two feet high. During the summer it produces fat clusters of red-violet flowers a little like rabbit ears, and not a bit like the lavender-blue spikes of *L. angustifolia.* The problem with lavender in this climate is not so much its hardiness but its intolerance of heavy, wet soils in the winter. NG]

Leucojum
[The small fall-blooming species of *Leucojum* are among the most delightful bulbs for the rock garden. *L. autumnale* is a reliable flowering plant (late summer and early fall) with very slender foliage and beautiful small white flowers. It does best in gritty soil in full sun. *L. roseum* is similar, but its fragrant flowers are rose pink and it is not such a vigorous grower. NG]

Lewisia
[This family of plants native to our western mountains presents a true challenge to the southern rock gardener. I have been delighted to discover two that will grow for me in part shade. The deciduous *L. nevadensis* is dormant for most of the summer and winter; it grows in late winter and spring and produces many lovely white

flowers in April. The other species, *L. cotyledon,* can take more sun and forms an evergreen rosette of succulent leaves. Both of these species want very good drainage and a collar of stones about the base of the plants to prevent excess water from rotting them at the neck. They are quite easy to grow from seed, provided it is sown in a cool greenhouse or in pots set in the refrigerator. NG]

Lilium

[*L. pumilum* is a charming orange/scarlet miniature turk's-cap lily appropriate for a sunny or partly shaded rock garden. It has slender leaves and grows to about eighteen inches. NG]

Limnanthes

L. douglasii (ann.), meadow foam or marsh flower, is one of the easiest and prettiest of the California wildflowers, but I have never seen it in any garden but my own, where it perpetuated itself for years after having once got a start in low, moist ground at the foot of a wall. Fall sowing for early flowers is better, but seeds sown at the end of February produce bloom by the middle of May. Flowers from seeds sown in November bloom by the first of April. The fragrant yellow-and-white flowers rest like flakes of foam among finely divided yellow green leaves that are as crisp and fresh as a spring salad. Meadow foam is said to prefer some shade, but it was lovely in full sun.

Lobularia

L. maritima (ann.), formerly known as *Alyssum maritimum,* should be sown at intervals, and the old plants pulled up as soon as they are shabby. Two of the best that I have had are 'Carpet of Snow' and 'Violet Queen.' Both are compact and free flowering.

Luzula

[Doug Ruhren says the luzulas, the woodrushes, are of easy culture, even tolerating dry shade. *L. sylvatica,* the greater woodrush, has a cultivar, *L. s.* 'Marginata' with a fine gold margin to its leaves. The snowy woodrush, *L. nivea,* has showy white flowers, and its dwarf form, *L. n.* 'Nana,' is the perfect size for a rock garden. NG]

Lychnis

[Last fall I added *L. alpina* to my scree bed in full sun. I was delighted with the many pink flowers in spring. The foliage is a tight tuft of grasslike leaves, and the plant is a perfect miniature. So far, it looks happy in our hot, humid summer weather, and seeds from my original plant have germinated with no special treatment. NG]

Lycoris

Lycoris is one of the classical names. Some say the genus was named for a nereid, and some say a Roman beauty. *L. radiata,* which we grew so long in our gardens as *Nerine sarniensis,* the Guernsey lily, is native to the southern part of Japan and the Yangtze valley of China and is hardy and satisfactory to Maryland and Tennessee. The jasper red umbels of long-stamened flowers, crisped and curled, appear in crowds that make a brilliant splash in the dull weeks of September. When the flowers have faded, the leaves follow to make a winter ornament. I do not know what to say about the culture of the red spider lilies. In most gardens they increase enormously and bloom extravagantly in any soil, in sun or shade. But like all amaryllids they are temperamental, and when they refuse to bloom I have never found anything to do about it. They are not suitable for pots.

Lysimachia

L. nummularia is in nearly every garden, whether it is wanted or not, and covers the ground so rapidly that it has its uses if kept away from valuable plants, though it is a little hard to get rid of. The almost round evergreen leaves make pleasing patterns and give the plant the name of moneywort, but I like to call it creeping jennie. I have known creeping jennie long and intimately without ever having seen a flower. However, it must bloom sometime, for the flowers are described as yellow and abundant.

[*L. n.* 'Aurea' is a form with yellow leaves that may brighten a dark spot, but it also must be watched because of its aggressive stoloniferous behavior. Pamela Harper recommends *L. japonica minutissima* as the best member of this species for a rock garden. As its name implies, it is the smallest and, incidentally, the best behaved. NG]

Mazus

M. reptans—which has no common name—is one of the best of the carpeters. Its habit is neat, its foliage is fresh, and the violet flowers are quaintly freckled. It blooms late in March as a rule, but I have found flowers even in February. Though mazus has a reputation for being a ramper, I have never found fault with it, for it comes from the Himalayas and does not like heat well enough to overdo—particularly in the sun. Even in the shade, where it is at its best, some patches dwindle while others increase. I would not recommend it for choice quarters; but to cover bare spots and grow between flagstones it is excellent.

[*M. miquelii* is a Japanese species similar to *M. reptans* which has a lovely white-flowered variety, *M. m. albiflorus*. Pamela Harper thinks that the two species are identical. NG]

Mertensia

[*M. virginica* is one of the lovely treats of spring. It makes only a brief appearance, producing clusters of blue flowers which are pink in bud. It disappears shortly after flowering but seeds around when happy in a fairly moist woodland setting. I am also trying the very beautiful *M. maritima* and will remember it for its beautiful glaucous foliage even if I cannot bring it to blossom. NG]

Milium

[*M. effusum* 'Aureum' is a bright golden grass for winter color. Native to Great Britain, it was made famous by E. A. Bowles and is known as 'Bowles' Golden Grass.' It is happy in part shade and remains about a foot high. The inflorescences in early summer are pleasantly graceful but not spectacular. NG]

Miscanthus

[Most of the miscanthus species, according to Doug Ruhren, are much too massive even for the largest of rock gardens, but he names one, *M. sinensis* 'Yaku-Jima,' which has an elegance and lightness as well as the shorter height (eighteen to twenty-four inches) so necessary in such a setting. The inflorescences, which may be over three feet high, are burgundy for a brief period, then remain attractive throughout the winter after they turn silver with flecks of gold. It forms clumps rather than spreading by solons and succeeds in either full sun or light shade on almost any soil, even heavy ones; however, it prefers moist over dry sites. NG]

Mitella

[Bishop's caps are easy to establish in areas suitable for growing tiarella. I have plants of *M. diphylla* which appear happy and have delicate white blooms in spring. NG]

Muscari

M. armeniacum is sometimes called the early giant, but it blooms in March. The spikes are up to eight inches and the flowers are deep chicory blue. The Armenian grape hyacinth blooms for a very long time—at least six weeks—and makes a nice patch of blue near the pale yellow rock garden daffodils.

One of the earliest of the little bulbs that bloom in the rock garden is *M. azureum,* formerly listed as *Hyacinthus azureus.* It has bloomed in my garden on February 14, but more often it puts in an appearance the first week in March. The three-inch spikes, flaring at the base and tapering to a point like tiny porcelain pagodas, continue to rise from the ground over such a long period that I have known two months to pass between the first and the last. At first they are the gray blue green of an old tapestry, but as the flowers open, the color changes to a blue violet.

[Formerly a member of the lily family, and now Hyacinthaceae, the grape hyacinths are diminutive enough to be included in most rock gardens; however, their rapid increase makes one wary. *M. botryoides* comes in both white and blue and blooms in late February or early March. *M. latifolium* has large, usually solitary, leaves and flowers that are pale blue at the top of the spike and dark blue violet at the bottom. *M. comosum* 'Plumosum,' the feather or plume hyacinth, is often found in old gardens. Because the bloom spike consists of only sterile flowers, the effect is of a fluffy mass of medium purple. NG]

Myosotis

The common forget-me-not, *M. scorpioides,* grows in any damp, shady place and blooms for a long time—especially in the variety *semperflorens*. Though it is not long-lived, it is easily replaced, for it blooms the first year from seed and in favorable places renews itself.

In this climate *M. sylvatica* (formerly *M. alpestris*) must be treated as an annual. I usually buy a few plants of both the blue and pink forms for early spring and pull them up in the first hot weather to make room for summer annuals.

[The cultivar 'Alba' is a beautiful, pure, white-flowered plant that is tighter in growth than the usual pink or blue ones. I grow them in areas distant from each other to keep the strains pure. NG]

Narcissus

N. assoanus (listed in catalogs as *N. juncifolius*), a native of the Pyrenees, gives its name "rush-leaved" to the jonquil group. It is a diminutive of the true jonquil and one of the most perfect little flowers in existence, exquisite in its proportions and delicately fragrant. There are from one to four flowers to a stem (usually one), and the stem is four inches or less. The flowers are about three quarters of an inch across, with a lemon-yellow perianth and a deeper yellow cup.

N. asturiensis, the smallest of the trumpets, is so adorable that you cannot believe your eyes when you see it for the first time in bloom with the very earliest spring flowers. Crocuses and snowdrops come no sooner, and only the winter aconite pushes ahead. This is the daffodil that E. A. Bowles calls "the neatest little gentleman in Europe."

N. bulbocodium, the hoop-petticoat daffodil, has been in cultivation in England for centuries. The variety *conspicuus* was introduced before 1560. It was in the early American gardens as well, having been planted by Thomas Jefferson at Monticello and treasured in other old gardens of the South, where it is still passed from one gardener to another. It seems to like our climate and in my garden is the most persistent, reliable, and free flowering of all the little daffodils. The flowers have wide crowns that are distended as though drawn over a hoop. The short perianth segments are narrow and pointed. The rushlike leaves are similar to those of the jonquils. It is a widespread species that is native to the western region of the Mediterranean from Portugal to France, and in North Africa reaches its southern limit high in the Atlas Mountains. It is extremely variable in size, form, and color, ranging from deep yellow to white.

N. b. citrinus is pale yellow and taller and earlier than the type. It grows in marshy ground and requires a moist soil mixed with sand and humus.

N. cantabricus is the rare and delicate white hoop-petticoat that blooms very early in the year and is very fragrant. It was called the Cambridge narcissus from having been grown there, about 1588, by Master Nicolas Belton, who fancied that the palsy could be cured if the patient were seated by an open fire and rubbed with the distilled water of these daffodils.

N. c. cantabricus, a native of Spain and southern France, is hardier than the Algerian form and blooms before Christmas. It persisted in my garden for ten years but bloomed only twice. That is, as far as I know it bloomed only twice, for the flowers might easily be overlooked when the leaves are falling. They are even smaller than those of the variety *monophyllus,* but they have the same air of jaunty fragility. They are not really pure white, as described in the books, but colorless and translucent like flecks of sea foam. The tube is greenish at the base; a faint greenish sheen travels up to the tips of the narrow, pointed segments; and there is a green shadow at the throat of the corona. The corona is only half an inch long, but even so it is longer than the petals. The anthers are golden. It has a subtle and penetrating fragrance, noticeable only when it is brought in from the chill December garden to the warmth indoors.

N. c. subsp. *monophyllus,* as its name implies, has but one leaf, rarely two, and is a white-flowered rarity found in Algeria and southern Spain. It is really too delicate for a garden, even a southern one, though one grew for me for two years, blooming the first season in January and the second late in February. After that they were seen no more. Peter Barr notes in his invaluable catalog of 1906 that this variety requires a warm, sheltered situation in hot sun and almost pure sand. I mean to invest in it again, for the fragile white flowers, lasting so well even in cold, rainy weather, are one of the chief pleasures of the rock garden in winter.

N. cyclamineus, the cyclamen-flowered daffodil, is like *N. triandrus* in that the petals are slightly shorter than the crown and a paler yellow. The flowers are solitary, nodding, and on slender six-inch stems. The species is native to Spain and Portugal, where it is found at the margins of mountain streams and in flooded meadows. In cultivation it is uncertain, sometimes thriving and increasing, and sometimes disappearing altogether. It is one of the bulbs everyone wants to bring to bloom at least once in the very early spring. It requires a damp pocket in the rock garden in a shady place where the soil is well drained but never allowed to dry out in summer.

N. × *gracilis*, a slender jonquil, is rather tall for the rock garden, but I would have it there, for the slight stems and rushlike leaves are not apt to interfere with the smaller plants, and it is nice to end the season with the last of the species to bloom. It usually comes along about the middle of April. It is a wild hybrid between *N. jun-quilla* and *N. biflorus,* though it is not found in the wild, the species having been so long in cultivation that the origin is lost. The scapes grow eventually to eighteen inches, but the flowers always have that tentative rock garden look. They are a clear, pale yellow, like those of the 'Queen of Spain.' There are two to a stem, and they are very fragrant.

N. × *johnstonii* 'Queen of Spain' is sometimes included with the triandrus hybrids, being a natural hybrid of *N. triandrus cernuus.* Though not one of the smallest, it has a delicate grace which sets it apart as a flower for a special place. It needs a little special attention, too, for it does not grow equally well in all gardens. It did not persist with me until I planted some bulbs in a shady part of the rock garden in soil well spaded and mixed with sand and leaf mold. Records kept over a period of nine years show great variation as to the time of the first bloom, from March 6 at the earliest to April Fool's Day at the latest. The pale lemon-colored flowers have a purity of outline and a smoothness of texture that exceeds almost any other daffodil. The flowers vary in the length of the trumpet, the way the petals are held (some sharply reflexed, others only slightly so), and the position of the flower, which may be drooping or at right angles to the stem. But all are exquisite. The stems are less than five inches at first but twice that later on.

N. *jonquilla,* the true jonquil, which Parkinson called the "Jun-quilia, or common Rush Daffodil," was brought to England from Spain in the reign of Queen Elizabeth, and thence to the New World. It still blooms in old gardens in the Carolinas and Virginia. The characteristic shining round leaves grow to about a foot, but they are short—as are the stems—when the flowers bloom. The golden flowers, in bunches of two to six, are intensely fragrant. The variety *minor* is a dwarf form with flowers smaller than those of the type, and the variety *simplex* is taller and later.

N. *minor* comes from the wooded slopes of the Pyrenees and has been in cultivation since the time of Parkinson. The small, very trim trumpets of primrose yellow appear on six-inch stems about the middle of March and last, even in bad weather, for two weeks. The form *nanus* is not recognized by all writers, but as it blooms in my garden it is a very distinct little trumpet of lemon chrome in proportion with its three-and-a-half-inch stem. The leaves are slightly longer than the stems, wide in proportion, and very gray.

N. *pseudonarcissus* subsp. *obvallaris* is a clear yellow flower of good form on a stiff stem of only six or eight inches if the soil is not too rich. The segments are shorter than the crown and of a paler yellow.

N. *pseudonarcissus* subsp. *moschatus,* which E. A. Bowles calls "the only really wild white daffodil known," holds its flower horizontally on a six-inch stem. It opens pale yellow and fades to the color of sea foam. The narrow crown is an inch and a half long, and the twisted segments are of the same length. There is a sturdiness in this small flower that all other small white daffodils lack, but my first experience of it displayed the fact that it had not a sturdy constitution. It bloomed one year, in mid-March, and thereafter was seen no more. Since then I have learned that it is a native to the high Pyrenees and that it should have cool soil in part shade, but having learned this, I have not been able to lay hands on it again. The South is filled with varied forms of this narcissus. The ones we call 'Silver Bells' have bloomed with me as early as the second week in February. These are of the swan's-neck type. The upright buds begin to dip as they open, so that the mature flowers are drooping, their pedicels curved like a swan's neck. The flowers are what the old writers called dog-eared; that is, the petals are swept forward as if blown by the wind. They are silvery at first, but as they fade they turn a curious shade of brown, like Indian pipe.

N. *rupicola* (sometimes noted as a subspecies of N. *juncifolius*), from Portugal, is even smaller than N. *juncifolius,* though that seems scarcely possible. The flowers are butter yellow on stems not above three inches. The six-lobed cup is characteristic.

N. *tazetta* subsp. *italicus* is the only dwarf daffodil of the Tazetta group. It is a perfect miniature of the type, with three or four crisp little flowers to a scape. The reflexed segments are very white in contrast to the globular and very yellow crown. The flowers have the heavy perfume of the bunch-flowered daffodils. The narrow, bright green leaves, a little taller than the six-inch scapes, disappear neatly when the blooming is over. The flowers bloom at the very end of March. The bulbs increase so rapidly that they must be divided frequently if they are to bloom. Otherwise this is an easy sort to grow in a sunny place, in a light soil that is moist in spring but dry in summer.

N. triandrus albus is also called Ganymede's cup because of the projecting crown, and angels' tears because the drooping flowers are like pearly drops. Parkinson called it the "Turning Jonquil" because of the twisted stem. The flowers are usually two or three to a stem, the stem six inches or less, and the narrow rushlike leaves about the same. The petals are sharply turned back from the cup. The triandrus hybrids are of three sorts: those with white flowers, those with yellow flowers, and the bicolors. Most of the white ones are rather large for rock gardens, but 'Pearly Queen,' 'Quince,' and 'Harvest Moon' are of an appropriate size.

N. t. loiseleurii (sometimes noted as *N. calathinus*) has snow white flowers nearly twice the size of those of the type, and on slightly taller stems.

N. t. pallidulus is said to be a native of the valleys of the Pyrenees. The flowers of this rare variety are a soft yellow.

N. t. pulchellus differs from the type only in that the flowers are smaller, with primrose petals and a creamy-white cup.

N. watieri is the only white jonquil similar in size and form to *N. rupicola*. The solitary flowers, an inch and a quarter (or less) across, are of a crystalline whiteness that can be likened to nothing but fairy porcelain. I have had this rare daffodil only once from Drew Sherrard, who offered it in her leaflet *Trowel and Typewriter*, but it disappeared without blooming. Drew Sherrard is much like me. I was never perfectly sure what I had ordered, and she was never perfectly sure what she had sent. And we would correspond for a year afterward trying to discover which of her treasures had bloomed in my garden.

Nemophila

N. menziesii (ann.), better known as *N. insignis,* another native of California, is the most popular annual in my garden. Everyone who sees it wants it. This is one of the dozen or so annuals that I plant regularly every fall because I have never had a volunteer, even though it comes from seed so readily. From fall sowing there is sometimes bloom by the end of February, and this will last well into May if the weather is not too hot. Seeds sown after Christmas, and even in February, may still give good results. This spring I had the happy thought of adding some seedlings of *Silene pendula* to the nemophilas planted on a dry wall, and I was delighted with the tangle of pink and blue flowers. Nemophila has the rare and desirable tone that is almost pure blue. It goes well with *Brunnera macrophylla* and *Bellevalia ciliata,* but it should be kept away from spring bulbs like *Anemone blanda,* grape hyacinths, and squills, which are in tones of blue violet.

In *Hardy Californians* Lester Rowntree says that *N. maculata,* which is called five spot, "in its native haunts makes just as lovely a picture as the shaded banks and grassy swards painted blue by the better known *N. insignis.* It has a huge flower, often two inches across, white with very fine purple veinings and a big striking blotch of dark purple at the top center of each petal. It is charming mingling with a sea of yellow-tipped Creamcups . . . or making a ground cover for foothill apple orchards 4,000 feet up, or in damp meadows in the mountains with clouds of *Limnanthes douglasii nivea* and *Lotus formosissimus.*" I have planted this one, too, but the seeds either failed to come up or turned out to be those of *N. menziesii.*

Nerine

I think I must mention the nerines—though I have had scant success with this South African genus in my own garden—for they are grown in southern California. I am not at all sure that some of the hardier species cannot be grown in other parts of the South with proper treatment, only I am not sure what the proper treatment is. In general, the genus is recommended only for nearly frost-free climates.

Of the smaller species, *N. undulata* alone has bloomed for me. Unfortunately it blooms in November when we are apt to have hard frosts, and unfortunately the leaves make their growth in winter, which means that there will be no flowers the following fall if they are too much injured. Even so I have had much pleasure from those frail scapes of rose-colored flowers that did escape all perils and bloomed with tender beauty on bright November days.

All of my attempts at growing *N. filifolia* have ended in failure either on account of the climate or my methods. Mr. James writes from southern California that

this species is a real find in milder climates. The thread-like leaves are evergreen, six to eight inches tall and of a pretty shade of light green. The dark pink flowers are widely funnel shaped with narrow wavy segments slightly reflexed near the tips, and with pistils and stamens longer than the segments. It blooms in the fall with six to ten flowers in an umbel on wiry stems twelve to fifteen inches tall. It seems to be indifferent as to culture. Bulbs which were watered once last summer flowered about the same time and as well as those which were planted by the edge of a lawn and were watered once or twice a week all summer. However, the foliage on those by the lawn was much better than that of the others. The bulbs are small and soon make nice clumps, and when planted should be covered only to the neck. I have moved them every month in the year, but have not yet been able to pick out which bulbs are certain to flower. It apparently does best after it is established and should be left undisturbed as long as possible.

N. masonorum is similar to *N. filifolia* but with smaller spidery flowers on six-inch scapes. I tried it once in Raleigh without success and have not been able to get it again, as it is so rarely listed. Cecil Houdyshel describes it as the first to bloom, often flowering in mid-July. For this reason, and because it seems to be comparatively hardy, I think it deserves a thorough trial in North Carolina.

Nierembergia

The cup flowers are tender perennials of the nightshade family with the solid bourgeois virtues of their relatives, the petunias. They thrive on heat and a long growing season and bloom without stint through wet summers and dry ones. Several species are grown in the South, but only two are appropriate for rock gardens. Both are from Argentina. The flowers are like small platycodons embossed with stars.

N. hippomanica violacea (formerly *N. caerulia*) is a half-hardy perennial that is hardy with us but not long-lived. The short duration does not matter, for the plants are easily raised from seed and, once started, are self-sown. Seedlings bloom the first year (though they are better the second season) from April until frost. The fine black seed can be scattered in October where the plants are to grow, and there will be bloom the following June. The hortense violet flowers are more than an inch across, and when the plants are in full bloom, they cover the fine pale green foliage. The low, compact, and wide-spreading plants are six or eight inches tall. This species thrives in full sun and dry, sandy soil. Seedlings that come up around the old plants are not always a good color, but good forms can be propagated from cuttings made in the fall. Seeds of the type and of the variety 'Purple Robe' are available.

The pearl cup or white cup, *N. repens,* grows along the Plata River in South America. In the garden it grows best in low, moist places in full sun, but it will endure even in dry soil in the shade. It spreads by fine stems that creep and root to make an almost, but not quite, evergreen carpet. It is said to be difficult to eradicate, and I can see that this might be, although it is too fragile to do much damage. In any case it is prettiest between flagstones or in stone steps where it can do no harm by spreading. The milk white flowers rest on the wavy deep green carpet of spoon-shaped leaves. The leaves are an inch long, and the proportionately large flowers are nearly two inches across. They appear about the middle of May and bloom at intervals all through the summer.

Oenothera

[This genus contains many beautiful species, some of which are extremely attractive but invasive, such as *O. speciosa* and *O. berlandieri.* These are to be planted only where they can be controlled or where nothing else will grow, which is where I have them and can enjoy their lovely pink flowers without worrying about their pesty nature. A delightful very large species for a good sunny site is *O. missourensis,* which can take dry conditions and still produce its yellow flowers in abundance. NG]

Omphalodes

[*O. verna,* or blue-eyed mary, is a fine low perennial which spreads slowly and is nearly evergreen in the South. In early spring forget-me-not blue flowers are produced about four or five inches above the soil. It is very happy in light shade in a rocky soil with some leaf mold added. NG]

Ophiopogon

[There are some attractive noninvasive members of this genus, often called mondo grass and formerly classed in the lily family, which are worth searching for. *O. planiscapus nigrescens* is my favorite. It has purple-black leaves, pinkish flowers, and blue-green fruit. The challenge is to find a site which enhances it, rather than losing it against a dark background such as mulch or rocks. It looks good when combined with other plants with good foliage, such as the Japanese blood grass, *Imperata cylindrica* 'Rubra.'

There is an attractive dwarf form of *O. japonicus* with green leaves, pale lilac or white flowers, and bright blue fruit. Doug Ruhren says *O. jaburan* 'Variegatus' is desirable primarily for its white-striped foliage. NG]

Origanum

The marjorams are called origanum, which means delight of mountains. The choice species prefer air that is purer than ours, though they cannot stand cold. *O. dictamnus,* the legendary dittany of Crete, is an ancient healing herb found in abundance on Mount Dicte. It was introduced into this country some years ago by the American Herb Society, but it is not much grown, probably because it is tender, and it was not until this spring that I found a source and set out a downy-leaved plant from a small pot. It has done well on the terrace in spite of the heat, producing a quantity of flowers which I shall allow to go to seed in case the plant does not survive the winter. But I hope it will prove hardy here, for it is regarded as a rock plant in England. The bright phlox-purple flowers emerge from little papery lavender cones hung on thin, wiry stems. The cones are as delightfully aromatic as the downy oval leaves, with a scent that is a combination of mint and thyme.

O. majorana, sweet marjoram, is also tender, but several plants on a sunny wall came through the last mild winter in Charlotte, and I have known it to survive ten degrees above zero in Raleigh. Even where it is not hardy it can be grown from seeds sown in place in the spring. In the rock garden it is better to shear the plants to keep them from blooming, for the inflorescence, though like that of dittany, is not so gay. The tiny white flowers hardly show, and the little green cones look like worms. They are also thought to look like knots, and give this species the name of knotted marjoram. Sweet marjoram is to me one of the nicest of all herbs because of the neatness of the foliage and the special quality of greenness of the leaves—in some way I cannot define they always seem to be greener than any other leaves. The delicacy of their fragrance is prized for potpourri and pomanders, and their flavor is a favorite in cooking.

O. onites, pot marjoram, is a shrubby, gray-leaved, permanent perennial that will grow anywhere that anything will grow. It spreads somewhat but is not aggressive, and it is one of the indispensable herbs of garden and kitchen, never spectacular but attractive in summer and for most of the winter.

Two other marjorams are offered. *O. pulchellum* is recommended by Elsie Hassan as a good plant for the driest and hottest places in southern rock gardens, and *O. vulgare,* as I have it, is indistinguishable from *O. onites.*

[*O. pulchellum* is one of the most delightful plants for a sunny rock garden. The decumbent habit of the flowering stems makes it perfect for draping over rocks. The showy pale green bracts form a beautiful background for the small pink flowers that appear in midsummer, and the foliage has overtones of purple bronze in winter. Similar but smaller in every way is *O. sipyleum* from Turkey. For a bright golden mass, *O. vulgare* 'Aureum' is wonderful. It is improved by shearing the top growth in midsummer, after which it comes back tight and close to the ground. I have one other whose name is unknown to me; it is not as vigorous as 'Aureum,' nor as bright. Instead, the leaves are variegated with soft shades of yellow, creamy white, and medium chartreuse. It may be *O. v.* 'Viride.' NG]

Orostachys

[These succulent-leaved plants are wonderful in a well-drained, sunny spot in the garden. *O. aggregatus* has green foliage and many tiny plantlets about the mother plant. My favorite is *O. furusei*, which has blue-gray foliage and flower spikes that look like small bits of coral with red bracts and white flowers. There is a very tiny one, *O. minutus*, and a spiky one, *O. spinosus*, which are both worth looking for. NG]

Paeonia

[Most peonies are too large even for the largest rock garden; however, *P. tenuifolia* is a choice species with finely cut dark green foliage and beautiful single crimson flowers. The ultimate height is only eighteen inches, and its blooming time is spring. It grows best in full sun but will do reasonably well in part shade. NG]

Penstemon

[The best and easiest penstemon I have grown in a shaded rock garden is *P. hirsutus pygmaeus*. It has performed for the past eight years by providing masses of tubular purplish flowers in late spring and by seeding about. The evergreen rosettes of leaves are deep burgundy green throughout the winter. I have tried others; *P. pinifolius* with its orange red flowers and fine foliage delighted me for a couple of years. This North American genus should be explored by all curious gardeners. NG]

Petrorhagia

The tunic flower, *P. saxifraga,* is one of the most valuable of rock plants for us because it blooms in summer, takes to heat, and is at its best in poor, dry soil. It not only blooms in summer but continues into the fall without being stopped by the early frosts. The fine pink mist of flowers takes the place of creeping gypsophila, which is difficult in this climate. There are white and double pink forms. The white one is beginning to appear in catalogs.

Phlox

[This genus has many wonderful plants for rock gardens that are either sunny or shaded. Most of them are North American natives and well conditioned to the rigors of a climate which may have intense heat and humidity in the summer and sudden drops to 0°F or lower in the winter.

P. drummondi (ann.) is my favorite of all summer annuals. This phlox, which is native to Texas, bears flowers in many colors. From a sowing of mixed seeds you can expect to have red, blue purple, white, buff, and pink flowers. I prefer to buy packets of seeds which have been separated as to color, and even then will have different hues within a color range. There are taller named cultivars, but the best for rock gardens are the smaller "unimproved" ones. I have discovered one tip not mentioned on the seed packets. They seem to require a cool period to stimulate germination, so don't wait until all danger of frost has passed; sow them where they are to grow in early spring.

Most gardeners immediately think of *P. subulata,* which, with its many colors and accommodating sprawling habit, is perfect for growing among and over rocks.

Two very desirable forms are *P. s.* 'Brittonia rose' and the beautiful, compact white *P. s.* 'Sneewichan.' Similar in habit but blooming a little later is *P. nivalis,* and this, too, comes in many colors; however, it is not as aggressive as *P. subulata,* and it tolerates poor soil and drought without complaint. Some desirable forms are pink *P. n.* 'Camla' and white *P. n.* 'Avalon White.' Another species for full sun is *P. bifida,* whose flowers have notched petals and lovely colors. Especially recommended are *P. bifida* 'Snee' with blue flowers, *P. b.* 'Colvin's White,' and the unusual blue-and-violet *P. b.* 'Starbright.' There are many hybrids, most of them spontaneous seedlings that appear unexpectedly in gardens. Some of my favorites are the ones which came originally from Lincoln Foster's garden in Connecticut. *P. ×* 'Coral Eye' is a lovely pale pink with a darker eye, *P. ×* 'Laura' is a very pale pink, *P. ×* 'Millstream Jupiter' is a fine blue, and *P. ×* 'Millstream Daphne' is a rich rosy red. One of the most beautiful hybrids is *P. ×* 'May Snow,' with its wide, round, pure white petals. A wonderful hybrid between *P. subulata* and *P. stolonifera* is *P. × procumbens,* which has fine dark evergreen foliage and beautiful wide-petaled pink flowers. This one prefers full sun, as does another chance hybrid which appeared in Lee Raden's garden in Pennsylvania. This one is *P. ×* 'O.G.K.,' and it has deeper-pink flowers.

For a shaded site, the many forms of our native *P. stolonifera* are superb, with their spreading habit and large flowers held about four inches above the ground. Their mats of leaf rosettes make a fine ground cover which is not too dense for little bulbs to penetrate. Try all of the colors, from white *P. s.* 'Alba' to pink *P. s.* 'Pink Ridge' to blue *P. s.* 'Blue Ridge' and *P. s.* 'Iridescent' to deep violet *P. s.* 'Sherwood Purple.' There are many shades of these basic colors, and chance seedlings are always worth keeping until they bloom. I grow them in the rock garden as well as throughout a bed of primulas in the woods, where they weave through the many different colors and species there, giving unity to the design.

There are other, larger species of native phloxes which grow well in woodland conditions. The many forms of *P. divaricata* are wonderful throughout the garden. I have them from the typical blue form to pure white. The one with notched petals is *P. d. laphamii*, and the white form of that is *P. d.* 'Fuller's White.' Their seedlings can be anything from a silvery blue to mauve, and although this species grows well in shade, it also tolerates full sun. Blooming at about the same time in midspring is *P. amoena*, with intense pink purple flowers. This one grows lower than the preceding species, only six to twelve inches, and it too does well in light shade but best in full sun. There are many beautiful forms available, from white *P. a.* 'Snowdrift' to *P. a.* 'Vein Mountain' to *P. a.* 'Pinstripe,' which has white pinstripes on the deep pink petals. A superb hybrid, which I believe to be of these two, is *P.* × 'Chattahoochee,' which has the deep blue of *P. divaricata* and the lower stature and red eye of *P. amoena*. Both *P. ovata*, with its beautiful pink to purple flowers ten to fifteen inches tall, and *P. pulchra*, with fragrant pink flowers, are worth having in a shaded rock garden or in the woodland garden.

One other group of phloxes, difficult but worth trying, comes from Chihuahua, Mexico. I tried them unsuccessfully in many parts of the garden, and nearly gave up before I planted them in a large iron pot filled with a very lean mixture of stones and sand. There is some question of the true species name; these are sometimes listed as *P. mesoleuca*, sometimes as *P. purpurea*, and sometimes just by their cultivar names. This year I am growing *P.* 'Vanilla,' a beautiful white form, and *P.* 'Arroyo,' a bright carmine rose, but I intend to acquire as many more as I can. They grow to about eight inches and want full sun. NG]

Phyteuma

[Members of the campanula family, phyteumas are unusual and beautiful for their late-spring display of spiky, globular blue flowers. They require a gritty soil and do very well in light shade. *P. scheuchzeri* and *P. betonicifolium,* two desirable long-lived species, have blue flowers and dark green basal leaves. They bloom for me in May after most of the spring flowers have faded and are much appreciated for that. NG]

Platycodon

[There are at least two good dwarf forms of this genus that are worth growing in a sunny rock garden. Their showy flowers and long summer blooming season make them especially desirable. *P. grandiflorus* 'Mariesii,' with its large, balloonlike blue flowers, grows to about eighteen inches; *P. g.* 'Apoyama' has equally large flowers but remains only about eight inches high. NG]

Polemonium

[*P. reptans* is a fine choice for a shaded rock garden. It is often called Jacob's ladder, perhaps because of the many leaflets which compose a leaf. In midspring beautiful blue, cupped flowers are produced at the tips of the stalks, which are about a foot high. NG]

Polygonatum

[A number of species of Solomon's seals make superb plants for a shaded section of the garden. The botanical name refers to the many joints of the rhizomes. The plants are lovely throughout the summer, with many opposite leaves to a stalk. *P. commutatum,* the great Solomon's seal, is very tall—up to seven feet—and is best planted in the woods. However, the lower *P. officinale* with its many clusters of white bells is charming; and *P. odoratum thunbergii* 'Variegatum' is a dramatic plant best loved for its superb variegated foliage. The bright pink buds in spring are one of the highlights of my gardening year. The Japanese species, *P. falcatum,* has an understated charm with its sculptured green leaves and greenish white flowers. *P. humile* is a fine low-growing plant, only six to eight inches, but its widely spreading rhizomes may make it too difficult to control except in the wild garden. NG]

Portulaca

P. grandiflora (ann.): In the South it is foolishness to be above growing such common dooryard flowers as rose moss and thrift and verbena in the rock garden—that is, if it is really a garden and not a collection of rare plants. Only these dependable plants provide solid and unfailing patches of color, rose moss and verbena in summer and thrift (*Phlox subulate*) in earliest spring. The full-blown double flowers and crude reds and yellows, though dominant, are not the only forms of portulaca, and some of the single flowers have the charm of anemones and the delicacy of shells. The difficulty is in securing these, for only the puffy double forms come in separate colors, and the only way is to sow a mixture and then weed out the undesirables—unless you are lucky enough to be able to buy plants in bloom. I found it in a pot in Mrs. Price's greenhouse, a fragile bit of porcelain with two rows of creamy petals marked with pale violet. Planted all to itself between the hot stones of the garden steps, it has the distinction of a choice alpine—and in the heat of the day there is still a morning freshness in the pallor of the shallow cups and the underwater color of the leaves.

Potentilla

[Having given up hope of growing the beautiful shrubby potentillas, I nearly abandoned the genus altogether. I am glad I didn't, for I am growing three worthy species which are excellent rock garden material. *P. villosa* is a low, silver-foliaged plant with bright yellow flowers which open whenever the sun hits them in early spring. It spreads slowly by producing rosettes of leaves at the edge of the mother plant. *P. tridentata minima* is a refined green-leaved species with smaller white flowers. The offsets are farther from the parent than *P. villosa,* which makes it a good weaving plant. The third truly desirable garden-worthy member of this genus is *P. alba,* with somewhat gray leaves and lovely white flowers in spring. These three species will grow happily in either full sun or part shade and aren't fussy about soils. NG]

Primula

While the South is not the ideal place for making a collection of rare and difficult alpine primulas, you can be fairly content (as long as you do not let yourself even think of *P. carniolica* of the Idrian Alps or *P. cusickiana* of the Wallowa Mountains) with the ordinary primroses, cowslips, and oxlips of Europe and with some of the more easygoing Asiatic primulas.

The solitary flowers of the true primrose, *P. vulgaris* (often listed as *P. acaulis*), are typically pale yellow, but there are garden forms in pink, rose, and purple, and even in blue.

Cowslips smell of spring. They are called *P. veris* because they show by their flowering the new spring coming on. The flowers are in one-sided umbels. They are yellow in the wild forms, freckled with tiny red dots. In the garden the colors range from apricot to orange to red.

The oxlip, *P. elatior,* is called *elatior,* "tall," because it is taller than the primrose and the cowslip. The flowers are pale yellow with an old-gold eye. They are said to be scentless, but to me they have a fresh, lemony smell.

P. polyantha is a garden primrose belonging to the same group as the cowslip and the oxlip. The form that is common in old gardens in these parts is pale yellow with a gold eye. It is one of the toughest of garden perennials, growing in the driest and most barren ground and blooming from earliest spring—sometimes even at the end of February—to late April or even May. The clumps can be divided indefinitely and replanted in all parts of the garden, even in the darkest corners, where they lie in the shadows like patches of pale sunshine. Gertrude Jekyll's 'Munstead Giants' endure long summers and heat with a stoicism equal to that of the common garden variety, and for the South they are among the most dependable, floriferous, and spectacular primroses that I have found so far. These bloom in many colors, palest pink to lilac and deep red violet, mahogany, and yellow. The florets are very large, to two inches across, and many in a bunch. 'Munstead's Cream' has large flowers of pale chalcedony yellow centered with stars of yellow ochre. This blooms for me regularly at the end of March, but this year I found bunch primroses in Mrs. Church's garden in Charlotte blooming in late February in drifts of ruby and amethyst.

P. juliae is a tiny early primrose from the Caucasus, less than three inches tall and with small flowers that are rosy red in the type. Even though it has been in cultivation for less than half a century, countless crosses with other species of the Vernales group have produced hybrids of all colors. Reports from members of the American Rock Garden Society show that it grows well in Maryland and Virginia, but I have no word of its flourishing south of Virginia, and my own efforts have not been encouraging. Still, I have not given up. As Robert Moncure said, "All of the *P. juliae* hybrids, as well as the regular form, do extremely well in the hot and dry summers of the South, if given plenty of humus and partial shade" (*American Rock Garden Society Year Book*, 1949, p. 22). I can account for one failure by the fact that I set the little plant out in ill-drained soil. Poor drainage is one thing that it cannot withstand. Probably the others were due to soil that became baked in summer. The roots of this primrose are near the surface of the soil, and a mulch to protect them from drying out is a necessity. The Juliae hybrids, being so small, are not such heavy feeders as the more robust primroses and should be given little manure. With these things in mind, I do not see why they could not be grown as readily in Charlotte as in Alexandria.

The most easily grown of the Asiatic primroses is *P. sieboldii*, a Japanese species which seems to adapt itself to a variety of climates and thrive in poorer soils with less moisture than most, but like *P. juliae* it is benefited by a mulch to protect the creeping rootstocks that lie close to the soil surface. It spreads slowly but improves with the years. The variety that I happened upon is called 'Southern Cross.' The large fringed flowers of Chinese violet are marked with silver. They have a faint and pleasant odor that reminds me of sweet lemonade. This form usually blooms late in March. A number of named varieties are offered in colors ranging from pink and lilac to rose, and there is a pure white one called 'Purity.' The flowers are in umbels on six- or eight-inch stalks among large wrinkled leaves with scalloped margins.

Although it comes from the grassy slopes of the Himalayas, *P. denticulata* has a good name for enduring the conditions of lowland gardens and is reported as flourishing in Maryland and Virginia. It is said to be an early bloomer, coming even in January in mild climates, but in its first year it did not put in an appearance until the first of April, and that was the last I saw of it. Balls of small round lilac flowers stand neatly above oval leaves that are small in early spring but grow large and lush later in the season. This group prefers a heavy soil.

The Chinese species *P. bulleyana* and *P. beesiana* did not respond to my efforts the only time that I had them, but their offspring, the bullesiana hybrids, have flourished for several seasons, blooming the last of April and winding up the primrose season. My plants came from Mrs. Chrismon, who raised them from seed, and I think that this may account for their success. The flowers of these hybrids are in barbaric patterns of red orange and red violet, combinations derived from the apricot and orange of *P. bulleyana* and the rich purples of *P. beesiana*. In one clump in my rock garden the florets are rose pink with an eye of Mars orange, and in another they are rosy red with garnet centers. The buds begin to open close to the ground, but one whorl of flowers rises above another, in the manner characteristic of the candelabra section, until the stalks are eighteen inches tall. Every year I am filled with wonder that any plants so splendid should bloom in my garden.

Mrs. Chrismon sent me these notes on her methods in Greensboro, North Carolina:

> The seed of *P. bullesiana* sown in mid-October germinated with "radish velocity"! The seedlings were transplanted to their permanent places the following April, into well-drained loam mixed with quantities of leaf mold and well-rotted compost. Asiatic primroses need less sun than the polyanthus, and morning sun seems best. Water in quantity is required from early spring to late fall, and a yearly mulch of leaf mold mixed with bonemeal. The tops die down in the fall, and do not appear again until late spring, just at the point when you have given them up as lost. In late March of the second spring the seedlings begin to send up blooming stalks. The flowers last well, and the plants bloom from six to eight weeks.

It would be discouraging to recite the list of primroses that have passed through my garden "like the snowflakes on the river seen but once and gone forever," but each year new names appear in the catalogs, and there is always the hope that some of these can be added to those that have already proved themselves fond of the South. But

Non-woody Plants

105

if they are to flourish, it is necessary to remember that primroses in general like deep, moist soil that is rich in humus, and that in these parts they require shade. Many, especially the Asiatic species, thrive on cow manure, and all are better for a spring and fall mulch of leaf mold mixed with sand.

[There are just a few more primulas which will tolerate the long, hot summers of the South. *P. kisoana* is perhaps my favorite, with its fuzzy pink stems and flower stalks rising from a pink resting bud in spring. This is a stoloniferous species, and so propagation is simple; new plants appear at some distance from the original plant by the second spring. I have only the white- and pink-flowered forms but have read that there are others. As with *P. sieboldii,* these plants simply go dormant under certain conditions.

P. pulverulenta, with red-purple flowers, and *P. burmanica,* two other candelabra types which are as easy as the ones Elizabeth Lawrence mentions, both prefer a moist site. I have had the latter in bloom throughout the summer, with flowers still good during the third week of August. *P. cortusoides* and *P. polyneura* are two other Asiatic species which I have found delightful. The former blooms in early spring with many flowers on a stalk in shades of rose purple, and the latter continues blooming well into the summer, with flowers in July and August this year. At a glance they look just about the same, but the blooming period makes it desirable to have both of them.

P. vialii is a short-lived species but definitely worth having. Late in the spring a spire of blooms rises from the furry leaves, and the combination of bright scarlet calyces and lavender flowers is wonderful. They are easily grown from seed and are absolutely winter hardy. When selecting *P.* × *polyantha* plants, avoid purchasing the large-flowered Pacific Giants unless you want only a spring houseplant. They are neither winter-hardy nor summer-tolerant. The 'Barnhaven Strain' is superb. Florence Bellis, author of *Gardening and Beyond,* worked for many years in Oregon to produce flowers of beautiful colors, perfecting a pink strain as well as a pale blue one. She also developed the 'Cowichan Strain' in many dark colors. These are *P.* × *polyantha* without the usual yellow or gold eye, and they have a rich, velvety look unlike any others. I am growing dark blue, garnet, purple, and a marvelous rich cherry red.

P. vulgaris subsp. *sibthorpii* is another excellent species that is especially good in hot climates. It is a beautiful pale pink. It is an early bloomer, making a good show in the first part of March and remaining attractive throughout the summer.

P. × *media* (or *P.* × *tommasinii*), the sterile hybrid of *P. elatior* and *P. veris,* is often found in big clumps in old gardens. It is a reliable performer in midspring, with many pale yellow flowers. It is this color which best illustrates primrose yellow. NG]

Prunella

Self-heal may be scorned by alpine gardeners, but not by me. I made several attempts to settle *P. grandiflora* in the Raleigh garden, where it bloomed well enough but did not live very long. Several years ago Carl Krippendorf from Ohio sent me potted plants of the variety *alba* which he had raised from seed, and these—whether they are a sturdier form or because Charlotte suits them better—are still with me. They bloom prettily in May and repeat later in the season.

Several other color forms in blue violet and red violet are available. Self-heal has a reputation for spreading, but with me it has never spread as much as I would like. As to soil, it is not particular as long as the spot is not too dry, and it grows best in shade.

Pulmonaria

The lungworts come so early, even before our own wildflowers, that it is always a surprise to me to see a spot of pink near the path and find the first buds all ready to open. These wildflowers of the European woods are related to the Virginia bluebells and have the same charming habit of starting out pink and ending up blue. In England this gave them the old name of soldier-and-sailor-flower, pink for the coats of the soldiers, blue for the coats of the sailors. All of the lungworts grow in shade in the acid soil that most wildflowers need.

P. angustifolia is the first to bloom, coming at its earliest in February and at its latest toward the end of March. The buds are a dark red violet. They open pink, and then the flowers turn the purest gentian blue. This is one of the earliest, bluest, and most permanent of rock plants. I have read that it should be divided often, but a single plant bought ten years ago has been spreading slowly ever since, filling empty crevices, but never encroaching, and forming a flat mat of oval leaves of medium green. It will grow and bloom in very poor, dry soil and in deep shade, but is much better in light shade with good soil and moisture.

The other species are more upright and bunchy, not trailing, and with me not long-lived. They usually bloom a little later than *P. angustifolia,* but still they make an early splash of color in the rock garden.

P. montana has flowers that vary from thulite pink to eugenia red when they open, but they turn to violet as they age. The foliage is not spotted.

P. officinalis, the spotted dog, makes large clumps of variegated foliage with pink-and-blue flowers.

P. saccharata, Bethlehem sage, produces large flowers that open out spinel pink and turn to soft blue violet but still with a trace of pink. The leaves are dark green with silver spots. In the variety 'Mrs. Moon' the flowers stay on the red side of violet and never fade to blue.

[*P. longifolia* is superb, with narrow pointed leaves that are dark green spotted with white. The intense blue flowers are beautiful in early spring. There are other forms or cultivars which may be garden hybrids of the above species. *P.* × 'Roy Davidson' has beautiful well-marked leaves and clear blue flowers. *P. argentea* has nearly white leaves that remain decorative all summer. *P.* × 'Highdown' has magnificent deep blue flowers and beautifully marked leaves.

P. officinalis in its white-flowered form, sometimes listed as *P.* 'Sissinghurst White' or *P. o. alba,* is beautiful planted in drifts. *P. o.* 'Cambridge Blue' is a fine form with light blue flowers. NG]

Pulsatilla

[This genus provides some of the most exciting early spring sights. I have not found them long-lived in my garden but continue to plant a few each year in an effort to have that annual excitement of seeing them unfurl their furry leaves in very early spring and then open their beautiful flowers to the sun each day. They require excellent drainage and full sun to be at their best. For years I had a large clump of *P. cernua* which produced drooping maroon flowers with cones of bright yellow stamens. The easiest species to grow is *P. vulgaris,* which has flowers in colors ranging from white through pink to deepest purple. Some of the better color forms are probably garden hybrids. *P. halleri* has been with me for about eight years now and has never failed to delight me with masses of violet flowers in spring. All of these species have elegant, feathery seed heads. Taxonomists have sometimes classified these as *Anemone pulsatilla,* which may be where you will find them listed in some catalogs. NG]

Puschkinia

P. scilloides has come into bloom in my garden as early as February 9 and as late as March 21. Its pale bells are washed and delicately striped with pale blue. Not the least of their charms is the fine spicy fragrance. I remember that the first time I had this little relative of the squills I thought it rather unattractive. The few-flowered stems were only four inches at their tallest and seemed to do most of their flowering underground. Later, Carl Krippendorf sent me a fine form with larger, bluer flowers, nine to an eight-inch spike.

Ranunculus

[Because our lawns are filled with *R. bulbosus,* I am wary of recommending other members of this genus for anything except a wild garden. There are a few species worth trying, but watch carefully lest they spread too vigorously. *R. ficaria* produces shiny leaves and bright yellow flowers in early spring. English growers have made many selections of desirable forms, one of the best being *R. f.* 'Brazen Hussy' with bronze leaves. I am also testing—in a pot first—a charming small-leaved Japanese species, *R. yakushimanus,* which, though vigorous, continues to bloom fitfully all summer. NG]

Rosmarinus

Rosemary (unlike lavender) is very long-lived in my garden. The one that I grow is the typical *R. officinalis,* which grows eventually to be a large shrub in congenial surroundings, but that would take a long time, and it has never seemed out of place among smaller plants. It is a wayward shrub that looks best when it is old and gnarled with sparse foliage like a mist from the sea. I planted it at a corner of the wall where the path is so narrow that you cannot pass without brushing against the leaves and being refreshed by their fragrance.

Elsie Hassan says that by far the best form is the small-leaved, low-growing Irish rosemary, which is almost everblooming. The real bloom of the rosemaries is in earliest spring. "Rosemary is a glory to behold right now," she wrote in February, "and the flowers are bluer than in summer."

The form *prostratus*, which now may be *R. lavandulaceus* comes from the island of Capri and is more tender than the type. This should not be a drawback in the South, although I have not succeeded in getting it established so far. Eleanour Sinclair Rohde said that it does not flower in England until April or May, while the type "flowers fitfully all through mild winters." This is the only variety offered in this country, but there are a number of other forms if only one could get hold of them. Miss Rohde complained that she searched for twenty years for a true fastigiate rosemary, but at last she found it. And so I shall not give up hope. The gilded rosemary is the one that I want most, but even if I should find it, the golden leaves may turn green if it is not in the poorest soil. Then there is a white-flowered rosemary, and one from Majorca with pink flowers, and one with double flowers. The latter Miss Rohde thinks mythical, for three centuries ago it was equally elusive. John Parkinson, author of *Paradisi* (1629), knew it "only by relation," which, he said, "I pray you accept, untill I may by sight better inform you."

Rosemary, like lavender, comes from warm Mediterranean countries where it grows on sunny cliffs near the sea. It needs to bask on open southern slopes in deeply dug, sandy soils made sweet by the addition of old lime rubble. In such places it will bloom best, live longest, and give forth its fragrance.

Salvia
[The only salvia I have grown successfully that has the correct proportions for a rock garden is *S. jurisicii*. It remains under fifteen inches and has finely divided leaves and attractive upside-down lavender flowers. NG]

Sanguinaria
[It would be an incomplete spring without bloodroot. *S. canadensis* unfolds as the weather begins to warm, and from the red roots come silver foliage and pure white flowers which open when the sun hits them. There is also a double form, *S. c.* 'Plena,' which blooms just a

little later than the single one. If left alone they will naturalize fairly quickly by self-sown seeds. Grow these in light shade where sunlight can get through in the spring and where tree roots don't take all of the available moisture and nutrients. NG]

Santolina

The generic name of these aromatic herbs is said to come from *sanctum linum,* an old name for *Santolina virens,* which is still called holy flax. Holy flax is the greenest of herbs both summer and winter. I believe it is my first choice for the rock garden. The plants spread to three feet or more if allowed but keep close to the ground; if planted on a wall, they veil the rocks in misty green. A yearly clipping keeps them in shape, and this is best done after the flowers fade. In June the pale yellow buttons and green leaves are as fresh and sweet smelling as a spring meadow.

S. *chamaecyparissus,* the gray-leaved santolina, is called lavender cotton. Like holy flax it is low-growing and wide spreading, but it is more vigorous and cannot so easily be kept in bounds. It is certainly the most beautiful of gray-leaved shrubs when at its best, but too much cold or humidity is apt to discolor the frosty leaves, and old plants have a tendency to break apart if they are not sheared often and thoroughly. On the other hand, Helen Noyes Webster of Lexington, Massachusetts, warns against reckless pruning: "Too much new wood taken off at once causes 'bleeding' and subsequent winter-killing." Although she wrote for the latitude of Boston, I think we should heed her warning somewhat, cutting back the old plants with the pruning shears only once a year—in early spring—to make them compact and keeping them so by frequent light clipping with the hedge shears. The temptation to do drastic pruning if they discolor in the muggy weather of August should be resisted. The same thing applies to southernwood, lavender, rosemary, horehound, and maybe some of the other herbs: one good pruning in spring and continual pinching and snipping all summer. I never let the lavender cotton bloom, for the brassy yellow buttons aren't attractive with the silver foliage. I often wonder where the idea came from that Nature has perfect taste.

Two other santolinas, S. *neapolitana* and S. *pinnata,* are listed in the Royal Horticultural Society's *Dictionary of Gardening*; the first one has white-felted foliage, and the other green foliage and white flowers. A friend sent me sprigs of a green one with much finer leaves than those of the holy flax (but it had not flowered) and a silvery one that she says is much finer of leaf and fluffy in growth.

The santolinas demand light soil, perfect drainage, and all of the sunlight that is available. They should always be grown on a wall or a bank or high up in the driest part of a rock garden. Although they live for many years, young plants are most ornamental, and as they grow so fast and root so easily, perhaps the best plan is to replace them every few years. Helen Mayer of Charlotte says that most herbs should be renewed at frequent intervals, and I am beginning to think that she is right.

Saponaria

In this part of the country *S. ocymoides* blooms from early April to late May, and we cannot count on it for summer color as in the North. Although this alpine from the mountains of central Europe is an old favorite on all lists of easy plants for beginners—requiring only good drainage and full sun—it is not always permanent. Neither Mr. Tong nor I could keep it in Raleigh, while it bloomed year after year in Nannie Holding's garden in Wake Forest, North Carolina, covering the rocks with clouds of mallow pink flowers.

[There is another summer-blooming saponaria that is worth seeking out. *S.* × *lempergii*, with pink flowers for much of the summer, is an excellent addition to the sunny part of the rock garden. Pamela Harper recommends *S.* × 'Olivana' as an easy, reliable rock garden plant. NG]

Satureja

Along with thyme, lavender, and santolina, the savories come from the herb garden to the rock garden, bringing with them the aromatic scent of summer. They resemble the thymes in appearance and habit—sometimes upright, sometimes creeping—but are more showy in flower. They require the same sort of situation: full sun and poor soil, high and dry on a rock wall. Coming from warm countries, they like heat and endure drought, but they are not so tolerant of humidity. From my own experience in Raleigh I should be inclined to skip them all, with the exception of our native *S. glabella*, but that

Elsie Hassan puts the two she has grown at the top of her list of good rock plants for the South.

The one that has done best for me is the Alpine savory, *S. alpina* (now *Acinos alpinus*), or at least the one that came to me under that name. There is so much confusion as to the names of the species, not to mention the genera, that I am not at all sure of it. My plant has gray and fragrant foliage and purple flowers throughout much of the summer, but I notice that Carl Purdy of California describes the leaves as deep green. He says that it grows in dry soil but does better with moisture.

Calamint is a European herb that was connected with several genera before ending up as *S. calamintha*. Now it has a genus of its own: *Calamintha,* and *nepeta* is the species name. It is a prostrate evergreen creeper as I have it, but according to *Hortus Third* should be from one to two feet high. [*Hortus Third* is probably describing *S. nepatoides*.] The plant in the trade is the first of the savories to bloom, with me in early May. In the North it blooms on through the summer, but here the flowering ceases with the hot weather. The flowers are bright manganese violet with a mist of fine purple dots. This, for a savory, is very gay. This species needs a gritty soil and lime.

S. montana, winter savory, sometimes listed as *S. cuneifolia,* is the one used in cooking. It makes a low gray mound and blooms in late summer and early fall. Elsie Hassan finds it very drought-resistant and easy to propagate. The flowers are white or pale lilac.

[I am not certain which of the several names for this attractive native shrub to use. You may find it listed as *S. georgiana, Clinopodium georgianum,* or *Calamintha georgiana.* I have selected the first of these because that is how it is listed in *Hortus Third.* It is tolerant of heavy soils as well as sand, requires good drainage, and makes a fine display of pink to lavender flowers throughout the fall. As the days become cooler and shorter, the fragrant foliage turns gradually purple. NG]

Saxifraga

After worrying with a number of the saxifrages that I saw in northern gardens and read about in rock garden books, I came to the conclusion that even those that are described as easy to grow are not for the South. But in Louisiana I found *S. stolonifera* growing in all of the corners that were too shady and too dry for any other plant. This is called the strawberry geranium and is usually considered a houseplant, but it is really perfectly hardy. Later I found it in gardens along the North Carolina coast and planted in the Deep South to cover the ground where nothing else will grow. I brought a piece home (a small piece is all that will be needed for a start—it did not acquire the name mother-of-thousands for nothing) to put in a prominent place in my garden, at the foot of the wall fountain.

I consider it one of the most ornamental of all the plants that grow among rocks. I thought of it at first as a foliage plant and did not expect to be pleased with the flowers, but they are small, white, and utterly charming. When they bloom, in mid-April, the open, airy sprays are as delicate as foam. The individual flowers are curiously designed. There are three tiny upper petals minutely dotted with pink and two exaggeratedly long lower petals that are tapered at both ends and attached by such a fine point that they are always in motion. The round, hairy leaves—pale green, striped with silver on top, and dark red beneath—are coarsely scalloped, and each scallop is pointed. They lie flat on the ground in a cool pattern of diminishing circles as the threadlike runners with tiny leaves at their tips spread farther and farther from the center. The plant is not quite evergreen when the winter is severe, but the foliage lasts until after Christmas, and by the first of April the new leaves begin to expand.

S. stolonifera is not to be found listed with the alpines, but it is one of the plants that the farm women offer for exchange, and you may come across it in a nursery or at the florist.

[There is a beautiful variegated form of *S. stolonifera* with leaves in shades of green, yellow, pink, and red which is just as easy to grow as the type but harder to find. I have had good luck with this one, though Pamela Harper says it is not reliably hardy for her in Virginia.

Our native *S. virginiensis* is the only other satisfactory member of this genus that I have found. It wants shade, but when happy will seed about and make a fine show with its spikes of tiny white flowers on stalks rising from the basal rosettes of leaves. NG]

Scabiosa

[There is one wonderful scabiosa that is perfect for any rock garden. *S. lucida* forms neat rosettes of finely cut foliage, above which rise stems to about four inches topped with dense heads of rose lilac flowers. It needs sun but can tolerate very light shade and will bloom continuously throughout the summer. NG]

Scillas

The delightful thing about squills is that they are so blue. *S. bifolia* has a pair of gray-green leaves with spikes of twenty or more small, narrow petals of cornflower blue. It blooms at the end of February or a little later and makes itself at home in the garden in either sun or shade.

Here in North Carolina *S. litardierei* (formerly known as *S. pratensis* or *S. amethystina*) blooms in mid-April with the English and Spanish bluebells. It needs a sandy soil in full sun and is one of the most satisfactory kinds for bloom and increase. It flowers in a blue-gray mist that lasts for three weeks.

Blooming at the same time as the small and early squills is a more robust species introduced from northern Iran in 1931 as *S. tubergeniana* but more correctly named *S. mischtschenkoana*. It is related to *S. sibirica,* but the flowers are larger and paler and rather more like puschkinias, with the same spicy aroma of woods in early spring. They come out looking as if they had been dipped in bluing, and with a sort of cold purity that results from having blue anthers and no trace of yellow. They grow paler with age, and the final effect is white. The flowers open at ground level, and as they mature, the threadlike scapes keep pushing up until they are four inches or more tall, several spikes crowding up from each bulb. The stout, short, pale green leaves arrive at the same time.

The small and early species, none of them over six inches tall, are followed when spring is at its height by the English and Spanish squills, or bluebells. The common English bluebell, *S. nonscripta,* blooms unromantically in my garden sometime in April. I always like to have a few in the rock garden, but they are beautiful only when planted in such quantities as to seem a sheet of color; individually they appear to me undesirable in all of the forms.

The flowers of the Siberian squill, *S. sibirica,* are pure blue-violet with a faint underlying tinge of rose on the inside. The penetrating blueness of the petals is heightened by the blueness of the anthers. There are from one to five small nodding flowers on short reddish stems, appearing in late February or early March. The varieties bloom earlier. 'Spring Beauty' is the first. It has been out as early as January 20, although in some seasons it is a month later. It is the most robust form of all, with six or more stout scapes and with flowers that are larger and of a deeper blue than those of the type. The variety 'Taurica' has bloomed in my garden for many seasons, at the earliest during the first part of February, and at the latest by the end of March. The flowers are a clear, pure blue that has no trace of violet in it. The dark blue hairline in the center of each segment is especially distinct in this form. There is also a white variety, 'Alba.'

The season of squills need not end with the spring, for *S. autumnalis* and *S. scilloides* bloom in late summer. The flowers on the former are small and are variable from pale lilac to deep purple. There is even a white form.

[*S. scilloides* is an excellent summer bloomer. It is a pink-flowering form with such tight clusters of small starry flowers that the effect is plumy. It is a wonderful plant for a rock garden or a lightly shaded site. NG]

Sedum

The sedums are sometimes called live-forever, but that name is misleading. As with other saxatile plants, the alpine species prized by collectors are difficult in all lowland gardens, and in climates like ours they are impossible. Mr. Tong and I once went down the lists of the specialists, and when we had tried them all, only the easy doers were left to us. I have never regretted the time spent on these short-lived mossy bits, as finely spun as cobwebs and as cold to the touch as dew, but I learned anew the lesson we all must learn, to turn our eyes from the distant mountaintops and look for the plants at our doorsteps. I found creeping between the stones in Mrs. Chrismon's garden as choice and thriving a collection as one could wish: a fat succulent one from a little seaside garden at Point Harbor, North Carolina, a fragile white-flowered one from Stone Mountain, and a number of others collected from gardens in the South and Southwest.

S. caeruleum (ann.) is an emerald green annual that bears blue blossoms and prefers a dampish situation. Although it is often mentioned as useful in the rock garden as a cover for shady corners left bare after the flowering of spring bulbs, I have never been able to get one seedling above ground. Still, it is considered one of the easiest annuals.

S. *sexangulare*, of European origin, is a delightfully dark and mossy evergreen carpeter that becomes a sheet of yellow when it flowers in late spring. I have had some difficulty with it in my garden, but I found it rampant on Elsie Hassan's shady terrace, where it was used to such good effect that I could see no need for rarer kinds. I saw it again, or one just like it—perhaps the ever-present Old World stonecrop, S. *acre*—on the increase with Mrs. Chrismon, and brought back to Raleigh a clump which settled down in a corner of the steps and already has gone into a number of other gardens. S. *sexangulare* is similar to S. *acre*, but it makes better and heavier patches and the flowers come a little later. These two are less than three inches tall.

S. *reflexum* is another evergreen yellow-flowered European species, but it is a little taller, growing to six or eight inches. It is valuable because the trailing cylindrical foliage takes on warm tints in winter. It forms a wide mat and looks well in all weathers.

Orland White of Charlottesville, Virginia, considers S. *dasyphyllum* one of the best species for the South, but I cannot keep it. It is the tiniest one of all, scarcely more than an inch tall, blue gray, and woolly. Crumbs of foliage fall off at a touch and root where they land. In cold climates this species is susceptible to dampness in winter, but here, after coming through the winter as fresh as a daisy, it damps off in midsummer.

S. *album*, the white stonecrop, is a species of wide distribution and many variations. Louise Beebe Wilder describes it in *Pleasures and Problems of a Rock Garden* as a ramper, but with me it stays quietly in its place, holding its own but never increasing more than enough to provide plants for visitors to the garden. The type is one of the best and most permanent stonecrops, but I doubt if the varieties would do so well in this trying climate. The only one that I have had experience with is the dainty purple-leaved variety, *purpureum*, which cannot stand our summers. The typical S. *album* grows to about six inches. The trailing pale green foliage is thick and waxy, and the flowers are white.

I have had a number of the western sedums, but the only one that takes at all to southern gardens is a Pacific Coast species, *S. spathulifolium*. It ranges from the foothills of California to an altitude of five thousand feet, and it may be that a plant's adaptability to lowland gardens depends upon where it comes from. The rosettes of gray, fleshy, spatulate leaves are individual and decorative. They keep close to the ground, not rising above four inches, and form slow-spreading clumps. The greenish-yellow flowers appear here at the end of April. This is a woodland plant, and, unlike the other stonecrops, it does best with some protection from the sun (but not in deep shade) and in an acid soil well supplied with leaf mold. [The purple-leaved form, *S. s.* 'Purpureum,' is equally easy in similar locations. NG]

I found *S. pilosum,* a minute and downy stonecrop from the Caucasus and Asia Minor, very much at home in Mrs. Chrismon's garden in Greensboro. Perhaps because it is biennial, this delightful wisp, which Louise Beebe Wilder called the brightest jewel in the sedum crown, is not offered by dealers in rock plants, but seed can be had from the British. The foliage is a delight in itself the first year, and the pleasure of pink flowers is added the next season.

The season of the sedums is long, beginning in April, with the flowering of our native *S. ternatum* and ending in November with that of the Japanese species, *S. sieboldii.* Von Siebold's stonecrop is called the nickle plant. The round silver leaves are delicately scalloped in dusty pink and come in whorls of three at intervals along the prostrate stems. The stems lie on the ground in neat circles. Late in October the small, flat heads of Persian lilac flowers pick up the pink of the leaf margins. Later, the tops die away, and in spring the delicately colored rosettes of the new foliage appear among the early flowers. This species is usually described as inured to any amount of heat and drought, but, in our climate at least, it requires some protection from the sun and a little more moisture than most sedums need. It is slow to become established, but once fixed it is lasting and has the desirable trait of remaining in a clump rather than traveling where it is not wanted. There is also a more difficult form with variegated leaves, *S. s.* 'Variegatum.'

I think that we should experiment with the numerous Mexican sedums, some of which are too tender for severe climates, but so far

I have been able to acquire only one. *S. diffusum* proved to be a very pretty stonecrop but unequal to our summers.

Most sedums have a preference for poor soil and strong sunlight, but in the South even the sun-loving kinds may need a little shade. All must be well drained, and although they are drought-resistant they will not go too long without water.

[I have found several more sedums that are delightful and easy to keep. Two similar natives for lightly shaded locations are *S. glaucophyllum* and *S. nevii;* the former has rosettes of linear, succulent leaves, and the latter has the same but in miniature. They both remain under three inches and have white flowers in late spring. *S. kamtschaticum* and its variegated form, *S. k.* 'Variegatum,' are fine slowly spreading plants with bright yellow flowers in late spring. They may prove too aggressive in sandy soil but remain well behaved in clay loam. *S. lineare* 'Variegatum' is a beautiful foliage plant with linear leaves striped with white. This seems very happy in a sunny site in heavy soil. A Japanese species similar to *S. sieboldii* is *S. cauticola,* which has beautiful whorls of round, succulent, bluish leaves in whorls of two often rimmed with rose and terminal flower clusters in rosy pink. Two related hybrids are desirable for fall bloom and good foliage throughout the summer. *S.* × 'Ruby Glow' has bluish leaves with purple overtones and a fine show of clusters of rosy flowers in early fall. It is probably one of the parents of *S.* × 'Vera Jameson,' which has even darker foliage throughout the growing season. Another hybrid, valued for its beautiful red foliage, is *S.* × 'Ruby Mantle.' It remains about an inch high and spreads slowly to form a mat of deep beet red leaves. Two other shade-tolerant sedums are beautiful throughout the year: *S. rupestre* and its cultivar, *S. r.* 'Minus,' have foliage similar to a blue spruce. They produce yellow flowers in summer, but their chief value is in their leaves. One of the most beautiful variegated-leaved sedums may be found under two names. The correct name is *S. alboroseum variegatum,* but it is often offered as *S. spectabile* 'Variegatum.' The cream-and-green leaves are wonderful when planted near yellow-flowered plants, and they are equally beautiful in sun or light shade. Even in winter the bright, creamy resting buds may be found near the ground. NG]

Semiaquilegia

[This genus is as easy to grow as columbines, but it has a charm and delicacy that sets it apart. The leaves are finely cut and seem thinner in texture than aquilegias, and the flowers are practically spurless and dusky violet. It wants the same conditions as columbines: part shade and good loamy soil. NG]

Sempervivum

The houseleeks cannot be too dry. I first saw them used as outdoor plants in Violet Walker's garden in Virginia. They flowed over the terraces like water and presented no problem. But when I brought home large clumps of all of the kinds she grew, they promptly died. I felt cheated by such behavior, for houseleeks are invariably recommended to the beginner as "kindly, plain-living, and indestructible." Even the name, ever-living, holds a deeper meaning than live-forever. I planted collection after collection, only to see the smug rosettes that looked so immovable when they were planted in their crannies in the fall, and which came through the winter with undiminished ranks, disappear almost overnight in the rainy season. I found a place at last where they have taken hold and seem to be on the increase. It is the top of a rock wall that is overhung by a pink Cherokee rose and where the soil is as poor and dry as a bone. It is dry even in the wettest weather. This confirms me in my belief that we could grow many more rock plants in these parts if we could devise ways to keep them dry in summer.

The nomenclature of the sempervivums is confused, for they hybridize so freely that most of the plants in any collection are unnamed and unnameable. The variety in detail is infinite, but there are a few outstanding types, and these will be found in any of the collections offered by nurseries. The common houseleek is called *S. tectorum* (of the roofs) because since time immemorial it has been grown on housetops to protect houses from lightning. The delicate colors of the coarse, stiff rosettes are as cold as jade and as warm as amethyst. The rosettes are rather flat and in some forms as much as three inches in diameter. The rosettes of the cobweb houseleek, *S. arachnoideum,* are small and globular and wrapped in gossamer. They are heaped in a mound, and those on the outside fall off and hang by a thin thread until they take root. The stragglers are very decorative as they cling to a wall, hand in hand, like mountain climbers. It seems to me that sedums and sempervivums, and succulents in general, are suited only to the more formal parts of the rock garden —the walls, pavements, and flights of steps. Aside from the exceptions that prove the point, they are awkward and uneasy among the casual plants that grow between rocks that hug the earth.

The flowers of the houseleeks are odd but charming. The little daisies at the tops of stiff stems clothed in fleshy sedumlike leaves are strangely like extensions of the foliage. They have the same waxy surface and come in the same tones of greenish yellow and reddish green. They bloom in the summer.

Setcreasea

[In many parts of the country *S. pallida* 'Purple Heart' is grown as a tender houseplant and valued for its beautiful purple foliage and rose-purple flowers. It has proven hardy in Zone 7 and warmer areas and is a beautiful perennial, similar to tradescantias. NG]

Silene

S. pendula (ann.) is one of those plants that are found often in gardens and seldom in the trade. I had it first from Elizabeth Rawlinson in Raleigh, and then, when I came to Charlotte, it found its way from Mrs. Black's garden to mine and from mine back to Raleigh. The original form was double, but the ones I have now are single, and these I like much better. They come in a variety of soft colors, which I have checked against my old Ridgway color chart as deep rose pink, amaranth pink, light rosalane purple, and Iyrian Pink. Thompson and Morgan offer the double-flowered forms in pink, white peach, salmon, lilac, and crimson. This is a flower that perpetuates itself indefinitely once it is established. Though there are never too many, there are enough seedlings to give away each spring, and some to move to bare spots where they are needed. They usually begin to bloom at the end of March, when they are a few inches high, and continue into May or June. I pull them up as they begin to get weedy, leaving always enough plants for seed. There is a selected form called *compacta,* but I rather like for them to spread.

[There are perennial members of this genus suitable for any rock garden, sunny or shady. *S. vulgaris* subsp. *maritima* 'Robin White

Breast' has beautiful gray leaves and white flowers for much of the summer. *S. schafta* blooms with lovely pink flowers on green-foliaged plants in either sun or light shade. *S. caroliniana* definitely prefers shade in my garden and has flowers which may be either white or shades of pink. The subspecies *wherryi* often has excellent pink flowers. *S. polypetala* has been difficult for me to establish, but it is worth trying in a sunny spot. It too may have either pink or white flowers. *S. virginica* is one of the showiest silenes, with brilliant scarlet flowers on decumbent stems. It seems to prefer part shade to sun and has been most permanent in really stony soil. NG]

Sisyrinchium

[There are many charming members of this group that are fine for rock gardens. They are said to prefer sandy soil; however, I have found that they grow well in a clay loam amended with stones. Our native blue-eyed grass, *S. angustifolium*, is a modestly delightful plant with its many small blue flowers. *S. macounii alba* is a beautiful plant with relatively large white flowers. *S. californicum* is wonderful, with yellow flowers produced for a long time in early summer. A splendid miniature, *S. mucronatum* 'Pole Star,' has proportions perfect for the smallest rock garden. From England we acquired a hybrid *S.* × 'Quaint and Queer,' only to learn that it was developed on the West Coast. It has flowers for most of the summer in an unusual shade of reddish brown. NG]

Smilacina

[The false Solomon's seal, *S. racemosa*, is a beautiful, easy-to-grow native plant which can tolerate considerable drought. It is appropriate for a large woodland garden and is beautiful in spring with plumes of small white flowers at the terminals of the stalks. It shows lovely dull red berries in late summer and then disappears for the winter. NG]

Solidago

[Most of the goldenrods are either too tall or too invasive to allow in any spot except a very large border or a wild meadow. *S. caesia* is an elegant, shade-loving species with slender panicles of the tiny yellow flowers so typical of this genus. It can be as tall as three feet, but its slender appearance qualifies it for inclusion in a larger rock garden. Pamela Harper recommends *S. japonica* 'Minutissima' as the best goldenrod for the rock garden. NG]

Spigelia
[The North American native species, *S. marilandica,* is an unusual plant for the edge of a woodland. The red-and-yellow up-facing flowers are produced at the tips of foot-high plants. They require adequate moisture but are not difficult. NG]

Stellaria
[The giant chick (I hesitate to say weed) is a beautiful evergreen perennial which has large, starlike white flowers. Its proper botanical name is *S. pubera,* and it is native to North America. Grow it in shade. NG]

Stylophorum
[There are two desirable species, and both are fine additions to the spring flower display. The native *S. diphyllum,* or Celandine poppy, is usually about a foot high and bears yellow two-inch flowers above beautiful blue-green foliage. The rarer *S. lasiandrum* from China has slightly smaller yellow flowers and greener leaves. They both do well in rich soil in part shade in a woodland garden. NG]

Tagetes
T. tenuifolia (ann.) is a favorite of mine. The variety *pumila* is a dainty dwarf marigold, and with its small button flowers and fine foliage is a good annual for late summer and fall. It dies hard, and only a very black frost can kill it.

Tellima
[*T. grandiflora* is a beautiful evergreen plant with hairy leaves and flowering stalks to two feet with many hanging greenish-white flowers in spring. It is similar to heucheras but prefers a moist, shady site among rocks. NG]

Teucrium
T. lucidum is a stiff little evergreen (or nearly evergreen) shrub that is very useful for edgings and low-clipped hedges. The prostrate shrub *T. chamaedrys* 'Prostratum' I have found offered as *T. prostratum.*

This one is hardier, more evergreen, and more of a rock plant. In the South some shade is recommended for both kinds, but they will not do well under trees, and in my experience grow well in the open.

T. orientale is another erect germander with shining evergreen foliage. The leaves are much larger than those of *T. lucidum.* These three are about a foot high. *T. flavum,* a gray-leaved species with yellow flowers, is twice as tall.

When I lived in Raleigh, Elsie Hassan sent me *T. marum,* which is called cat thyme. "I had two fine plants and the cats have torn them to bits," she wrote. "The scent seems to drive them crazy." Although Mr. Cayce, our springer spaniel, allowed no cats in the garden, I could never get this beautiful little shrub to grow. I should like to try it again in Charlotte, but I have no source for it. It makes a neat, compact, oval shrublet, eight inches tall or a little more. The minute spade-shaped leaves are sage green on top and silvery beneath. The general effect is a misty gray which is charming, especially when the plants are dotted with tiny amethyst flowers. The scent is a bitter one to human beings—more bitter than wormwood—but at the same time strangely refreshing. Elsie Hassan recommends cat thyme for full sun in the highest and driest parts of the rock garden.

[I recently received a beautiful plant labeled *T. scordium crispum marginatum,* which I believe to be more correctly named *T. scorodonia* 'Crispum Marginatum.' It is a beautiful foliage plant for shade. The crimpled yellow edges give it lightness, and the deep yellow veins make it a bright spot in a darker setting. NG]

Thalictrum

[There are some charming small thalictrums which will do well in a partly shaded rock garden. *T. kiusianum* from Japan is my favorite, with tiny purple flowers on plants only five inches high. It has a pleasantly stoloniferous habit and slowly spreads underground. The dark green leaflets have a delicacy which adds lightness to the edge of the border. Another species with proportions appropriate for a rock garden is *T. alpinum,* which grows to ten inches and has inconspicuous flowers but attractive fernlike foliage. *T. koreanum* is an unusual species in that it has shield-shaped leaves and pale yellow flowers in spring. Like *T. kiusianum* it is stoloniferous but not aggressive. NG]

Thymus

There is a soothing monotony in the gray-green foliage and gray-violet flowers of this genus. It grows wherever the soil is poor and the sun is hot but endures only where the drainage is thorough.

Thyme must be in all gardens, for it gives courage to the heart and opens the eyes to fairies, besides being very desirable in the kitchen. There are many sorts: upright, prostrate, and creeping. All are more or less evergreen, blooming from late spring to midsummer and smelling of all sorts of nice things like anise, pineapple, lemon, and geranium. With a few exceptions the species do well in my garden and in the South generally. They like hot weather.

The upright thymes are gray-leaved and bushy. Common thyme, *T. vulgaris,* is the one used in cooking. The English form has a broader and darker leaf than the French thyme, whose foliage is narrow and dusty. These are at their best for flavor and fragrance when grown in poor soil that has been well limed, and I have read that they should never be pruned except when sprigs are pinched off for soups and salads. Since my kitchen garden and rock garden (and all other gardens) are one, I find the use of the shears necessary for the sake of appearance.

I have an idea that the fragrant little gray herb grown in this country as *T. nitidus* is not the Sicilian thyme, which is described as having a shining dark green leaf. However, its identity matters little to the gardener, for it is a pretty plant whose only fault is that it is not very long-lived. A narrow-leaved, round little shrub about a foot high, it resembles lavender rather than thyme. The pink flowers are produced freely in April, and the silver leaves are untarnished in summer.

At the Plantation Gardens Mrs. Bruce Chalfin has the red-stemmed thyme of southern Russia, *T. cimicinus.* It is a trailing plant with small leaves that turn purple in winter and heavy-headed lilac flowers that bloom in summer. It is not an outstanding species, but the foliage is good for flavoring.

Two species should be investigated for the South, and I mean to do so when I can get my hands on them. *T. membranaceus* "from the hot hills of Spain" is desirable particularly for the flowers, which are striking because of the large, colored bracts. *T. longiflorus,* introduced from Spain, is similar, with tubular flowers and colorful calyces. It is recommended for rock gardens only in a favored, warm, and sunny climate, and that sounds like Charlotte to me. Unfortunately the pair is still rare even in England, where they seem to be mostly grown in the alpine house.

The embroidered thymes, *T. vulgaris* cultivars, though they look more robust are as impermanent as the creepers. They are the golden cultivar 'Aureus' and the silver cultivar 'Argenteus,' so called because of their variegated leaves. They look like very dirty pieces of embroidery to me, and I never miss them.

Except for the type, the lemon thyme, *T.* × *citriodorus,* is the most satisfactory and enduring kind for the South. It is erect and bushy but spreads so fast that there is always plenty to give away. I have read that it prefers some shade and good soil, but it flourishes in full sun on a dry wall, and the only attention it gets is severe and frequent clipping. This is a delightful labor, for the scent of the dark green foliage is as refreshing as that of a freshly cut lemon. And finally, the best form for flowers is the cultivar 'Pulchellus,' though I have never had this one myself, never having found a source for it. I found fragrant masses in bloom at the end of May in the Thompson Memorial Rock Garden at the New York Botanical Garden. The flowers are a pale but definite rose color. The flowers of *T.* × *c.* 'Roseus' are larger and more colorful, a clear red-violet called mallow purple. This blooms at the end of July and winds up the season. The large leaves are pleasantly aromatic, with a scent peculiar to this variety.

The other erect thymes that I have grown cannot be recommended for this climate—or at least not from my experience—but they are so tiny and so delightful that I cannot bear not to mention them with the hope that someone else will have better luck. *T. ericifolia,* now *Micromeria ericifolia,* came to me from Elsie Frye's garden in Seattle. I tried setting it out both in spring and in fall, but I could never get it to survive a summer or a winter. It is a minute, compact ball of brassy heathlike foliage and rose-red flowers, the sort of miniature that you feel you cannot live without once you have seen it, and I certainly would not do so if I could discover a way of keeping it. *T. erectus* ("a listed name of no botanical standing"), from the same source, has green beadlike leaves and bluish white flowers. *T. broussonetii,* a native of Morocco, came to me from Carl Purdy in

California. It grows to about six inches tall and has small leaves and bright heads of rose-colored flowers.

These thymes are many and varied, and most of them are easily grown in the South—more easily than in cold climates, for some of them are tender. Mother-of-thyme, *T. praecox* subsp. *arcticus,* is a coarse and sprawling and indestructible species much used between flagstones. The man who used to help keep our paths weeded called it the best-smelling weed in the garden. There are a number of forms and named varieties.

The prostrate types with tiny leaves and flowers are the most delightful, but even with copious watering it is difficult for me to keep these through the midsummer drought. Still I continue to plant them, hoping to find a spot to their liking. They grow very quickly, covering the flagstones with a green film that is dotted with flowers in early summer. The white flowers of the cultivar 'Albus' sparkle like drops of dew, and in winter the foliage is the greenest of all. It is so fragrant that Louise Beebe Wilder "encouraged great mats" to grow in her rock garden for her to sit upon while weeding. Mrs. Bruce Chalfin could use the white moss thyme for a weeding pad, for it grows luxuriantly at Lynchburg, Virginia, but in my garden I am grateful for enough to carpet the lawn of a doll's house if it grows at all. The flowers of the cultivar 'Coccineus' are described as crimson. Either I have the wrong plant, or all other gardeners are color blind, for with me they are the typical pale lilac, though perhaps a little rosier than those of the type. I have read that this form grows even in shade, and I wonder if all of these little ones would not be better off with a little protection from the midsummer sun. I think I shall try them at the foot of the birdbath in the shadow of the pine trees. Another exquisite but even rarer form is 'Annie Hall,' a discovery of Mr. Hall of Harrogate. I have seen this flourishing at Nik-Nar, and I imagine that like the other small carpeters it does best in a cool climate. This one has shell-pink flowers.

The woolly thyme, *T. lanuginosus* is the most adorable of all, a tiny mat of silver down like a fine cobweb; but it is sensitive to dampness in winter and summer, and I find it impossible to keep.

One of the best thymes for the South is a Balkan species, *T. thracicus* (now *T.* 'Long-leaf Gray'), which came to me from Carl Starker. It is of open habit, about as tall as *T. praecox,* and grows, blooms, and spreads in a heartening manner. The light pinkish lilac flowers are showy and numerous, and they bloom for several weeks beginning at the first of April. The leaves are gray and hairy.

Another good one came from Carl Starker as a stowaway, a tiny seedling in a clump of achillea. He identified it as *T. balticus* (a "listed name of no botanical standing"). It is a low creeper with fine ruddy stems and tiny aromatic leaves that have a purplish tint. It is said to bloom freely, but so far has not bloomed at all. Its chief value is that it is colorful in winter. It seeds itself freely and is often found at a distance from the original planting.

T. herba-barona is called caraway thyme, but to me it smells strongly of anise. It is a creeping sort from Corsica that requires a sheltered position and thorough drainage. I had it a number of times before I finally got it established in a south-facing, dry wall. The light roseine purple flowers are later than those of most of the species and a rosier color. It comes into bloom about the middle of May.

[One of the smallest, most compact thymes came to me as *T. drucei minus,* but *Hortus* says it is more properly called *T. praecox* subsp. *arcticus* 'Minor.' It makes a wonderful tight mound of small, round, fragrant leaves. There are several slightly woolly ones which grow well here: *T.* 'Bressingham Pink,' which has mauve flowers and gray-green foliage and stays very close to the soil, and *T.* × 'Longwood,' with gray foliage and a long blooming season in early summer.

T. × *citriodorus* 'Bertram Anderson' is taller growing than the preceding ones and has golden-tinted foliage from fall through winter. *T. necefferi* is unlike all others with its small, narrow gray leaves and mauve pink flowers. One of the most beautiful flowering thymes is the shrubby *T. pallasianus* 'Peter Davis,' with gray foliage and mauve flowers. I have one other tiny one, *T. minimus,* which isn't listed in *Hortus* but makes the most compact growth of any I have seen. I wonder whether this is the same as *T.* 'Doretta Klaber,' which I received from Joyce Fingerut in Pennsylvania. *T. camphoratus* smells only vaguely of camphor to me and is a good shrubby thyme with gray foliage. *T. mastichina,* from North Africa, is hardy here and is a beautiful, fragrant, shrubby type with suggestions of purple and red in the winter foliage. NG]

Tiarella

[There is no genus that can provide a more beautiful, airy aspect in the shaded spring garden than this one. I would hate to be without any of the tiarellas. *T. cordifolia* has a bad reputation that is unjustified in my garden. It is barely stoloniferous and not a bit weedy. The variety *T. c. collina* is beautiful, often with pink, usually fragrant flowers. From Roxie Gevjan in Newtown Square, Pennsylvania, I received *T. wherryi,* which was authenticated by Dr. Wherry himself. This plant has deeply cut leaves which turn a dark bronze in the winter light and fragrant pinkish flowers. It is unlike any *T. wherryi* I have ever purchased and is one of my most cherished plants. The Oriental counterpart, *T. polyphylla,* is a pleasant addition to the woods garden, but it lacks the showy elegance of our native species. I have a beautiful form which appeared in my rock garden. I suspect that it is a hybrid of the nonstoloniferous form of *T. cordifolia* and *T. c. collina.* The leaves are somewhat shiny with beautiful dark markings in spring and winter, and the flowers are pinker than any other forms I have seen. It has the added asset of blooming in May after most of the other species have finished. NG]

Torenia

T. fournieri (ann.) is called the wishbone flower, I suppose because of a fancied resemblance between a wishbone and the black velvet U that stands out at the base of the gray-violet corolla. I always get a few plants in the spring, for the seeds do not germinate out-of-doors until the first of June or later, and plants from seeds sown early under glass lengthen the season. By midsummer there are plenty of volunteers. Torenias revel in heat and thrive on humidity. They will even stand drought, but they are at their best in the low, shady part of the rock garden and with plenty of water. The plants begin to flower when they are a few inches high, but even with continual pinching and plucking they get quite leggy before frost touches them. There is a variety called *alba,* but it is not a pure white, and to me it looks dirty.

T. flava, a smaller species with brown-and-yellow flowers, is the best of summer annuals, but after the last war even English seed merchants dropped it from their list, and the Royal Horticultural

Society's *Dictionary of Gardening* says it is of no horticultural merit
—probably the person who wrote that libel had never seen it.

Tradescantia

[Most tradescantias are either too tall or too weedy and sprawling for any rock garden, but there is one beautiful native species
worth acquiring for a sunny site. *T. hirsuticaulis* remains from eight
to twelve inches tall and produces beautiful deep violet flowers in
late spring, after which the foliage dies down only to reappear in late
summer. NG]

Tricyrtis

[I have never met a tricyrtis I didn't like; however, I don't especially
like the common name, toad lily. They are all deciduous perennials,
and most of them bloom in late summer or early fall and are best
suited to the larger garden. They require shade and are relatively
easy to keep happy.

T. *macropoda* is one of the earlier species to bloom here, with pink
flowers spotted with purple. The other species I have grown bloom
in late summer or fall. The easiest one to acquire and grow is *T. hirta.*
The passionflowerlike blossoms at each of the leaf axils make this
species a delight. They are white with many purple spots, giving a
purple impression at first glance. There is a white form, which often
has bits of pink in it, and a lovely variegated-leaved one. In the latter
the variegation consists of a stripe of yellow at the leaf margins.
Several species have upward-facing yellow flowers. Thus far I have
been able to try two of them: *T. flava,* with beautiful yellow flowers
spotted with red, and *T. perfoliata,* which is similar but has leaves
with bases surrounding the stem. *T. latifolia* is another early species
to bloom for me, and it too has up-facing yellow flowers, but spotted
with purple rather than red. It is a tall plant, often reaching three
feet. I am growing two other species, which are considered by Brian
Mathew to be forms of *T. latifolia. T. puberula* has foliage covered
with minute silvery hairs, and *T. bakeri* has the typical yellow flowers
but is a lower-growing, more sprawling plant. I have recently added
T. dilatata, a Korean species with pink flowers spotted with purple.
One of the most spectacular species of this genus is *T. formosana,*
with flowers up to one and a half inches across and usually white

with spots of red. There is considerable confusion over whether *T. stolonifera* is a synonym or a variant; certainly it is similar. NG]

Trillium

[It was a difficult decision to include these beautiful plants in this book, for the temptation is great to purchase collected stock, and the wild populations are rapidly dwindling. A few nurseries such as We-Du Nurseries in Marion, North Carolina, propagate their stock, but most offer wild-collected plants. The genus is filled with beautiful woodland plants; they usually have three leaves, and three sepals and petals to each flower. They grow from rhizomes and bloom throughout the spring. The showiest species is *T. grandiflorum,* with its pure white flowers up to three inches in diameter. The much rarer double form is marvelous but has been reluctant to flower for me. One of the earliest species to bloom in my garden is the low *T. pusillum,* with beautiful up-facing white, changing to pink, flowers. Imagine this same flower in its pink phase nodding beneath the typical three leaves on a stalk to one and a half feet and you have *T. catesbaei. T. erectum* displays its relatively large maroon flowers on short stalks just above the leaves. Probably the easiest species to grow in profusion is *T. sessile,* which has maroon flowers that look as if they never quite open. There is also an easy-to-please yellow-flowered one which is sometimes listed simply as *T. luteum,* and sometimes as *T. viride luteum.* Hybrid seedlings often appear with flowers in shades between yellow and maroon. The mottled foliage of these species is attractive and lasts throughout early summer. The only other trillium I have grown successfully is *T. cernuum,* with fragrant, nodding white flowers. This one requires growing on a bank in order to see it at its best; otherwise, one has to make an effort (which is certainly worth doing) to see the flowers. I have not succeeded with *T. undulatum* or *T. nivale* and am reluctant to try again until I am certain that I have a source for nursery-propagated material. NG]

Tulbaghia

Tulbaghia is a South African genus named for Tulbagh, a governor of the Cape of Good Hope in the eighteenth century. It is closely related to agapanthus and sometimes is called the pink agapanthus.

Some botanists place both genera with the amaryllids. *T. violacea*, the species usually listed, is a newcomer to my garden, but so far it has proved itself hardy and acquitted itself well. The bunches of lavender flowers on eighteen-inch stems remind me more of an allium than an agapanthus, and the leaves have a garlic odor. The scapes appear with me at monthly intervals from June to September. In California they bloom in summer and winter. They make a large clump when established, and the flowers are more effective en masse. Tulbaghias are not hardy in the North, but they are recommended for spring planting if they are dried in the sun before being stored for the winter. In the garden they like a light soil and will grow in either a dry or a moist situation if they are in full sun. They are easy to grow in pots, can be potted at any time, and are long in bloom.

[It was a wonderful discovery that these South African plants are fully hardy in the South. *T. violacea*, with violet-blue, bell-shaped flowers, is often called society garlic. This one has bluish-green, strap-like leaves, while *T. v. variegata* has longitudinal stripes of white along the leaf margins. They want a good, sunny site with fairly moist soil. Pamela Harper has not found the variegated one hardy, but it came through −12°F for me. NG]

Tulipa

Species tulips come from Mediterranean and Oriental countries where the summers are not only hot but very dry. I plant the bulbs in light, rich, and limy soil, in raised beds where they get maximum sun. I keep the foliage of nearby plants from overshadowing them, and I keep the hose away from the places where they are planted.

In these parts, the species that bloom late seem on the whole to be the most reliable. *Tulipa batalinii* produces yellow flowers with the smoothness of texture and delicacy of outline that seem to be peculiar to very small flowers. The urn-shaped buds are like the tulips in old prints. They stand about six inches above the pale, red-rimmed leaves.

One year the first to bloom was *Tulipa biflora*. There are usually two flowers to a stem, but there may be more. The ones I had were creamy white inside and vinaceous outside. They started blooming close to the ground and looked at first like very small crocuses. Later, the stems reached three or four inches, and the two pale, tapered leaves stretched up to six inches.

T. hageri has proved one of the easiest and best. It blooms regularly in early April, the original clump increasing in girth and flowering more freely each year. The flower is a cylix and of a dark, rich red that makes the clear primary colors of spring seem garish and crude. The anthers are a dull plum color when the flower opens, and then they split and turn out a coat of rust-colored pollen. The bright green buds, slowly turning red, and the narrow curled leaves are a part of the pattern.

In April I have in bloom a much tinier red tulip, *T. linifolia,* with scarlet petals and narrow, gray, wavy-edged leaves that lie flat on the ground. The contrast between the intensity of the color and the minuteness of the blossom kept my thoughts returning to it all summer.

Uvularia

[The bellworts are fine native plants for shaded locations. Two of the species—*U. perfoliata* and *U. grandiflora*—have leaves that clasp the stems and pendulous yellow flowers in spring. *U. sessilifolia* has leaves attached at a single point on the stem and greenish-yellow flowers. Most of these species are quite short when flowering occurs but grow taller later in the season. They are all easy in woodland conditions. NG]

Vancouveria

Vancouverias, like their Old World relatives, the epimediums, are low, leafy ground covers for acid soil in moist, shady places, but also like their relatives, they endure under less favorable conditions and come through hot summers even in soil that is poor and dry. I find them somewhat difficult to establish, but once there they are there to stay, flowing in green ripples from one rock crevice to another. They need not be checked, for the light foliage and thin roots are not apt to interfere with other small plants, and little bulbs planted among them will not be imprisoned.

I had taken for granted that the genus was named for the city, but I find that both are named for the eighteenth-century explorer Captain Vancouver, commander of the *Discovery*. I am still puzzled by the common name, inside-out flower. Upside-down flower would be more appropriate for the small, inverted blossoms that are like those of shooting stars (dodecatheon).

When the plants are set out, the leaf stems should stand up but the slender runners should lie flat with a covering of three inches of soil.

There are three species, all native to our northwest coast. *V. chrysantha* grows in the open on rocky slopes. The yellow flowers are larger than those of the other species, and the leaves are thick and leathery.

V. hexandra of the coniferous forests is called redwood ivy. It blooms with me at the end of April or very early in May. The small flowers are off-white and bloom in delicate, few-flowered panicles just above the even foliage. With me this species grows only a few inches tall, but I have planted it in a very dry place. The three pale leaflets of the pinnate leaves are rounded hexagons.

The flowers of *V. planipetala* are white or faintly tinged with violet. They are smaller than those of *V. hexandra* but in larger panicles. The leaves are evergreen.

Verbena

In the South no garden of any kind can afford to be without its verbenas, and the one best suited to the rocks is the one listed as *V. tenuisecta* (now *Glandularia tenuisecta*). It is a tender perennial from South America that blooms the first year from seed and travels very rapidly because the branches root as they go. It makes a wide mat in a single season but cannot be called invasive, for much of it is killed back in winter. Usually a few plants are left for early spring; if not, there are always seedlings in a garden where this verbena has once been planted. I have only sown seed once, in the middle of March, and the seedlings flowered in the middle of July. The plants that over winter bloom in May, or sometimes even in April. They bloom all through the summer, often until Christmas. This is called the moss verbena because the finely divided, pale green leaves form a soft mat. It demands nothing but sun. The flowers of the type are bright violet purple. This year that color disappeared from my garden completely, and the flowers all bloomed out pale amaranth pink. Elsie Hassan says she has a form with flowers of a good clear red.

Another excellent verbena is a somewhat tender, lacy-leaved, white-flowered one that came into my garden without a name and disappeared from it still nameless after about fifteen years. I once had masses of it, but a series of severe winters took it off. It has the longest season of any flower that I know. [The lacy-leaved white verbena is probably *V. tenuisecta* 'Alba.' NG]

V. rigida, listed as *V. venosa*, is a coarser, stiffer, and slightly taller species, with flowers that are petunia violet in the type and a more delicate tint in the cultivar 'Lilacina.' It blooms from seed the first year and is permanently perennial thereafter, blooming continuously from early May into November. It is, however, aggressively stoloniferous.

V. tenera, another South American species, should be in our rock gardens (and probably is without my knowing the name for it), but I have never been able to find a source for either the type, with its lilac flowers, or the Italian variety, *maonettii*, whose petals have wide white margins.

[Pamela Harper has not found *maonettii* hardy in Virginia, but it has come through winters in Raleigh. There are at least two other verbenas suitable for sunny rock gardens. *V. peruviana* is a superb ground cover, creeping slowly but surely throughout an entire summer regardless of drought or heat. It continues to produce heads of bright red flowers on stalks to about three inches even after light frosts and freezes.

V. canadensis is another valuable species. It is larger in all respects and comes in many shades from pink through mauve and violet to deep purple. The flower heads may be up to three inches across, and it too will bloom from the first mild days in spring until a hard freeze ends the year's display. Both of these species require full sun, but they do not demand anything else. NG]

Veronica

Notes on veronicas invariably begin with the statement that all species are easily grown in any soil. This may be true in the North, and perhaps in the cooler parts of the South, but it was not true in Raleigh—or at least not in my garden in Raleigh. Some veronicas, however, are easily grown anywhere, and there are a number of easy and satisfactory dwarf kinds for rock gardens at low elevations. There are also some choice alpines that will endure humid summers, but only under special conditions, or, as far as my experience goes, not at all. In the North rock garden veronicas are relied upon for summer bloom. In the South their blueness is the property of spring. None that I have grown bloomed after July 1.

The most popular low-growing veronica is the rock speedwell, *V. latifolia,* which is known in the trade as *V. teucrium.* The latter is descriptive, for the oval leaves are very like the foliage of *Teucrium chamaedrys.* The best-known form of this species is 'True Blue.' It is erratic as to time of bloom. With me the first flowers sometimes appear at the end of March and sometimes not until the second week in May. The flowers are of the blueness of lakes in the mountains or chicory by the roadside. There are a number of other good forms. The species *V. prostrata,* sometimes listed as *V. rupestris,* is daintier and more prostrate than most. The flowers are the bluest of blues or the snowiest of whites. The white-flowered one is as beautiful as a rock plant can be, but I have never been able to keep it for more than two or three springs. The blue one is permanent.

V. peduncularis, a rather coarse species from Asia Minor, is one of the most dependable, although not one of the showiest. Still, the white flowers, finely striped with pink, are very pretty when they come into bloom sometime between the end of March and the end of April. The comparatively large oval leaves are coarsely toothed. This is one of the taller species, growing to six inches or more in height. It is one of the few that do at all well in the shade, although several are described as shade-enduring.

The comb speedwell, *V. pectinata,* blooms at the same time. It is not long-lived but does well for a time in gritty soil in a dry wall; it requires full sun, though it comes from dry, shady hills in Asia Minor. The flowers are deep blue with very white centers and white anthers. The leaves are woolly. In the cultivar 'Rosea' the flowers are a tint of red violet and the leaves are grayer than those of the type.

There are three flat ground covers of practically no height at all. *V. repens,* the tiniest speedwell, is a Corsican alpine which has never found this climate congenial. In cooler gardens and in soil that is neither too wet nor too dry it is an excellent creeper. *V. nummularia,* from the Pyrenees, dies out in the hot weather, but it is such a vigorous little plant that there is always a portion left to make a fresh start in the cool weather and provide a patch of smooth, oval, pale green leaves over the winter. It is neat and pleasing, but the flowers, which appear at the end of March, are minute and insignificant. *V. filiformis* has the same habit of disappearing in the middle of the summer unless it is in very rich, moist soil and in the shade. For this reason I have not found it a very satisfactory ground cover, although it is a nuisance in good soil and should never be allowed in the rock garden proper. *Hortus* says it is a pernicious weed in central New York. It is splendid to plant between the flagstones of a walk or terrace, where, if the foliage burns in hot weather, it can easily be raked away. A film of round green leaves is sure to appear again in the fall, and in early spring, often in March and occasionally in February, there are quantities of pale blue and white flowers. As long as it is kept where it can do no harm, this veronica is indispensable.

Several of the upright species are low enough in stature to be suitable for the rock garden. The woolly speedwell, *V. incana,* is a good one for the South. In a well-drained, sunny situation it grows to perfection, and at the end of April or early in May spikes of dauphin's violet stand above the silver rosettes of the foliage. If the faded spikes are cut back, there will be a second flowering in early summer. The metallic leaves remain to decorate the rocks in winter, and altogether this gay species from the mountain regions of Siberia is one of the most satisfactory as well as one of the most desirable veronicas for these parts.

The thread-leaved speedwell, *V. filifolia,* is much less spectacular but pretty and entirely dependable, with very slender stalks about nine inches high and starry flowers of pale blue violet—a lovely clear color like blue glass with light shining through it. They bloom for several weeks, beginning in April. *V. multifida* is a closely related species and evidently very similar, with pale, feathery flower spikes and fine divided leaves. It is available, but I have somehow overlooked it. Both these species are easily grown, even in poor soil, and both survive the long dry periods of summer as well as the overly wet ones.

V. gentianoides is said to be the easiest of alpines, but all of my attempts to grow it in Raleigh ended in failure. It never tarried long enough to bloom. Since it comes from wet mountain meadows in southern Europe and is recommended for the gritty soil of a wet moraine, I thought I would try once again in Charlotte, in a damper place. By keeping it watered in summer, I think it can be established —if it is worth the trouble. Tufts of wide glossy leaves, like those of *Gentiana acaulis,* form handsome gray-green mats and give the species its name. This has been called the earliest veronica, but *V. fili-formis* comes first in my garden. Still, early March is early enough, and it blooms on until the end of April. When the plant came last fall from Carl Starker there were a few flowers, and I hope a second flowering will be a habit here. The flowers are comparatively large and of a pale blue violet color with deeper violet veins, on stocky spikes about eight inches tall.

V. spicata, from the hill pastures of Europe and northern Asia, is one of the most reliable perennials for southern flower borders, and in several dwarf forms is equally good in the rock garden. The cultivar 'Corymbosa' and the cultivar 'Nana' both produce stout six-inch spikes of vivid blue violet in the late spring. They are long-lived and easily grown in any soil, but for the best effect they must be divided now and then.

[There is a very beautiful cultivar of *V. prostrata* known as 'Tre-hane,' which has bright chartreuse foliage throughout the year and spikes of blue flowers in May. Mine is growing near the bright gold–flowered *Coreopsis auriculata* 'Nana' and my bluest form of *Festuca ovina glauca,* and the combination is wonderful.

Veronica spicata 'Icicle' is a green-leaved plant which forms a clump and produces pure white flowers from late May into July. It is well behaved and asks only to be divided about every three years or so.

From England come two hybrids of *V. spicata* and *V. incana* which are suitable for larger rock gardens in sun. *V.* × 'Sarabande' shows some of the gray color of the leaves of its *V. incana* parent while it produces the showier blue flower spikes of *V. spicata. V.* × 'Minuet' has a creeping habit and produces lovely pink flowers throughout the summer and fall.

V. liwanenesis is an attractive creeping ground cover with small, rounded green leaves and bright blue flowers in spring. Mine has yet to bloom, but it is a fine plant—spreading but not invasively so.

V. orientalis was added to the garden only last spring, but it has come through a very difficult summer beautifully. It has gray foliage something like a rosemary and a prostrate habit. To have cobalt-blue flowers in early summer is a splendid bonus. This one is growing in a scree mixture consisting primarily of stones and sand, for it was described as a dryland plant from Turkey.

V. 'Mrs. Holt,' which I believe to be a cultivar of *V. prostrata,* is a diminutive form of this species with attractive bright pink flowers. NG]

Viola

In spite of the fact that sweet violets are almost a symbol of the sentimental South, they cannot be grown in all sections with equal success. In my garden they require more care than I am willing to take, although I was ashamed to admit it until the indefatigable Elsie Hassan wrote, "I have tried innumerable varieties of *Viola odorata,* and lost them all. Mrs. Evans in Ferriday, Louisiana, says that they need deep soil, and judging by the eighteen-inch roots of those she sent, I believe she is right. They have to go deep to withstand our heat and drought. She also says that the plants will produce too many leaves and too few flowers if the runners are not cut off and reset. Following this advice meticulously would be a never-ending task if one had many sweet violets."

V. odorata occurs in a number of forms in its wide range in the Mediterranean region and Asia, and there are numerous horticultural varieties, both old and new. An old-fashioned single purple called 'Princess of Wales' was once a favorite, but since it has been supplanted by the superior flowers and inferior fragrance of the modern variety, 'Royal Robe,' I no longer know where to find this sweetest of all violets, except in my own garden. 'Charm' is a delicately tinted blue form, and the cultivar 'Rosina' is called the pink violet, though in reality it is almost magenta. 'Rosina' grows well in various parts of the South. I have seen great mats of it in South Carolina, and Mrs. Evans has a good word to say for it in Louisiana, along with the warning that its shallow roots must be kept covered with dirt or it will dry up and die. In Greensboro it blooms for nine months of the year, and this winter I found a clump in bloom in January in my own garden. This is one of the loveliest of violets as to scent and color, and it also has the best foliage. The round, dark, evergreen leaves cover the ground thickly and evenly and never become rank and unruly. A white form of *V. odorata* opens in the gardens of Pinehurst and Chapel Hill on the springlike days of late winter. Double forms of the sweet violet are difficult but delightful. There is an old one called 'Swanley White,' one with pale lavender flowers called 'Lady Hume-Campbell,' and the fine, sweet, dark-flowered 'Double Russian Violet.' Anyone who is willing to take the trouble to grow these lovely old violets will find some of them listed by dealers on the West Coast.

V. jooi, from southeastern Europe, is one of the nicest violets that I have ever had, but I am not sure how reliable it is in the South, or at least in this part of the South. On the first trial it bloomed well while it lasted, beginning in early March and carrying on through the summer, but it did not last long and did not reseed as it is said to do. The spring before we left Raleigh I had more plants from Claude Barr, and they looked thrifty when we went away at the end of October. I planted them in sun and limy soil because they come from the limestones of Transylvania, but an acid soil in shade is recommended. Some experimenting may be required to get this species established, but it will be worth the trouble, for it is a charming violet, small and trim with wonderfully fragrant lilac flowers. The round, smooth, dark green leaves grow close together in little mounds about three inches high. They keep their spring freshness throughout the summer.

V. rupestris is a European species that is native also in the northern United States and Canada. The cultivar 'Rosea,' which is the form found in gardens, has never done well with me, but Elsie Hassan reports that it flourishes in Birmingham, Alabama, surviving even in poor soil and blooming from March to July and again in the fall. This is another so-called pink violet that is not really pink. The smallish flowers are purple.

Only those who like the minute will care for *V. riviniana,* the common European wood violet. As I have it, it is as small as *V. walteri* —so small that it was in bloom for several days before I found it. This happens now and again, though I spend most of the spring on my knees peering behind bushes and searching beneath the leaves.

V. riviniana is a satisfactory species, blooming from May through the summer and thriving in the shade in a woodsy soil. The pale flowers are light wisteria violet. They are half an inch across, and the round little leaves are not much more than an inch in diameter, though *Hortus* says the leaves are to three inches wide.

V. sororia is a horticultural name for a large and very beautiful pure white violet with nice healthy leaves. It endures heat and drought and a low altitude, blooming profusely late in March and seeding itself freely but not to excess. The leaves are like the leaves of the common violet, but the flowers are very different. They are long-petaled and narrow, of a crystalline whiteness with a hint of green.

I have had two Asiatic violets, one difficult and one very easy. The difficult one is *V. dissecta chaerophylloides,* a Japanese species similar to our bird's-foot violet. It bloomed for me once—the first to bloom that year—coming with the crocus species early in March. In the form that I had the flowers were large and creamy and marked with hairlines of bright violet. There is also a variety with rose-colored flowers. The finely cut leaves disappeared as soon as the weather became warm, and, alas, they never appeared again. I am not sure whether the difficulty was altogether with the climate. I had planted this violet in shade, according to the grower's instructions, but I later read that it should have had full sun and a little moisture. The acid woods' soil provided was correct.

The Chinese violet, *V. patrinii,* blooms early and late in my garden, making a violet pool in the pale shade of bare branches. It blooms in the spring in March and April (or even in February in an early season), and again in the fall from October into December. The neat round clumps spread by underground runners, and seedlings come up generously—too generously to allow it choice quarters in the rock garden. But for its invasiveness, I should place this violet high on a list of good plants for the South, and even though I pass it on with a warning, nearly every visitor to the garden wants it. Being very drought-resistant and not particular as to soil, it is a useful ground cover in shade, but it is most beautiful in full sun when volunteers are allowed to bloom in the stones at the edge of the gravel path. In the spring, when the flowers push up ahead of the leaves, each clump is a solid mass of hyssop violet. The leaves are long, finely scalloped ovals at first, but in summer they lengthen to narrow spears four inches long. They are immune to disease and red spider mites, and so keep a spring freshness into the fall.

In Raleigh, Loulie Busbee brought us plants of *V. tricolor*, or Johnny-Jump-Ups, one spring in a strawberry basket, and they kept themselves going from that time on. When we came to Charlotte, my niece and nephew begged them from Elizabeth Clarkson and planted them beneath the pine trees before there was any garden to put them in. These survived much leveling and scraping, and they spring up cheerfully each season between the rocks and in the path. Sometimes we find them in bloom in February.

[*V. cornuta* 'Molly Sanderson' is one of the most remarkable of all violas. It originated in a garden in Kent and then was discovered in Mrs. Sanderson's garden in Ballymoney, North Ireland, by an official at Wisley who gave it its name and introduced it into the British nursery trade. It crossed the Atlantic in the early 1980s. Its flowers are as black as a charcoal briquet, except for light touches of gold and purple at their throats. It blooms heavily in spring and fall and sporadically during the heat of summer. It is hardy to Zone 4, at least, and propagates easily by cuttings taken in late summer. AL]

[*V. corsica* is one of the best and most beautiful of the heat-tolerant violas. In areas with cool summers it will bloom continuously except during winter, but in the hot South it blooms throughout the winter and into July. It self-sows, but not reliably, and is best maintained by collecting and sowing fresh seeds each August. The petals are violet blue and the flowers are larger than Johnny-jump-ups but smaller than pansies. It grows well in light shade or full sun.

V. labradorica is worth growing for its bronze-purple leaves alone, which remain beautiful and fresh all summer. It grows happily in light shade and produces small purple flowers in spring.

V. pedata and its form, *bicolor* are exquisite natives. The problem is finding exactly the right location for them. They are often found growing along roadsides in part shade or full sun and are wonderfully drought-resistant plants. Some authorities and nurserymen recommend growing them in acid sand, while others suggest clay. I think the critical factor is good drainage. The flowers come in various shades of violet or a combination of pale violet and deep purple.

V. selkirkii has delightful long-spurred red-violet flowers in spring, and again when the weather is cool in fall. This is a deciduous species with long white roots and bright green leaves. It is remarkably drought-resistant, and although it seeds about, it has not become pesty.

V. tricolor, or Johnny-jump-up, has charming flowers and might be better considered as an annual or perennial annual in the South. Most of them are bicolored purple and yellow or blue and white, but my favorite is 'Bowles' Black,' a black purple one which breeds true and begins blooming early in the fall and continues throughout the winter and into early summer, until the heat ends the display. I let it grow wherever it will, and this is most often in full sun. NG]

Zephyranthes

The name of the zephyr lilies means flowers of the west wind. They are also called fairy lilies and rain lilies, the last because, like cooperias, some of the species bloom after summer rains. This is an American genus, and a number of the species are natives of the South and Southwest. Our own Atamasco lily, *Z. atamasco,* is the most beautiful. It is native as far north as Virginia and is probably hardy beyond its range. The flowers, which are like solitary white lilies, bloom here in April, sometimes at the end of March. *Z. candida* is the hardiest, although native to the Argentine. It is said to winter in protected places as far north as New York. The late white flowers are small and crocuslike. With me they come in late August and September, but in wet summers they may begin earlier and continue into the fall.

Abies

Ernest Yelton of Rutherfordton, North Carolina, considers the balsam fir, *A. balsamaea hudsonia,* one of the indispensable plants in his rock garden. It has been recorded as growing ten inches high and twenty across in fifteen years, thirteen by twenty-three inches in seventeen years, and by Mr. Hillier in his *Manual of Trees and Shrubs* as less than three feet tall and more than three feet wide in thirty years.

The true balsam of the southern Appalachians is *A. fraseri,* which grows in the boreal forest at altitudes of five thousand feet and more. A cultivar, *A. f.* 'Prostrata,' a low, wide-spreading shrub rarely exceeding four feet, was introduced into the trade in 1938 by the Kelsey-Highlands Nursery.

[Unfortunately, the firs have yielded few dwarf selections that will thrive in the drought and heat of a typical southern summer. However, in addition to the variety *hudsonia* cited by Elizabeth Lawrence, the balsam fir offers the comparatively successful cultivar 'Nana,' which is similar in habit. The leaves of 'Nana' are held radially, giving it a starry appearance that I prefer, but both are admirable, though slow to establish in our southern climate.

A. concolor 'Compacta' is a miniature facsimile of the white spruce of the southern Rockies that establishes nicely. Described as grayish blue, in the warm South it manages a soft pastel green.

A. lasiocarpa arizonica 'Compacta' is a selection of Alpine fir that ultimately grows too tall for all but the largest rock garden, but the pace is so slow that it makes a valuable addition to the garden for many years. PJ]

Acer

[Maples are generally thought of as large trees, but several are small enough or sufficiently slow growing to make splendid additions to large-scale rock gardens. The best selections are the cascading cultivars of the dissected-leaf variety of Japanese maple, *A. palmatum dissectum*. These are typically small, dome-shaped trees that slowly mature to four to six feet or more while developing at least an equal spread. The branches are clothed with delicate, deeply divided leaves that give outstanding autumn displays, and in many cases outstanding spring displays as well. In winter the architecture of the branches, which are often subtly colored, is attractive.

Dissectums can be arbitrarily divided into two groups based on leaf color during the growing season: cultivars with green leaves and those with red or burgundy leaves. Variegated selections also exist, but I have yet to see one that impressed me. Some good green cultivars are 'Viridis,' 'Waterfall,' and 'Palmatifidum' or 'Paucum.' 'Filigree' has faint green leaves with darker veins, and 'Ornatum' has magnificent color displays at both ends of the growing season.

My favorite of the red selections is 'Tamukeyama,' a vigorous cultivar of darkest burgundy color, which it holds through the hottest summers. It also has good stem coloration, adding winter interest. 'Garnet,' 'Ever Red,' and 'Crimson Queen' are proven selections that are similar to 'Tamukeyama' in most respects. 'Red Filigree Lace' is a novel new cultivar with a leaf surface that is so reduced that not much more than veins remain. I have found it difficult to establish.

Dissected Japanese maples are propagated almost exclusively by grafting and may be purchased with the graft made at various heights on a standard. High grafts are often useful in preserving precious ground space in smaller gardens. I find that autumn color is as significant on shade-grown plants as it is on those sited in full sun. Shade protects the thin, fragile leaves, which readily die back from the tips when under duress.

A. palmatum 'Shishigashira' is the best Japanese maple for small rock gardens. This short, stoutly branched cultivar has a natural bonsai look that blends well into an alpine setting. The small leaves are crowded toward the branch tips and are especially visible in their good autumn colors. 'Shishigashira' is tolerant of, and remains more compact in, full sun. My specimens are planted in good soil, but in order to avoid unnecessary growth I do not fertilize them.

Several years ago I was given a young *A. orientale,* and it has become one of my favorite maples. Its grayish green three-lobed leaves are about thumbnail size. In autumn the leaves turn apricot and persist well into December. *A. orientale* is variable from seed, which is how it is most often acquired, but is typically a twiggy, much-branched shrub that grows only two or three inches per year. My plant is now around ten years old, and it is less than two feet tall. Coming from the eastern Mediterranean region, this species prefers high light and is tolerant of summer drought. PJ]

Arctostaphylos

[*A. uva-ursi* is a prostrate native shrub similar in effect to the creeping blueberries. In its habitat bearberry, as it is commonly known, makes a dense, lush ground cover up to a foot tall in open, sandy woods or on exposed ridges. When initially planted, long, trailing stems are produced that wind like scouts about the garden. In time, these runners branch and create a handsome, leafy carpet. PJ]

Berberis

The dwarf evergreen barberries are bristling, angular shrubs with character and distinction, but hostile to weeders. Never go near one without gloves. A little research in the catalogs, both East and West Coast, will bring to light several species and varieties of great individuality, and this is the kind of armchair gardening that I approve of. The barberries like open situations and, with the exception of *B. empetrifolia,* they like lime in the soil. But the ones that I know seem to grow as well in acid woods' soil and considerable shade. The soil should be light and well drained.

The Chinese species are the ones that I am familiar with. Two of these are small and slow growing. *B. candidula* is of neat, dense habit, with very dark spiny-edged leaves and solitary flowers like little golden lanterns. It grows eventually to a little more than two feet.

B. × *stenophylla,* a garden hybrid, is considered to be the most beautiful barberry by William J. Bean, author of *Trees and Shrubs Hardy in the British Isles*. The type is a large shrub, but there are a number of small forms, one of which Robert Moncure of Virginia praised as "one of the most symmetrical and attractive dwarf shrubs, reaching an ultimate height of about ten inches, with small glossy leaves, laden with dainty yellow and gold blossoms in early spring. It is a most worthy addition to the limited number of dwarf shrubs suitable for the small rock garden."

B. verruculosa, the warty barberry, is said to be nearly hardy in Massachusetts. In four or five years a small plant from a pot has grown to nearly eighteen inches and spread about the same amount. It blooms here at the end of April, and the small pale yellow flowers are pretty though not conspicuous. The very narrow leaves are a little over an inch long and as shiny and prickly as holly. They are light green above and very pale beneath. The new growth has a bronze tinge. The fruit is black.

[*B. thunbergii,* the Japanese barberry, is one of the deciduous members of this extensive group of shrubs. It produces reasonably conspicuous pale yellow flowers in late April, but it is more note-worthy for the excellent autumn colors and masses of showy red fruits that persist well into winter. The variety *atropurpurea* has a scarlet property about the leaves and stems when grown in full sun. 'Crimson Pygmy' is a handsome dwarf selection of this variety which develops into a dense, low mound up to eighteen inches high by as much or more across in fifteen years. It blends in well with similar mounding specimens, especially conifers such as chamaecy-paris, adding contrast in both color and texture. It is often found in nurseries under the pseudonyms 'Little Gem,' 'Little Beauty,' 'Little Favorite,' and 'Atropurpurea Nana.' PJ]

Buxus

I would never think of box in connection with a rock garden, but the tiny and charmingly individual plants would be perfectly acceptable in such a setting. A miniature of the Japanese species *B. microphylla* 'Compacta' has all of the good qualities a tiny evergreen can have, and no faults—unless slow growth is considered a fault. It never be-comes more than a foot tall, but it increases in girth about an inch a year and in time becomes at least twice as wide as it is high.

[*B. m.* 'Kingsville Dwarf' is a hint faster and broader than 'Compacta' but otherwise similar. Both of these selections are excellent dwarfs, but they are not without faults. In winter many of the younger leaves discolor to an awful muddy brown. The problem is seldom extreme, though, and seems less evident on shade-grown plants. 'Green Pillow' is a dwarf of similar dimensions that has larger leaves and better winter color.

B. m. koreana is a hardy geographical form of the little box. 'Tide Hill' is a beautiful selection of this variety that also retains good dark green winter color. Though it may reach only fifteen inches, 'Tide Hill' spreads moderately fast, to as wide as three feet in fifteen years. PJ]

Calluna

From my first dealings with heather and disparaging reports from Birmingham (Alabama, not England), I felt discouraged about its value in the South, but after seeing established plants in the paved terrace of the Sarah P. Duke Gardens and in a nursery in the sandhills, I decided that it has no aversion to heat.

There is only one species of heather, *Calluna vulgaris,* but a plant so widely distributed—from northern Scotland to the Mediterranean, and from the mountains to the sea—must have forms for all sorts of climates and situations, and fortunately the best of these are available. However, my work with them was interrupted by the move from Raleigh to Charlotte, and at present I can do little more than sum up the possibilities.

The blooming season of heather is long—from early summer into winter, and perhaps until spring. One of the first I acquired was the form 'Tib' because it is said to bloom into December in New Jersey. But 'Tib' met with an accident before the summer was out.

In size they vary from spreading shrubs three feet tall to tiny tufts of two or three inches. 'Alportii' is one of the taller ones, with dark foliage and bright red violet flowers, and another is 'Mair's Variety,' outstanding among the white-flowered forms. Two little ones that I had in Raleigh, *C. v.* 'Pygmaea' and *C. v.* 'Foxii Nana,' were like deep-piled mats of bright green moss. Neither one bloomed, though they settled down at once and looked very healthy when I left Raleigh. I gather that they are not free flowering in any case, and I shall try 'Mrs. Ronald Gray,' which has a reputation for flowering.

I think that I am going to like the double-flowering forms best, if they are anything like 'H. E. Beale,' which has bloomed in the terrace wall through two of our driest and hottest summers. The American nurserymen seem to call this heather 'Mrs. Beale,' a mistake (if it is one) that I can readily understand, for it is as dainty as a lady in a dress of sprigged muslin. From early July into September the long, slenderly tapered spikes are crowded with lilac flowers that look like minute roses. The shrub is of medium height—up to two feet—and rather sparse and angular, with very dark leaves. It is not one of the best for foliage, but you cannot have everything, and even those dark branches are a welcome sight in winter.

I shall not go into the matter of colored foliage, as I detest the type, but for those who like them there are forms with silver, copper, and gold leaves.

Heather is at its best in poor soil. Ground that has not been under cultivation before is best for them, but few of us can manage that. An open situation is essential for their well-being, for they will not grow in the drip of overhanging branches, but in the South they do need some shelter from the afternoon sun. Once established they need no further care except for the shearing of dead blossoms in spring (and this is advised against by some gardeners) and a topdressing of sand and leaf mold when their bloom is over.

Cedrus

The Atlas cedar (*C. atlantica*), the Deodar (*C. deodara*), and the cedar of Lebanon (*C. libani*) are all trees that flourish in the South, and I should think their dwarf forms would do as well. The only one I have ever seen was in the old Fruitland Nursery in Augusta, Georgia. The nursery was acquired in 1857 by Prosper Jules Berckmans, who spent the rest of his life introducing and propagating fruits and ornamental trees and shrubs for southern gardens. In January 1937 my mother and I spent a warm, sunny afternoon with Towne Hall, the nursery's horticulturist. The yulan (*Magnolia heptapeta*) was in bloom, though it normally blooms in March, and the fragrance of the large white flowers mingled with the perfume of sweet olive and Japanese apricot. We saw many rare shrubs in the arboretum, and in the fields there was a row of little cedars, *C. atlantica* 'Pygmaea,' that had been growing there for a long time. They were sturdy little shrubs, oval in shape and about two feet tall, with a stout trunk and bristling gray-green needles. Mr. Hall said they could be propagated only by grafting. I have never seen this cedar elsewhere or found any reference to it.

C. deodara 'Pygmaea' was found in a California nursery by Mr. Gotelli, and the original plant is now in his collection in the National Arboretum. It is reported to be twelve inches tall and seventeen inches wide after seventeen years.

[Although only a handful of the cedar selections are useful to rock gardeners, all of them are desirable. They grow more attractive with age and require very little pest control. *C. deodara* 'Nana' is a low-growing pale blue shrub with a relaxed, sprawling habit, with its seasonal flush of foliage in midsummer instead of spring. It has the look of a dwarf deodar, which is so reduced that it hardly resembles the species, in contrast to its sibling selection 'Pygmaea' cited by Elizabeth Lawrence. The specimen I saw in a Long Island garden had spread four feet in width and remained less than a foot tall after fifteen years. My own plants grow decidedly faster but retain the low stature.

C. libani 'Minuta' grows a couple of inches a year and matures into a miniature replica of the species. Even as a young plant its stiff, open habit and short, crowded needles suggest many years of meticulous training, a pleasant deception in any garden.

C. brevifolia and its cultivar 'Epsteinianum' ultimately become small trees, but for at least ten to fifteen years their slow growth makes them wonderful specimens. 'Compacta' and 'Bergmani' make wide, stiff, irregular cushions a foot in height in ten years. PJ]

Cephalotaxus

Mr. Hall told me that the dwarf plum yew at Fruitland was *C. drupacea,* which is now considered a variety of *C. harringtonia.* Since it suckers, I take it to be *C. h.* var. *d.* 'Nana,' which Ernest Wilson sent from Japan to the Arnold Arboretum in 1916 and is the only form I know of that does; if so, it must have been a young plant in 1937, for it did not cover much ground when I saw it. In my garden, after twenty-five years, three suckers have come up a few feet from the trunk, which is only seven inches tall. From the trunk the suckers stretch out horizontally to eight feet, lying flat or slightly ascending. The tips of the branches are sometimes three feet above the ground.

The needles are in two ranks; they are a bright and shining green and to an inch and a half long. It is hardy in Zone 6.

At one time Mr. Tingle of Tingle's Nursery in Pittsville, Maryland, grew, as *C. repandens,* a dwarf form of *C. harringtonia fastigiata.* When I saw it in the nursery, a six- or seven-year-old plant that had never been cut was still less than a foot tall.

[*C. h.* var. *d.* 'Fastigiata' is a multiple-leadered, narrowly upright selection, well composed in youth but spreading apart with age. It is applicable to larger rock gardens if regular pruning is begun at an early age. Its tendency to produce horizontal basal offshoots has undoubtedly led to the introduction of similar plants with assorted names. The cultivar 'Repandens' cited by Elizabeth Lawrence probably originated in this way. The genus is remarkably pest-free and culturally undemanding. PJ]

Chaenomeles

A dwarf Japanese quince that has grown in my garden for more than ten years was eighteen inches high and twice as wide when I planted it and is the same height now, although it has grown wider. It came without a name, but I think it must be *C. japonica.* The small flowers are half the size of those of *C. speciosa.* They are coral red, a color that is good with the pale yellows of the little daffodils but bad with squills and periwinkle. The color must be carefully considered, for this shrub has a way of blooming at all seasons. It flowers freely in March and often blooms again in midsummer or fall or in mild parts of the winter. It will flower even in shade and in the poorest, driest parts of the rock garden, but of course it does better in good soil and in sunlight. The fruits are small and pale yellow, and sometimes there are flowers and fruits at the same time.

Chamaecyparis

"As to the dwarf conifers I would not want to be without in my rock garden," Ernest Yelton said, "my first choice must go to *C. obtusa* 'Nana,' the true form of which is a green tennis ball of tightly packed foliage. It reaches about six inches in fifteen years. *C. pisifera* 'Squarrosa Minima' is apt to revert to nonjuvenile foliage, and must be constantly manicured; it is very lovely and will stay in scale if given a regular haircut."

Ernest Kellam has *C. obtusa* 'Pygmaea,' a low, spreading shrub, and *C. o.* 'Reis Dwarf,' which is upright. He also has *C. pisifera* 'Squarrosa Aurea Nana,' twelve by fifteen inches after ten years (the smaller the plant the longer the name), which has yellow-green juvenile foliage, and *C. p.* 'Pygmaea,' which I had in Raleigh. In an unusually dry summer it was the freshest-looking shrub in the garden. It is a plump little ball of fine blue-gray needles.

[Chamaecyparis, the false cypress, is perhaps the most valuable conifer for the southern rock gardener. This group of trees is composed of five species and has yielded hundreds of selections with annual growth rates from imperceptible to vigorous, widely spreading to strictly upright habits, and coloring that ranges from silvery blue to bleached yellow. The best selections are of the Japanese Hinoki (*C. obtusa*) and Sawara (*C. pisifera*) false cypresses.

C. obtusa 'Nana Gracilis,' mentioned by Elizabeth Lawrence, is among the oldest and finest selections. Cup-shaped sprays of dark green foliage tier loosely in this narrowly pyramidal selection. However, after twenty-five years it may reach six to eight feet in height with a three-foot spread at the base and is therefore appropriate for only the largest gardens. Variant seedling selections of 'Nana Gracilis' include 'Caespitosa,' 'Minima,' 'Juniperoides,' and 'Intermedia,' all wonderful diminutive green buns. These and similar Hinoki buns are the supreme rock garden conifers, often maturing into dense cushions less than a foot tall and more than a foot wide. They are susceptible to summertime scorching and should be chosen straight from the nursery in early autumn when scorch from the previous summer will still be obvious. They are available only from collector or specialty nurseries. Additional cultivars include 'Chilworth,' a very dark green with growth habit much like a tiny tree, and 'Verdone,' which resembles a short, bushy, orange-hued 'Nana Gracilis.'

'Nana Lutea' is one of the many popular golden forms of Hinoki false cypress. Others include 'Golden Sprite' and 'Lynn's Golden Ceramic Christmas Tree,' the former a bun and the latter a small shrub easily as colorful as its title. 'Nana Aurea' is a larger shrub whose branches appear to have been dusted with yellow. 'Kaamani-Hiba' is a golden dwarf with curiously stubby branchlets. The golden dwarfs are particularly prone to sun scorch and must be watered meticulously and heavily mulched.

C. pisifera, the Sawara false cypress, has produced far fewer true dwarfs. Most slow-growing selections tend to send up faster reversions, but if these are removed as soon as they appear, several of these dwarfs develop into truly beautiful specimens. 'Tsukomo' and 'Minima' are two such cultivars, differing primarily in that 'Tsukomo' has a blue quality. 'Minima Variegata' carries scattered yellow blotches like dripped paint. 'Hime-Sawara' is similar to 'Minima' but has a slower growth rate and finer texture. With occasional pruning it is easily maintained as an attractive little ball.

C. pisifera also produces, in addition to juvenile and adult foliar types, an intermediate "plumose" leaf type. 'Plumosa Compressa' is the best and most readily available. It is a low, flat-topped shrub with many upthrust branches, reaching two feet in height by as much or more in width in ten years.

C. p. 'Golden Mop,' a yellow thread-leaved cultivar, is the brightest false cypress available. It is a mound of screaming yellow, quite durable, and must be sited in full sun to reach its most iridescent quality. Though drought-tolerant, the foliage suffers without plentiful moisture.

C. thyoides, the white "cedar," has produced few rock garden dwarfs, 'Little Jamie' being perhaps the best. If faster reversions are kept in check, it develops into a tight cone a foot or so tall in ten years. 'Andelyensis' is a commonly available slow-growing small tree that is often erroneously sold as a dwarf in nurseries. *C. thyoides* occurs naturally in and along swamps and shallow ponds and should not be sited in dry conditions.

C. lawsoniana, the Lawson's false cypress or Port Orford cedar, does not yield selections that are happy with the southern life, though they are some of the most strikingly beautiful of all garden trees and shrubs. For the persistent enthusiast, however, 'Erecta Filiformis' is a wispy, upright, thread-leaved selection that is unlike any other conifer I know. With luck I was able to establish this selection for several years in a cool spot of my garden. 'Torulosa,' a fine blue-green form with curiously twisted branches, has been the most durable dwarf Lawson's cultivar I have attempted. I have, however, sacrificed several to the elements in the search for a proper site. I am growing it in a site which has full sun during the middle of the day and light shade the rest of the time. The roots are well shaded and moist at all times, with a good layer of mulch. PJ]

Chamaedaphne

[*C. calyculata* is the lone member of this native shrub from the eastern United States and northern Europe. Commonly known as leather leaf, chamaedaphne is a sparse, gaunt, evergreen shrub that relishes moist peaty soil and high light. In midspring small, white, urn-shaped flowers are borne among the leaves at the apex of the previous year's branches. Leather leaf blends well into naturalistic landscapes, but for rock garden use the selection 'Nana' is one of the best dwarf shrubs to be found. 'Nana' is low and spreading, with tiny leaves set on prominent, shiny, cinnamon-brown stems. It supposedly can reach eighteen inches in height, but after ten years my plant is less than ten inches tall. PJ]

Cistus

The rock roses are grown on the West Coast but not much in the East, where they are considered tender, though those that I had in Raleigh seemed hardy enough for the length of time that I had them. They are valuable for quick effect and for resistance to heat and drought. Though they are sometimes difficult to establish, pot-grown plants can be successfully set out in late spring. Plant them in poor soil in open, sunny places where the drainage is sharp.

Most species are too large for rock gardens, but I had from Carl Starker a prostrate form of *C. incanus* that does not grow taller than eight or ten inches. It spread to a diameter of three feet, however, before the year was out, and made a charming cushion of gray in the wintertime. The flowers, like little wild roses but of solid substance and a porcelain whiteness, bloom in the middle of April. I like the white-flowered rock roses because the colors are apt to be muddy-red violets.

Although *C. incanus* is considered one of the tender species, it wintered well in Raleigh. Where a slightly taller plant will do, *C.* × *corbariensis* might be a better choice, for it is one of the hardiest. This has the same pure white flowers but not the same gray leaves. The foliage is not striking, and though the leaves persist through the winter, they look rather shabby.

Convolvulus

It is hard to believe that *C. cneorum* has been in cultivation for three hundred years, for it looks like a modern ornament designed for indoor gardens and outdoor living rooms. It is as soft as silk, as bright as metal, and as brittle as glass. Not that it is out of place in a less formal setting, for the flexible branches hang gracefully over a dry wall and follow the contours of the stone with the fluency of quicksilver. It seems to have found just the right place in the dry wall at the edge of the house terrace, although I would not have put it on the north side if there had been a choice. Here it has grown for two winters, one extremely cold and the other unusually mild, and two miserably hot summers, and it has been the best of the gray-leaved shrubs in the garden, glittering in the winter sun and shimmering like a silver fountain in the summer heat. Even if, in the end, it is not long-lived, it will be a valuable shrub, for it grows easily and rapidly from cuttings. A plant from a small pot covered four feet in one summer. This spring I cut it back severely before new growth started, and I think a yearly pruning will be necessary to keep it from sprawling too much.

The silky silver leaves are narrow, with nothing to suggest a morning glory, but the small shell-like flowers are typical. They are pearly white with a touch of pink and rest so lightly on the tips of the branches that I thought a butterfly had lighted there when I looked up one morning in April and saw the first one in bloom. In California the shrub blooms all summer, but here only in the spring.

Cotoneaster

As far as I know them, there is so little to choose between the prostrate cotoneasters that I doubt whether I would tell one from another without labels. There is a sameness about their small oval leaves, small white flowers, and dull red berries. But all are neat, pleasing, and give little trouble, while their branches trace such dainty evergreen patterns over stones and rock walls that it is easy to see why they are called rocksprays. They are easily grown in any soil, even if it is on the poor, dry side; their only requirements are full sun, good drainage, and perhaps some lime in the soil, though that does not seem to be necessary.

The true *C. buxifolius,* according to William J. Bean in his *Trees and Shrubs Hardy in the British Isles,* is an evergreen shrub from one to two feet tall. However, Henry Hohman, a nurseryman of Kingsville, Maryland, says that it is only partially evergreen, low, and compact. I have not grown it myself.

C. congestus is sometimes considered a pygmy variety of this species. It is described—as you would expect from its name—as a shrub of dense, compact habit and very slow-growing. With me it is of open growth, and a tiny pot plant has thrown out eighteen-inch branches in two years. Fortunately I was glad to have it grow like this. It has flattened itself very picturesquely against a low stone wall, and the pliable, densely clothed, rust-colored stems are extremely decorative.

William Bean says that *C. conspicuus* is known in two forms, one erect and three to eight feet tall, the other "very prostrate and stiff," which he saw at Exbury "growing flat on the ground spreading widely and covered with the scarlet fruits in autumn." I had under this name a very pretty one which came from Fruitland and was described as six feet tall. In one growing season it spread three feet but was still perfectly flat and clearly had no intention of ever growing any taller. I think that this is the species grown in this country as *C. decorus* and called the necklace cotoneaster because the red berries are hung on the branches like beads on a string. It is different from the others, which are mostly stiff and angular, in that its branches are finer and more numerous, and the effect is soft and graceful.

C. dammeri, from central China, is very slow-growing. In the ten years that it spread itself over a sunny wall in Raleigh it grew little more than *C. congestus* has grown in two years in my new garden. It could easily be kept to any size by gentle pruning. The white flowers with pink-tipped buds and fuzzy stamens are rather pretty in April, but the small fruits are dull and inconspicuous.

C. microphyllus is a low-growing but most vigorous shrub, quickly spreading out to a radius of three feet. It is rigid and ungainly, and decorative neither in fruit nor flower. In the right place its stiff horizontal lines are effective, and it is good to know about such an easy doer for poor soil or rough places.

C. thymifolius is prostrate, compact, and the smallest-leaved of all. *C. microphyllus* and these forms are all alpines growing at high elevations in the Himalayas, and therefore perfectly hardy, but they adapt themselves to mild winters and hot, humid summers.

Among the tender evergreen rocksprays I have found only one dwarf form. It is known in the trade as *C. pannosus* 'Nana' and is described as forming a compact bush a foot tall. The typical silverleaf rockspray is a handsome Chinese species with quantities of small dark red berries. The foliage is grayish, especially in spring when the new leaves come out. A dwarf form of this should be particularly good for the South.

Cryptomeria

"I am unhappy with *Cryptomeria japonica* 'Vilmoriniana,'" Ernest Yelton said, "because it is now approaching the exile stage; *C. j.* 'Lobbii' was removed long ago." 'Vilmoriniana' was brought by Philippe de Vilmorin to France from Japan about 1890, and in his garden near Paris it grew in twenty years to be a perfect globe two feet in diameter. I had it in Raleigh from the old LeMac Nursery in Hampton, Virginia, but I left it behind four years later. Joel Spingarn in New York State gives it ten inches by twelve in ten years; Helene Bergman, of the Brooklyn Botanic Garden, gives it about two and a half feet in height in forty years.

[*C. japonica,* the single species of the Japanese cedar, is seldom seen in southern landscapes or available from southern nurserymen, though the dwarf forms are of easy culture and disease and pest free.

The cultivar 'Compressa' and the similar 'Vilmoriniana' discussed by Elizabeth Lawrence represent the tiniest of Japanese cedars. After twenty years in the garden they remain dense and composed, and probably under two feet. 'Tsuga' and 'Nana' are equally slow but less dense and more irregular in habit. Their attractiveness lies in their natural tendency toward grotesqueness.

'Globosa Nana' is a somewhat larger cultivar that develops into a luxuriant, compact dome three feet across after twenty-five years. For those with ample space, there are few more handsome plants. 'Elegans Nana' is similar to 'Globosa Nana' but less refined. It has a tufted, uneven composure and covers itself with clusters of male cones which resemble tiny yellow flowers. 'Spiralis' is a unique form with leaves that spiral ropelike around the stem. PJ]

Daphne

[Daphnes are small, handsome shrubs that produce wonderfully fragrant flowers in reliable profusion, often throughout the year. It is often said that daphnes, the eastern European species especially, require soils with a high pH, but I have not found this to be critical. All of the species I grow are planted in the slightly acidic woodland soil of piedmont North Carolina, which I amend with well-rotted pine bark. Daphnes generally do not transplant well, and the sooner that young daphnes are set into place, the more likely they are to establish themselves.

D. × *burkwoodii* is a hybrid of *D. cneorum* and *D. caucasica*. The selection 'Carol Mackie' is a small, upright shrub with decorative leaves outlined by creamy yellow margins, and it produces whorls of fragrant pink flowers, borne abundantly in spring and infrequently thereafter. This is a first-rate garden plant, perhaps the prettiest variegated shrub available. In the South it is best protected from hot summer sun. I also find that it, as well as *D. cneorum* 'Eximia,' responds favorably to the incorporation of wood ashes.

D. *caucasica* is a durable species with a tolerance of cultural extremes. I have grown this Caucasian shrub with equal success in dry, gravelly soil under shade and in an enriched sandy loam in full sun. A friend has a specimen planted on a mound of poor clay in full sun, and it is thriving. It is continuously laden with flower buds, easing into heaviest bloom during the first warm month of spring, with occasional flowers throughout the year. I enjoy this plant most in the bleakness of winter when, during a brief warm spell, a lone flower will open and remind me with delightful fragrance of the season soon to come.

D. *cneorum* 'Eximia' is one of those rock garden plants that you know you must have when you see it in flower for the first time. I have found it to be one of the most difficult daphnes to establish, but perseverance has been rewarded. 'Eximia' is a procumbent shrub six inches to a foot high, with fragile branches and thin, narrow leaves. It looks common enough until early spring, when whorls of rich pink flowers burst forth from crimson buds. A white-flowered selection, 'Alba,' is available, as is a more dwarf selection, 'Pygmaea.'

D. *collina neopolitana,* a Mediterranean native, is yet another species that is satisfied with the climate of the South. This little gem grows to a height of three feet and bears petite flowers that are rose purple outside and white within and resemble tiny lights set among the abundant dark green leaves.

D. *genkwa* is the only species in my garden that is entirely deciduous. This Chinese native bears lavender flowers in clusters that surround the upper two-thirds of most branches, profusely in May and occasionally throughout the summer. This is one of the largest daphnes, easily reaching four feet when grown in full sun, but in shady, dry conditions it survives just as well and grows much more slowly, up to three feet tall and three feet wide.

D. *odora* is the most commonly grown daphne in the South. It remains a choice plant for many years, but very old specimens are rarely seen. The form with yellow-edged leaves, 'Aureo-Marginata,' deserves its popularity. This selection is visually most striking not in flower but during the late winter when the vivid pink flower buds sit swollen across the surface of the plant. The heavy fragrance during flowering is unequaled. It matures to five feet, spreading to two to three feet.

D. *retusa* is another Chinese species, and one that I find easy to propagate and cultivate. This stocky evergreen has thick, glossy leaves with revolute margins and rosy lavender flowers that open glistening white. It appreciates a sunny position in any good soil and will grow to three feet with a width of two to three feet. PJ]

Deutzia

[Deutzias are popular summer-flowering shrubs of moderate to large size, with at least one notable exception. D. *gracilis* 'Nikko' is a foot-tall shrub with relaxed arching branches that spread up to three feet in ten years. In June it covers itself with an abundance of pure white flowers as if it were laden with snow. In addition to rock garden possibilities, this is a great shrub for mass planting. Like most deutzias, 'Nikko' is of easy culture, preferring full sun and good drainage and requiring little maintenance. PJ]

Enkianthus

[Enkianthuses are charming, unimposing shrubs with small bell-shaped flowers and conspicuous autumn display similar to those of the common blueberry. I do not know of any that are small enough for the scale of an alpine scree, but E. *cernuus* 'Rubens' remains under three feet for ten years and often longer. The flowers of many of the enkianthuses may go unnoticed, but the red flowers of this species hang between rigidly tiered branches and are readily obvious and very pretty. The autumn color is good, though not spectacular. PJ]

Epigaea

[The name *Epigaea* is derived from the Greek *epi* (on) and *gaea* (Earth) and alludes to the ground-hugging habit of this interesting evergreen shrub. *E. repens* is one of only a handful of native southern shrubs small enough to be suitable for use even with the tiniest alpines. It is commonly known as trailing arbutus or mayflower, a title that tradition attributes to the Pilgrims, who, impressed by the great masses they encountered, honored it with the name of their ship.

In the wild, mayflower is occasionally found in association with large rock outcroppings or in dry upland woods. I often find it skirting around the bases of old beeches on a steep ridge. During May sweetly scented pink flowers peek from beneath stiff, leathery leaves. Successful cultivation requires a rather sterile, acidic soil with very good drainage and no disturbance once it is established. It is drought-resistant when grown in shade but tends to dry out in full sun unless supplemental water is provided. Transplanting container-grown plants is difficult but possible. I have found the period just prior to the onset of new growth to be the best time to work with this species. In addition to the typical species, a larger tetraploid selection and a double-flowered form are available. *E. asiatica* is the equally desirable Japanese counterpart and the only other member of this genus. PJ]

Erica

The ericas are the best of the heaths for our climate. The typical *E. vagans,* the Cornish heath, seems to be little planted because of the dull color of the flowers, the cultivated forms being far superior. The cultivar 'Mrs. D. F. Maxwell' is one of the best small shrubs in my garden. Its habit is neat, and the foliage is bright and cheerful throughout the year with the yellow green tips of the new growth making a gay pattern against the old dark leaves. It blooms here from the end of May to the end of August, producing spikes of clear rose-colored flowers. It gets to be a foot or more in height and much wider in breadth. A fifty-cent plant out of a pot has spread to nearly two feet in two years, and probably would have covered more territory if I had not planted a large santolina practically on top of it. It roots as it goes. The tiny cultivar 'Nana,' only four inches high, is most appealing and is one of the most flourishing heaths that I have had. The stiff spikes of parrot green are colorful against the dark metallic leaves of the bronze bugleweed. The flowers of this and the cultivar 'Lyonesse' are pure white.

E. carnea, from the mountains of central and southern Europe, is called the spring heath, but in climates as mild as ours it blooms in winter, and sprays can be picked with the Algerian iris and stray violets even on the chilliest and darkest days. 'Winter Beauty,' 'King George,' and 'Alba' bloom before Christmas. The English boast of earlier kinds, but I have not found them in this country; 'Vivellii' is a late one, blooming on into spring. According to the descriptions there is much variety in the colors, but as I have known them they are mostly either white or a medium red-violet. However, I have no quarrel with that, for it is delightful to find any flower so delicately blooming in the frosty weather.

E. × darleyensis, a hybrid between *E. carnea* and *E. mediterranea,* grows with me to about a foot and a half and spreads a little more than that. There are many named cultivars. All through the late winter the prettily shaped bushes are sprinkled with tiny lilac bells that come into full bloom in February. In summer they are still colorful with the dark tones of the old branches, the bright tips of the new growth, and the pale green of the buds. As far as my experience goes, which is not very far, for it takes many more years than I have given to it to learn the ways of a group of plants, this is one of the best heaths for the South. I have seen it thriving in gardens other than mine, and it is easily grown in any soil.

The heaths as a whole dislike stiff, heavy clay soils that become water-logged, as well as soil that becomes too dry. They require a light, acid, moisture-holding medium of rotted leaves, peat, and sand.

Escallonia

E. rubra pygmaea came to me this spring as *E. nana rubra.* I had never seen it listed before. I lost no time in sending for it, and by June 12 a tiny sprig had made good growth and begun to bloom. This miniature originated in Ireland as a witches'-broom on *E. rubra* and if left unchecked has a tendency to revert to the typical form. I can see already that it needs to be pinched back soon and frequently to keep it small and shapely. *E. rubra* is the hardiest of the genus, and since several other escallonias are being grown in Charlotte, I can see no reason to believe that it will not survive our winters. It will grow in sun or part shade and requires moisture. The light green, finely toothed leaves—like tiny rose leaves—and the red stems of the new growth are decorative even without the small tubular flowers, which are produced very freely. The flowers are described as red, which I find a difficult color to fit into a general rock garden scheme. I was much relieved to find them in reality a warm, soft rose color that is very pleasant with the pinks and lavenders that seem to prevail with me in summer.

Forsythia

[*F. viridissima* 'Bronxensis' is a twelve-inch-high, wide-spreading selection of this early spring-flowering shrub, which is known in the South as yellow bells. The pale lemon yellow flowers are small in comparison with larger cultivars of forsythia, but they are freely produced and attractive. Cultivation in any good garden soil is suitable, and as with most flowering shrubs, full sun promotes more flowers. 'Bronxensis' is an excellent companion plant to use among upright dwarf conifers, which enhance and accentuate its flower display. PJ]

Fothergilla

[*F. gardenii* is a shrub of the coastal Southeast which may occasionally be found growing in the proximity of *Rhododendron atlanticum.* As a young plant fothergilla has an upright habit, generally no taller than thirty inches, but it spreads in time into a neat, rounded shrub. In early spring dense, thumb-sized spikes of white flowers are borne along the tips of leafless branches. Although without petals, the inflorescence is showy because the numerous stamens have conspicuous white filaments (stalks). The foliage, which promptly follows blooming, is large and handsome and turns orange and scarlet in autumn. Fothergilla prefers a peaty, sandy loam, but any well-drained organic soil seems sufficient. In the wild it is most often seen in at least partial shade, but more flowers and superior fall colors are produced when it is grown in full sun. PJ]

Gardenia

The greatest treasure of the southern rock garden is the dwarf Cape jasmine, *G. jasminoides* 'Prostrata.' It is much grown in California and the Deep South, and in the middle South as far north as Norfolk, Virginia. It is perfectly hardy in Raleigh, coming back in time for summer bloom even if it is partly killed back by a severe winter. I do not know how much farther inland it will grow, or how much farther north than Norfolk. This is where some experimenting needs to be done.

The plants are low and spreading, not more than a foot tall but eventually spreading to three or four feet in diameter. The shining, pointed leaves and the deliciously scented flowers are like those of the type but much smaller. The pointed buds, greenish and furled spirally like the buds of morning glories, open into double white flowers two and a half inches across. They bloom in June and all through the summer.

Like the big gardenia, the little ones need a good acid soil rich in humus. They should be planted in the shade and mulched with leaf mold in summer.

Gaultheria

Since our native evergreen *G. procumbens* is on some lists for beginners, it must grow well in some gardens—but not in mine, where three years is the limit of its stay. Now that it has been abroad and come back as *G. procumbens* 'Holland Import,' a much larger-fruited wintergreen than the Eastern form, I may be able to keep it longer than the plants that come straight from the mountains.

I have given up on the other American species after a halfhearted attempt, for it does not seem likely that I can grow these little shrubs from the high Cascades, which are difficult in cultivation even on the West Coast, but I think the Oriental sorts should have a trial. For a while these were not available, but now a few nurseries offer several. I picked *G. miqueliana,* a Japanese alpine described by William Jackson Bean as handsome in flower and fruit and hardy to zero, as first choice, and the Himalayan creeper, *G. nummularioides,* as second. If these fail, there are still *G. veitchiana* (now *G. hookeri*) and *G. cuneata,* both from western China. *G. wardii* from southeastern Tibet is probably too tender for us as it does not stand even the south of England.

All species require shade and a light soil with plenty of humus and, above all, constant moisture. The last is the stumbling block in my garden.

Genista

[Genistas are various-sized, mostly European shrubs, often armed with vicious thorns, that freely bear yellow pealike flowers in summer. They are closely allied to the brooms, cytisus, and have similar cultural requirements. Genistas are relatively unknown to southern gardeners and probably represent an undiscovered treasure.

G. *pilosa* 'Vancouver Gold' is a recent introduction that makes a dense mat of wiry stems and small leaves. It covers itself with flowers in early summer. I have only recently added this selection to my collection, so I cannot address how well it ages. I am told that it increases slowly and remains an attractive mat for many years and that it is particularly well suited to rock-wall culture.

G. *tinctoria* 'Plena' is a semiprostrate, double-flowered form of this species, which is popular in southern European landscapes and grows well in the South. PJ]

Hedera

The sharply defined patterns of the small-leaved ivies show up best against stone, especially where there is a stone wall or a paved area. When I saw how charming they were in Elsie Hassan's garden, like darker shadows on a shaded terrace, I realized anew to what good effect they can be used between the crevices of flagstones or growing up from the base of a wall or spilling over the top of a rocky ledge. There are forms of the English ivy, *H. helix,* that are stiff and shrubby in habit, and forms that are trailing or climbing. Two of the shrubby ones can be used as individual plants without support, or they can be trained against a rock or a wall. The cultivar 'Erecta' is a charming little shrub with small, dark, sharply pointed leaves in two rows on the stout stems. The cultivar 'Conglomerata,' called the clustered ivy, is similar except that the margins of the leaves are very wavy and the lobes are blunt. It grows very slowly—eighteen inches or less in five years—and does not spread laterally. Another shrubby form, the cultivar 'Meagheri,' has climbed to the top of a six-foot wall and started down the other side in the same amount of time and has branched out to cover at least five feet in either direction. The narrow lobed leaves make a delightful pattern.

One of the most decorative of the climbing forms is the cultivar 'Deltoidea.' It is slow growing, traveling perhaps three feet in five years, and very little branched. The pattern of the dark leaves is very distinct and interesting. They are heart-shaped when young and shield-shaped when mature.

The small, distinctly lobed leaves of the cultivar 'Pedata' make a pretty pattern on rocks. The leaves of 'Sagittifolia' are shaped like little arrowheads.

The much-branched forms are desirable for a ground cover or for planting between flagstones. The best of these, and one of the most delightful of the small-leaved types, is the cultivar 'Maple Queen.' It spreads quickly but remains bushy and compact. The leaves are square at the base and bright green. Another dense and low-growing sort is the cultivar 'Pittsburgh.'

Ivies with variegated leaves add to the interest of a collection. The foliage of 'Green Quartz,' a variant of 'Pittsburgh,' is marked with yellow green. In the cultivar 'Cavendishii' the creamy margins are the same in all seasons. The leaves are small and varied in outline. In the cultivar 'Discolor' the white or cream-colored marking spots and streaks the leaves, and in the cultivar 'Tricolor' the margins of the leaves become red in the fall.

Among the forty-five species and varieties that George Lawrence sent me from the collection at Cornell, these are the ones that I have found best suited to the rock garden. In five years none of them have become too vigorous to be kept easily in place or considered undesirable companions for choice plants. Most ivies are at their best in shade, preferring northern and eastern exposures, but the cultivar 'Deltoidea' does as well facing south or west. All are greedy plants that like moist leaf mold, but they will tolerate poor, dry soil.

Helianthemum

I must mention the sun rose, if only to say that it will not grow for me—at least not for long. While it lasts, it blooms beautifully from April through June, and I have had named varieties in all sorts of lovely colors: lemon yellow and gold; apricot and nopal red; shell pink, rose, and wine; but sooner or later (three years at most), perfectly healthy-looking plants suddenly dry up in midsummer, and for no apparent reason. I wondered if I had watered them enough, and then I wondered if I had watered them too much. And then I wondered if they had too much sun, for Mr. Fowler says that though sun lovers, they need some shade in this section; and then I wondered if they had too little sun. Well, they won't grow for me, but perhaps they will do better with someone else.

Hypericum

[Among the best shrubs for sunny locations are the low, sprawling hypericums. *H. cerastioides* is a low, prostrate plant with blue-gray foliage and bright golden-yellow flowers which make up in number for their relatively small size. The way the leaves clasp the seed pods in winter is attractive, and the tight clusters of new growth buds give promise for the following spring.

H. olympicum in the form I have remains under a foot high and has attractive gray-green leaves. In early summer it is covered with showy, bright yellow flowers with the characteristic stamens protruding like powder puffs. NG]

Ilex

The only really dwarf holly that I know is *Ilex crenata* 'Helleri,' a prostrate form of the excellent Japanese holly that is as easily grown as the type and one of the best rock garden evergreens. It will grow anywhere—in sun or shade—but an acid soil rich in humus is preferable. The oval, crenate leaves are dark and very tiny. The berries are black like those of the type. This is a stiff, twiggy, closely woven little shrub that forms an impenetrable mound of glossy green. It grows very slowly, never getting much more than a foot tall and spreading to about eighteen inches in ten years.

I am on the lookout for *I. rugosa,* another prostrate Japanese holly, which has the advantage of red berries and is of interest because of its wrinkled leaves. It has been grown at the Arnold Arboretum, but I cannot find any other reference to its cultivation in this country.

[The evergreen hollies are generally similar to boxwood in their effect in the garden. I know of only a few more that are rock garden worthy. *I. crenata* 'Dwarf Pagoda' is a compelling dwarf form of this Japanese species. The most alluring aspect of this plant is the raiment of tiny thick leaves, which resemble little green coins crowded onto the stems. Its habit is stiffly upright with widely spaced branches, and with age it develops a tremendous amount of character. Culture is easy, but full sun is necessary in order to obtain the smallest leaves and most compact habit. Pamela Harper says that *I. c.* 'Mariesii' is smaller than 'Helleri' and that the cultivar 'Piccolo' is smaller still.

Another holly, only recently introduced, is *I.* × 'Rock Garden.' This is a hybrid involving large and spiny-leaved parents that resulted from controlled crosses made in the early 1970s. Trials to date suggest this cultivar will be low-growing and at least twice as wide as high. It is a female selection with the potential to bear attractive red fruits, but typical gardens may not have appropriate pollinating shrubs. PJ]

Jasminum

[*J. parkeri* is a tiny, summer-blooming, evergreen jasmine native to the western Himalayas. It is listed as hardy to Zone 8, but a specimen in a Hillsborough, North Carolina, garden (Zone 7) is growing just fine. (This particular specimen, however, is annually sparse of flowers, which may indicate cold tenderness in the flower buds.) The thin bright green stems and leaves make a colorful addition among rocks and serve as the perfect background for the sweetly scented bright yellow flowers. It is a beautiful rock garden subject, suitable for even the smallest collections where the proper niche can be found. PJ]

Juniperus

"In spite of many opinions to the contrary," Joel Spingarn said many years ago, "I cannot detect any appreciable difference between *J. procumbens* 'Nana' and *J. squamata* 'Prostrata.' Undoubtedly time will prove me wrong." Time must have done so, for he subsequently listed them as separate plants, and as such they are grown in Charlotte, although I am not convinced that they are properly named. In Donald Kellam's garden *J. procumbens* 'Nana' is four inches tall and three feet wide; in mine *J. squamata* 'Prostrata' has grown to a height of ten inches in eighteen years, and there is no telling how far it would have crept, rooting as it went, if I had not cut it back frequently and drastically to keep it from covering a gravel path as it fanned out from the foot of a tall pine tree.

[There are only a few dwarf junipers that are reliable for use in the rock garden. The best is *J. chinensis* 'Echiniformis,' one of the elite of the dwarf conifers. Extremely slow growing and impenetrably dense, this urchinlike hummock grows one and a half feet tall by as much or more wide in twenty years. It is a brittle plant and should be placed where straying feet cannot easily damage it. 'Echiniformis' is occasionally listed as *J. communis*.

J. communis 'Berkshire' is a superb selection of the common juniper that forms a low, compact, widely vase-shaped shrub. It must be sited where it will receive long periods of full sun if it is to maintain the compact form. *J. communis* forms work best in lean soil without fertilization. *J. c.* 'Compressa' forms a short, dense, narrowly vertical column of crowded shoots and tiny leaves unlike any other dwarf conifer. It is, however, prone to disease and pest problems and requires a lean, open, airy site and careful attention to caterpillars. It occasionally produces reversions to faster growth, which should be promptly pruned back. This rewarding plant requires work and dedication.

J. squamata 'Blue Star' is a low, mounding cultivar with soft awl-shaped leaves that are equally sky blue on both surfaces. Full sun is required to effect this appealing and unique saturation of color. The rather soft foliage has shown some susceptibility to rotting when lower branches lie in contact with frequently moist soil or mulch. High-grafted specimens, which will solve this problem, are increasingly available but at a high price. 'Blue Carpet' is similar to 'Blue Star,' but, as the name implies, more spreading.

Numerous prostrate and low-spreading selections are available that, though dwarf in height, grow much too vigorously sideways to be suitable for average rock garden use, but where there is space, they are impressive when trained to clamber over rocks. Included in this miscellany are many beautiful cultivars of *J. horizontalis, J. communis* 'Repanda,' and several other mountain forms of the common juniper found listed under a variety of names. PJ]

Leiophyllum

[*L. buxifolium,* or box sandmyrtle, is another small-leaved evergreen shrub that is native to the eastern United States. This species is often prostrate where it occurs in higher elevations of the Appalachians, and it is this form that is usually sold as a rock garden plant. Whether this variety remains flat when brought into cultivation I cannot say, but I have been told that it does not. However, as a prostrate plant or a dwarf shrub box sandmyrtle is eminently well suited to the rock garden. It is a plant for a hot, sunny position, where it will thrive once established. In late May, as the weather turns hot, leiophyllum covers itself with small flowers that are, as author Michael Dirr aptly described it, "a froth of white." The flowering season is long and quite an animated period for the garden as hordes of insects parade among the flowers. PJ]

Leucothoë

The leucothoës are little appreciated—perhaps because they have no common name, though they are fittingly named for a king's daughter. If they were called sweetbells, as one of the deciduous sorts is, everyone would want to plant them. Perhaps another reason for their being in disfavor is that they need moisture and cannot be left to fend for themselves in times of drought.

Although the leucothoës are among the best and most satisfactory of the native broad-leaved evergreens, we have none small enough for the rock garden. The two low-growing species in cultivation in this country are from California and Japan.

L. keiskei, the Japanese species, is an erect shrub to about three feet, but there is a flat, spreading sort not more than eight inches tall. I seem to have the latter, for the zigzag branches spread horizontally and seem to have no tendency to grow upward. The leaves are prettily tapered like those of our native *L. catesbaei* (probably *L. fontanesiana*). They turn red in the fall, and the new twigs are reddish, too. The flowers—which I have not seen—are the largest of any cultivated species.

Leucothoës need an acid soil rich in humus and partial shade.

Lithodora

[One of the advantages of rock gardening in the South is our ability to grow *L. diffusa* 'Grace Ward,' a very beautiful subshrub with gentian blue flowers in midspring. Plant this in a well-drained, partly shaded location. The dark green foliage is evergreen and is injured only in severely cold winters. My stock plant survived a terrible winter when our temperatures reached −12°F. NG]

Lonicera

L. pileata, the privet honeysuckle, with its small oval leaves, horizontal habit, and prostrate branches, is not conspicuous in flower or fruit—if it flowers at all, for it is said to be chary of its blossoms—but any low evergreen is useful, especially one that will grow in the shade. The dainty leaves and slender branches are much like those of *L. nitida,* but this shrub may not prove as perfectly evergreen, though so far it has come through severe weather in good condition. This species is from western China and is not hardy much below zero.

Mahonia

Two barberries of the Mahonia group are used as evergreen ground covers in shade where there is room for them to spread, as they do by underground stems. Both grow to a foot tall, more or less, have spikes of yellow flowers in spring followed by blue fruits, and decorative pinnate foliage with leaflets like holly leaves. I have seen *M. nervosa* at Blandy, but at present I have no source for it. It comes from the lower mountains and is a little taller than *M. repens,* which comes from the higher mountains but seems just as ready to settle down at lower altitudes. I had the latter in Raleigh. It was a beautiful plant when it came to me from the Rocky Mountains, but after a while it became leggy in spite of my pruning. However, I had planted it in wretchedly poor and dry soil under oaks, where most shrubs became dispirited. In Virginia Robert Moncure found it "most adaptable and useful on a shady bank of heavy and poor clay, and for large rock gardens, wild gardens and exposed rocky places."

Mitchella

[*M. repens,* partridgeberry, is a tiny, unobtrusive ground cover that is suitable for undisturbed, shady areas of the rock garden. The delicate strands of this native evergreen wind randomly through and over the leaves, mosses, and lichen-encrusted rocks of the forest floor and might go unnoticed were it not for the bright red fruits that appear in autumn. Successfully rooting or dividing pieces is as simple as making the effort, provided the new home is similar to the old. PJ]

Muehlenbeckia

Very few plants from New Zealand have survived in my garden, but I have hopes for the wire-plant, *M. axillaris*, which came to me from Elsie Hassan and is already beginning to spread itself about. It is a matted vine of no height at all, about as minute as a plant can be and still be visible. The microscopic but leathery leaves are on stems that seem to be made of the finest wire. It is hardy at least as far north as New Jersey, where it flowers in June and July. It has not flowered for me yet, and I rather think that the small greenish yellow flowers do not amount to much. This is an easy rock plant, growing in any soil as long as it is in the sun.

"I have *M. complexa* in a pot," Elsie Hassan wrote, "because it is so decorative, but I believe it would survive out-of-doors. I first saw this species in a garden in Ohio, trailing over a huge boulder. The spattered effect of the tiny leaves against the stone was lovely. I must acquire a boulder and try some that way. It was not supposed to be hardy in Ohio, but this was a protected situation." There seems to be some confusion about these two species, and both may be listed as *M. nana*. *M. complexa* is called the maidenhair vine because of its fernlike foliage. In California it climbs to the tops of chimneys.

Paxistima

[*P. canbyi* is a native evergreen that makes a low, shrubby ground cover. It is found on calcareous slopes in the Appalachians of northern Virginia and West Virginia, but in cultivation it seems to tolerate any well-drained organic medium. In landscape effect it is similar to bearberry, and like that plant prefers to be sited in high light. PJ]

Picea

"*P. abies* 'Pumila' is the best spruce for me," Ernest Yelton says, "reaching one foot in fifteen years. *P. a.* 'Pygmaea' is a lovely little bun about six inches tall. *P. a.* 'Nidiformis' makes a bush four feet in diameter over three feet high but is excellent and will withstand our climate. *P. a.* 'Remontii' is a better form for me. *P. pungens* 'Montgomery' is a lovely soft blue plant about a foot in height, and is not greedy. *Picea glauca albertiana* 'Conica,' in spite of getting larger with the years, is wonderful as a peripheral plant for the rock garden."

"Some plants grow very slowly at first," Donald Kellam says, "but when they find they like it here they begin to grow rapidly; one of these is *P. a.* 'Mucronata,' a compact globe when young, but eventually becoming a tree."

[Variants of *P. abies,* the Norway spruce, are limited for rock gardeners in the South because of the tendency of most to grow considerably faster than in the northern latitudes where they were selected.

P. abies 'Little Gem,' the most dwarf cultivar I have grown, is an appropriately named compact shrub with short needles crowded onto short, congested branches. When sited in full sun it will grow to about a foot high and wide in ten years. Though it is prone to partial or complete dieback for no apparent reason, I feel it is worth the risk. The one specimen I have succeeded with is one of my most prized beauties. Three other cultivars—'Repens,' 'Tabuliformis,' and 'Procumbens'—are spreaders which, when pampered, are capable of exceeding a ten-foot spread in fifteen years, so cautious siting is essential. They grow more slowly in partial shade but are more pest prone than those grown in full sun.

P. glauca, the white spruce, performs well in the South. The now-common dwarf Alberta spruce, *P. glauca albertiana* 'Conica,' mentioned by Elizabeth Lawrence, is among the most durable, useful, and well-groomed dwarf conifers, tolerating light shade as well as full sun. Given ten years of happiness, though, it will outgrow very small gardens and develop into a perfectly symmetrical cone six feet or higher, so once again, siting is critical. Though it has severe mite problems in the Northeast, I have seen little evidence of that in the South. The similar cultivars 'Alberta Globe' and 'Little Glove' are slower-growing, more rounded facsimiles.

P. glauca 'Echiniformis' is another of the very best dwarf conifers; it is a handsome little plant suitable for even the smallest rock gardens. After eight years, my specimens, which are in full sun, are less than a foot tall and twice that in width. A stressful summertime may cause partial dieback, but rarely will the entire plant succumb. Thorough mulching and watering are recommended. 'Cecelia' is a much less common recent discovery. It is a congestion of beautifully bright sea-green foliage that is atypically short and fleshy for white spruce. 'Elf' and 'Monstrosa,' also recent introductions, have typical species foliage and produce about an inch of new growth a year.

P. omorika 'Nana,' the Serbian spruce, through its compactness intensifies the effect of the glossy green leaves with prominent white undersides. Though spherical for at least ten to fifteen years, 'Nana' ultimately takes on an upright posture.

P. orientalis, the Oriental spruce of the Caucasus, is the most handsome spruce of all, but unfortunately the dwarf forms are suitable for only large rock gardens. 'Connecticut Tpk.' thus far in my garden has increased a couple of inches a year and carries sleek leaves that are closely held along reddish stems, resulting in a refined, tidy appearance. 'Gracilis,' or 'Nana,' is a desirable selection that slowly forms a large shrub or small tree. A fifteen-year-old specimen in the Coker Arboretum in Chapel Hill has endured shade and competition from large trees, yet it remains attractive and under three feet tall.

The popular powdery blue form of *P. pungens*, the Colorado blue spruce, has produced several dwarfs that are wonderful rock garden shrubs and valuable complements to the predominantly green tones of a garden. 'St. Marys' is the smallest selection that is readily available. My specimen produces less than two inches of new growth per year. Like many picea dwarfs it is slow to gain an attractive shape, but it becomes more dense with age and develops into quite a charmer. 'Globe,' silvery green, and 'Gotelli's Broom,' steel blue, are compact mounds increasing an inch or less annually. Now in nurseries on the West Coast, they should soon be readily available. 'Compacta,' 'Glauca Nana,' and 'Thume' all form flat-topped shrubs and expand two to five inches a year. Prostrate selections, listed as 'Procumbens' or 'Glauca Prostrata,' are also available; the resulting plant develops into a gorgeous ground cover but will be slow only in those cases where the lateral branch was secured from a dwarf cultivar. Upright reversions must be immediately removed. Most of the *P. pungens* selections are of easy culture in full sun or modest shade, with no significant pest problems. Drought stress is perhaps the most damaging enemy. PJ]

Pieris

[There are a few species in this genus with forms small enough to add structure to the larger rock garden. At least two selections of *P. japonica* are excellent. *P. j.* 'Bisbee's Dwarf' is a compact plant with slightly twisted leaves and reddish new growth in spring. The pendulous white flowers are graceful in spring. *P. j.* 'Pygmaea' is a very small form with small, linear leaves.

P. phillyreifolia is a stoloniferous plant with the same delightful flowering habit. Although it remains under two feet high, it has the potential to spread beyond that, and this needs to be remembered when selecting a site for it.

P. taiwanensis 'Snowdrift' is a delightful miniature which blooms profusely and thus far has remained less than one foot high. It too has the drooping racemes of white flowers.

P. yakushimensis is variable in growth habit, but the best are superb with large clusters of white flowers. Although listed as growing to eighteen inches, mine is now twenty-four inches after about eight years. NG]

Pinus

"Among the pines," Mr. van Melle said in our rock garden bulletin in 1949, "the nicest thing known to me is *P. strobus* 'Nana,' an utterly dwarf, compact mass of gray white pine foliage of irregular form and indefinite width." I saw it long ago at the Tingle Nursery in Pittsville, Maryland. The tallest of a row of eight-year-old specimens was eighteen inches, and most were not over twelve inches.

Ernest Yelton says that "*P. cembra* makes a very soft small tree but eventually gets out of scale. I have a lovely dwarf pine in an elongated shape which I have lost the name for; it was obtained from the Raraflora Nursery near Philadelphia and has stayed in scale on the top of a tufa ridge for three years."

[Few species of pine are sufficiently low or slow growing to be suitable for rock garden use. Most dwarf forms are the product of seedling selection or propagation of the witches'-brooms that pines frequently produce, leading to interesting new cultivars that often come to market as unnamed dwarf seedlings.

P. mugo, the mountain pine from higher elevations in central and southern Europe, is the most common of the naturally slow-growing pines. As seen in a typical garden center it is a wonderfully appealing dark green mound of short needles because mass producers shear them numerous times before marketing. But once planted in the garden, a seemingly docile cushion quickly lusts for all the space it can consume. These clones also vary from region to region, so that a northeastern genuinely slow-growing clone may accelerate when brought to the South. If you can find them, 'Gnom' and 'Teeny' are two dependably slow cultivars for southern gardens. They may reach a foot across in ten years.

P. parviflora 'Adcock's Dwarf,' from the Japanese white pine, is one of the best pines available for southern rock gardens. It is typically single trunked with widely spaced upturned branches crowded with short bluish-green needles. It grows at most a couple of inches a year and enjoys full sun early in the day and partial shade thereafter. Through the winter it carries small golden candles that will develop into the following season's growth.

P. pumila 'Draijer's Dwarf' and 'Dwarf Blue' are two selections of the dwarf Siberian pine that have grown well for me for several years, in spite of their origins in the cold, exposed regions across northern Asia. 'Draijer's Dwarf' has an open, irregular habit and is extremely slow growing. 'Dwarf Blue' grows at least twice as fast (though still slow-growing) and ultimately forms a striking compact shrub. The foliage of these cultivars is dark bluish green and slightly twisted, attractively exposing a modest white stomatal banding.

P. rigida 'Sherman Eddy' is a very nice selection of our native pitch pine, growing low and wide with large, coarse needles.

P. strobus, the North American white pine, commonly produces witches'-brooms with viable seeds, thereby providing tremendous potential for the selection of dwarf forms, and this has led to the introduction of many very similar forms. Use of the cultivar name 'Nana,' cited by Elizabeth Lawrence, has been abused in this way. However, if you see a cultivar 'Nana' that suits your needs, then by all means buy it.

In addition to 'Nana' there are several other selections of white pine that can't be resisted. The dearest of these is *P. s.* 'Horsford,' an extremely dense little bun with short, thin needles and an annual growth rate of an inch or less. *P. s.* 'Merrimack' is similar but slightly more coarse and wide-spreading. Care should be exercised in siting these diminutives, as they do not transplant well. The tightly clustered branches and needles can cause twig girdling or needle rot during warm and humid summers, resulting in severe damage or death. Periodic cleaning to improve air circulation will help to avoid this problem, as will avoiding the selection of the most Lilliputian in favor of slightly faster varieties. All white pines have a difficult time with pests and climate in the warm South.

P. sylvestris, the Scotch pine, is rarely seen in southerners' gardens but offers several useful dwarfs. For me it has proven exceedingly pest free and of easy culture. I have succeeded best with lean soil and light shade. 'Girard's Dwarf' is the prince of a very good list of selections. It forms a tidy, narrow green cone that increases about an inch a year. The prostrate form, 'Repens,' is a useful ground cover that slowly clambers along at a couple of inches a year. For large rock gardens 'Saxatilis,' 'Nana Compacta,' and 'Beuvronensis' are all excellent shrubby forms. The first two are low and wide, and the last tends to be about as wide as high. 'Globosa Viridis' is distinguished by its long, stiff, somewhat twisted needles and dense, widely rounded habit. PJ]

Polygala

[*P. chamaebuxus* is a splendid low evergreen shrub for lightly shaded sites with excellent drainage. It has rounded bright green leaves and usually remains less than eight inches high. There are a number of attractive forms with yellow or white flowers, and a showy one, *P. c. grandiflora,* with purple-and-yellow blooms. It spreads slowly into a dense mat and blooms in spring. NG]

Rhododendron

My few attempts at growing the pygmy rhododendrons have very promptly ended in failure, but Elsie Hassan wrote me that *R. intricatum* was lovely and long blooming in Birmingham. This Chinese species is also a favorite with Carl Starker, who says, "three fat old dowagers thirty years old are now three feet high. They are glorious in April and show a flower or two all seasons." Though many of the dwarf species are alpines and difficult at best, I am sure that there must be others that will endure heat and drought. But it is among the azaleas that we will find those best suited to our needs.

Several years ago I saw a low shrub, not more than a foot high, used as a ground cover in the Fruitland Nurseries and found that it is the azalea 'Viscomte de Nieuport.' It is a coarse plant by rock garden standards, for it has the large leaves and flowers characteristic of the Indian azaleas, but it can be used if height is the only consideration.

'Gumpo,' on the other hand, has small, shining dark green leaves, and only the white flowers are enormous. The flowers of 'Flame Creeper' are not at all like flame but of a soft color called rose dorée. All of these bloom early in May, and all are flat little shrubs only a few inches high, very slow-growing, and with tiny leaves. They are not as easily established as the large azaleas and should not be allowed to dry out in the summer.

R. atlanticum grows in low, damp pine woods from Delaware to South Carolina. It is like the wild honeysuckle (*R. periclymenoides*), deciduous and with sweet white or pink flowers, only it spreads by stolons to form mats from six to eighteen inches high. Moisture, sun, and a light soil are essential to its well-being, and I find that it will not bloom in heavy shade. There is a rare fall-flowering form which grows a little taller and blooms from late September into November but does not bloom in the spring. I found this in Mr. Clement's garden and with difficulty persuaded him to share it with me.

R. indicum 'Balsaminiflorum,' which I prefer to call *Azalea rosaeflorum,* is a stiff shrublet with small double flowers of that beautiful clear pink described as salmon but really a tint of spectrum red. It must have constant moisture.

[Scores of selections of the rhododendron genus, in which the azalea has now been classified as a subgenus, have been made since Elizabeth Lawrence considered those appropriate to the rock garden, far too many for a complete discussion here. I suggest the American Rhododendron Society as a source for more complete information.

R. hyperythrum sets flowers well as a young plant and is pink in bud before opening to white. Though listed as ultimately growing to five feet, a seven-year-old specimen in my nursery at Sarah P. Duke Gardens has grown two feet wide but is only fourteen inches tall.

R. makinoi, my favorite species, forms a round shrub four feet in diameter and pleasantly dense, but its size limits its use to only the largest rock gardens.

R. metternichii kyomaruense is the slowest growing of the large-leaved species that I have found to perform exceptionally well. My five-year-old specimen continues to hug the ground, though I suspect that, being well established, growth in subsequent years will be somewhat faster.

R. yakushimanum, the prince of the large-leaved species, blooms in late spring with rich pink flower buds that slowly open into large white bells with a delicate, sweet fragrance. The species may grow to three or four feet in ten years or remain much lower and spreading, depending on the source. It has undergone much hybridization in recent years, resulting in smaller plants. 'Yaku Angel' is a good example.

All these species grow well in a mixture of decayed pine bark and coarse sand with very little else added. An acidic, organic mixture that drains very well is beneficial. Exposure in full sun may result in more compactness and better flower set but will also increase water demand. Planting for full morning sun and moderate light afterward is a good compromise.

The small-leaved evergreen rhododendrons are much better suited to sunny landscapes and readily blend into alpine constructions. *R. impeditum* and *R. fastigiatum* are two closely allied Asian species that are among the best. *R. fastigiatum* survives in my garden, but in light of the condition of the plant I do not recognize this as a success. On the other hand, a friend has an impeccable specimen of *R. impeditum.* The trick appears to be in finding just the right site, as is so often the case. Both species mature to under two feet and have small but very attractive violet flowers. 'Ramapo' and 'Purple Gem' are two frequently recommended *R. fastigiatum* hybrids.

R. ovatum and *R. yungningense* are seldom-seen species that I have found pleasing. The former is not particularly exciting, but it does well, grows slowly, and has pretty pink flowers. *R. yungningense* is an odd-looking shrub with an open and sparse habit. Small plum-colored flowers are borne in clusters near the branch tips late in the spring. The leaves of this species are densely covered with rusty scales and glands that emit a pleasant odor similar to that of eucalyptus.

Azaleas are well represented in sizes suitable to rock gardens, and, on the whole, the small cultivars perform as admirably in the South as their larger counterparts. 'Rukizon' is undoubtedly one of the smallest and most handsome. This selection has tiny, dark green leaves and salmon-pink flowers. It stays under ten inches high while slowly spreading as little as fifteen inches in ten years. 'Chinzan' is another very attractive cultivar that is similar to 'Rukizon' in size and flower. Its leaves are larger and are often described as being heart-shaped, though that requires a stretch of the imagination.

R. kiusianum, the azalea that I most desire to succeed with, has proven to be the most obstinate. It is a native of high mountain meadows on the Japanese island of Kyushu, where in summer thousands of viewers are attracted to its mosaic display of purple, pink, and red. It typically grows about a foot tall, though it may be twice as high in the South. It has small flowers but is a twiggy shrub, so there are lots of them. The leaves are oval and densely covered by cinnamon-colored hairs.

R. nakaharai is an uncommon azalea native to the mountains of northern Taiwan. It is a prostrate or slowly mounding species which has largely been popularized in the United States through the efforts of Polly Hill at Barnard's Inn Farm near North Tisbury on Martha's Vineyard, and she has introduced a selection of the species, 'Mt. Seven Star,' as well as a group of hybrids in which *R. nakaharai* is a key element. These are collectively known as North Tisbury hybrids and are typically low-spreading or mounding in habit. *R. nakaharai* flowers are red but may be tinted orange or purple. PJ]

Rosa

R. arkansana 'J. W. Fargo,' which came to me from Claude Barr, is a western rose that has flourished in my Charlotte garden. It keeps close to the ground, blooms freely (with me in early May, but in South Dakota not until July), and is dainty in flower and foliage and decorative in fruit. If there is a fault, it has not shown up, but I suspect it is about to do so. After four mannerly years of slow increase, I have noticed just this spring a tendency to throw out runners that come up some distance from the original plant, so I feel I must temper my praise with a word of warning. The clusters of rosy buds and delicate pink flowers are delightful against the soft gray foliage. The buds, like the buds of moss roses, are caught in a filagree of slender mossy sepals, and the wide, many-petalled flowers are wonderfully fragrant. The polished hips that follow the flowers last all summer, and I sometimes pick them in the fall for little winter bouquets. The leaves are like the leaves of burnet—gray-green ovals with such finely toothed margins that drops of water cling to them after showers and early in the morning.

R. chinensis 'Minima' was first brought to England from the island of Mauritius when it was taken from the French in 1810. Sweet named it *R. lawranceana* for the painter of roses, Miss Mary Lawrance. From this came the fairy roses, which were much in vogue for a time. None was over a foot tall, and the smallest—so it is said —could be covered by half an eggshell.

Wars have twice brought miniature roses to the notice of gardeners. They again became popular after the First World War when M. Correvon, a Swiss nurseryman, introduced the tiny form of *R. chinensis* sent to him by Major Roulett as *R. roulettii*. Major Roulette had found it during the war in a cottage window in the Swiss village of Mauborget. The villagers had cherished it for so many generations that no one could remember how it had come there. In their windows it bloomed all year and was only three or four inches tall, but in gardens it blooms only in summer and is a little taller.

R. chinensis, the monthly rose, is one of the best and most easily grown roses in the South. The only one that I have had is *R. roulettii,* now known as *R. chinensis* 'Minima,' which produced a few pale, pointed buds and wan little flowers and then perished from too little moisture and too much shade. I never acquired more because they seemed to fit neither the rock garden nor the flower borders. Elsie Hassan solved the problem by planting them to themselves in a raised bed against a garage wall. A large part of the soil was pure sand, and she kept them well watered. They grow well where they are open to the sky but protected from the sun much of the day.

'Pixie' seems to be the best and most readily cultivated of the named varieties. The bud is really the size of a grain of wheat; it is a warm white color and shaped like that of a tea rose. The flowers are more double and more compact than those of most of the fairy roses.

'Oakington Ruby,' another favorite, is a true miniature, but the red flowers are not so well formed as those of 'Pixie.'

Elsie Hassan finds 'David of Doncaster' and 'Baby Lillian' of uneven growth, and 'Sweet Vivid' a lovely color and a good bloomer but of weak growth and given to black spot.

The flowers of 'Sweet Fairy' are a delicate pink with buds of a deeper color, and the long, pointed buds of 'Pom-pom de Paris' are deep rose.

Ruscus

[*R. aculeatus,* butcher's-broom is an attractive dark green shrub for light to full shade. Its tight growth makes it especially appropriate for smaller rock gardens. Male and female plants are usually required for the production of berries; however, Elizabeth Lawrence had the rare hermaphroditic form, which she generously shared with her gardening friends. The common name was acquired because butchers used it to clean off their chopping blocks. This is easy to imagine when you feel its stiff stems. NG]

Sarcococca

"Gardens of earlier times were sweeter than ours," Louise Beebe Wilder lamented in *The Fragrant Path.* "Why do garden makers of today so seldom deliberately plan for fragrance?"

It seems to me that rock gardeners are particularly insensitive to the pleasures of the nose. Perhaps this is because rock plants have so long been associated with the brilliant but mostly scentless flora of the pure cold air of great heights. In mild climates the air is nearly always heavy with the odor of flowers. On summer nights a southern garden sleeps beneath a blanket of the perfumes of gardenia and cooperia and tuberose. On warm winter days it basks in the sunny fragrance of sweet olive and sweet box. Sweet box is redolent of honey and of something indefinable but well suited to the deceptive air of false spring.

Sweet box is the name that the English gardeners give to sarcococca. We would do well to use it in place of the harsh Greek name, which smells of the tomb and even in translation (fleshy fruit) is unaesthetic. The genus, it seems, is a very natural one—which means that the species are so much alike as to be indistinguishable at times even by taxonomists. This need not bother the gardener, especially in this country, where only two species are commonly planted, and the difference between them is plain enough once you are acquainted with both. They are excellent shrubs with shining, healthy foliage that lasts well through cold weather, drought, heat, and humidity. They will grow anywhere in sweet or acid soil, prefer moisture but endure drought, like shade but tolerate sun if the soil is not too dry, and can be counted on in a northern exposure. With me neither species has ever fruited, though both flower profusely in February.

S. hookeriana comes from the Himalayas and is hardy on Long Island. The form in cultivation in this country is the variety *humilis*. It is described as growing no more than a foot or two in height and spreading by underground stems to make a wide mat. In my garden it is very slow growing and so far has shown no tendency to spread. The leaves are narrow like willow leaves, the flowers creamy with pink anthers, and the berries, which I hope to have in time, should be black and shining.

S. ruscifolia, from western China, is described as rather tender, especially when young, and Walter B. Mayer says he has lost his young plants twice in Charlotte, North Carolina. I cannot understand this, as Henry Hohman grows it at Kingsville, Maryland, where I have seen large well-established plants, and I had it for a number of years in Raleigh. It may be that Mr. Hohman and I had the variety *chinensis,* which has smaller leaves and is more rigid in habit and hardier than the type. This species makes a round, compact bush that eventually grows to two feet or more. But it does it very slowly, taking a good many years to reach twelve inches. The leaves are oval and pointed, as the specific name suggests, like the cladodes of butcher's-broom. The berries are red.

Serissa

"I think a small shrub on my garden wall deserves enthusiasm," Elsie Hassan wrote from Alabama. "When it is in full bloom it looks as though someone had dropped an apron full of stars. An aunt in North Carolina sent it to me, and the Arnold Arboretum identified it as *Serissa foetida.*" Since the stems root wherever they touch the ground, there are always plants to give away, and so the serissa has traveled from garden to garden, especially along the coast, from Florida to Norfolk. As Henry Hohman lists it without comment, it must be hardy near Baltimore. In the Deep South serissa is evergreen, but in my garden the small oval leaves drop in severe weather, and there are no new ones until late spring. This shrub blooms profusely in May and is seldom out of bloom during the summer and fall. In spite of the name, the small white violet-tinged flowers are sweet smelling, and the leaves and the wine-colored twigs are fetid only when crushed. Plants bloom best in full sun and when watered and fed, but they grow and bloom in shade and submit to any abuse. A variegated form with gold-edged leaves is the one usually offered as a houseplant. There is also a form with double flowers, but this I have never seen and I doubt whether I would like it. In time serissa gets to be three feet tall and spreads as far as it can, but it is easily kept in place.

Skimmia

S. reevesiana had been growing in my Raleigh garden for two years when we left there, and though I cannot say that it was flourishing, it was at least existing when we came away. The advantage of this Chinese species is that it is hermaphroditic, while the Japanese skimmia has male and female flowers on different plants. It is also best for the rock garden because it is the most dwarf species, usually not more than two feet tall. It bloomed with me late in April but did not fruit. The flowers are white, abundant, and fragrant; the berries are red, and the leaves are long and narrow and very thick.

I once saw *S. japonica* growing in a Maryland nursery, but I have never been able to get it for myself. There seems to be much difficulty about the berries even if plants of both sexes are present. Walter B. Mayer has brought *S. j.* 'Foremanii,' described as a free-berrying hybrid between the two species, through two trying winters. In the garden it does not look very flourishing at the present moment, but a plant from the greenhouse is handsome indeed. It would be desirable for its bold lacquered leaves even if there were never any berries.

All of the skimmias are compact and slow growing. They need a light soil, humus, moisture, and shade. I think that moisture is especially important in our climate.

Spiraea

One of the very best shrubs for the southern rock garden in summer, and for rock gardens almost everywhere for that matter, is the quaint and deserving and entirely dependable *S. japonica* 'Bullata' (formerly *S. bullata*, a Japanese species which is round and compact and about twelve inches tall. Where spring comes late it does not bloom until

July and August, but in my garden the first little bunches of raspberry blossoms begin to open in early May and continue throughout the summer. The leaves are small, thick, and crinkled; it is easy to see where the synonym, *S. crispifolia,* came from. Part shade and a slightly alkaline soil are recommended, but I do not think it matters very much.

S. × bumalda 'Norman' is a form of *S.* × bumalda of the Anthony Waterer strain but is nothing like that hideous and commonplace shrub. 'Norman' is scarcely more than six inches tall, a dense mat of wiry stems and bronze leaves that turn bright red in the fall of the year. The flowers are rosy pink in early summer.

Elsie Hassan sent me a small white-flowered spiraea, less than two feet tall and spreading, which I think must be another dwarf Japanese cultivar, *S. japonica* 'Albiflora.' She said she had it from a neighbor who brought it from a farm in Georgia. "The flowers are lovely and most profusely borne from May until November. The buds are like bunches of seed pearls. Add the profusion of bloom, and it is a perfect dwarf shrub for rock garden or terrace," she wrote. It will grow in any soil and will bloom in shade, but it does better in the open.

S. decumbens, a choice white-flowered alpine from the Dolomites, is prostrate in habit, spreads slowly from underground runners, and eventually reaches a height of less than twelve inches. It does not flower until it is well established. This little shrub bloomed for me once in the middle of May. It was not a success with me, perhaps because it did not like the climate but more probably because I had it in shade in acid soil with a western exposure, and I have since read that it requires lime, a gritty soil, and a northern slope.

['Alpina' and 'Little Princess' are similar selections of the Japanese spiraea, *S. japonica,* that grow to about one and two feet, respectively, and bear rose-pink flowers. Both are densely twiggy mounds, eventually wide spreading, and grow vigorously in any well-drained garden soil. They flower heavily in early summer, with continued touches of soft color until frost. Every three to five years the Japanese spiraea, and especially 'Little Princess,' benefit from selective pruning to remove older branches. Pamela Harper says that there are gold-leaved counterparts, 'Gold Mound' and 'Golden Princess.' PJ]

Taxus

The most satisfactory yew for the South is the English species, *T. baccata*. There are numerous low-growing forms, but the only one I have grown is 'Repandens,' which came from Tingle's Nursery and grew in my Raleigh garden for a number of years without getting to be more than two feet tall. When I came to Charlotte, Mr. Tingle sent me another; it had evidently been growing in the field for some time and was already four feet tall; in spite of being cut back, it is now about eight feet tall and sixteen feet across. I have learned that in seventy-five years it may grow to ten by thirty feet, and I had better begin dealing with it more severely. In addition to putting up with heat, it is said to be the hardiest English yew, withstanding temperatures well below zero.

The most beautiful dwarf yew I have ever seen is *T. baccata* 'Prostrata' in Mrs. de Forest's lovely garden in Santa Barbara. It is a low, neat, slowly spreading ground cover, two feet tall or less, with bright green needles. My visit to California was long ago; I have searched in vain ever since, but I have never found a source for it.

In the *Bulletin of the American Rock Garden Society* (January 1968) Anna Sheets says another dwarf Japanese yew, *T. cuspidata* 'Minima,' one of the very smallest, is easy to grow in sun or light shade in piedmont North Carolina. It was raised in 1932 from a seedling selected by B. H. Slavin, director of parks in Rochester, New York.

Thuja

The Oriental arbor-vitae is better suited to the South than the American one. *Thuja orientalis* (now *Platycladus orientalis*) 'Aurea Nana' is sometimes listed as Berckmans Golden Arbor-vitae. "It is popular on the West Coast, deservedly so," H. J. Welch says, "and should be in every collection, however small; it is seldom over sixty centimeters high." Most nurseries still list it as *Thuja*.

T. orientalis 'Juniperoides,' a compact and columnar form, may grow to a height of eighteen inches or more in seven years. Mr. Welch gives its mature height as less than a meter.

[The cultivars of *T. occidentalis* from eastern North America and *T. orientalis* from Southeast Asia are so commonly used as utility plants that people perceive them as low-cost items and are therefore unwilling to pay the price necessary for nurserymen to turn a profit. For that reason good selections may be difficult to find. Thuja, however, is very easily propagated by cuttings during the winter months, so obtaining appealing clones is only as difficult as finding a specimen to snip a cutting from.

T. occidentalis 'Hetz Midget' is one of the most popular dwarf selections, and deservedly so. This narrow globe of dense, vertically held foliar sprays may ultimately reach waist height but will take many years in doing so. A specimen I rooted is after eight years still less than a foot tall. This cultivar also bronzes less in winter cold than many selections of arbor-vitae.

'Milleri,' 'Holmstrup,' and 'Globosa Nana' are similarly good cultivars differing in their almost perfectly rounded habit and slightly more accelerated growth rate. 'Recurva Nana' is a favorite of mine, with loosely held horizontal sprays that slowly layer to form a broadly conical specimen. In twenty-five years this cultivar may reach forty inches in height.

'Umbraculifera' is a fine selection that forms a wider-than-high mound of thin dark green foliage with a unique bluish cast that bronzes little in the winter. Two specimens in the Sarah P. Duke Gardens measure two feet high and three feet across after thirty years. The leaves have a fragrance of the Great North Woods.

The cultivars 'Tiny Tim,' which increases by millimeters per year, and 'Hoseri,' only slightly more rapid, are useful for smaller rock gardens. Unfortunately, however, both discolor to an unattractive brown in winter, a time when conifers are most prominent in the garden.

T. orientalis, recently reclassified as *Pladycladus orientalis,* may be found in nurseries under either name. It is a species especially well suited to hot climates. In addition to the selections cited by Elizabeth Lawrence, the cultivars 'Sanderi,' 'Meldensis,' and 'Rosedalis' are narrowly upright in youth and broaden with age. However, their growth rate of four to six inches per year reduces their useful life in all but the largest collections.

'Westmont' is a relatively recent introduction that closely resembles 'Aurea Nana' in color but is perhaps a trifle more compact. It is very colorful year-round when sited in full sun.

T. plicata 'Cuprea' is a pretty dark-green selection with growing tips that are creamy yellow as they emerge. I grow it in light shade, where it becomes open and upright with the contrasting yellow tips still evident but pleasingly speckled throughout. At the Arnold Arboretum in Boston there is a fifteen-year-old specimen growing in a similar location which has remained under two feet. PJ]

Thujopsis

[*T. dolobrata* is an uncommon Asian conifer similar to and closely allied with *Thuja*. This beautiful species is no dwarf but is often shrubby and can easily be kept under four feet for many years with a little judicious pruning. For rock gardens, *T. dolobrata* 'Nana' grows at a fraction of the species's rate, ultimately forming a broad mound one to two feet in height by twice as wide. This handsome dwarf prefers light shade and protection from desiccation in our climate and will pale and die back if grown otherwise. PJ]

Tsuga

Donald Kellam gets all his dwarf conifers from the Mitsch Nursery in Oregon. He has some interesting small hemlocks that are cultivars of *T. canadensis:* 'Gentsch White,' with silver white tips, new and rare; 'Jeddeloh,' very fine, stays low; and 'Nana'—Mr. Mitsch was not sure of the name, as the same plant is listed as 'Nana Gracilis' and 'Gracilis,' but it is a beauty. 'Pendula' is a weeping form for large gardens.

T. diversifolia, a forest tree in the mountains of northern Japan, is a puzzle. In cultivation in England, H. G. Hillier says, it is a small horizontally branched tree. I first saw it in Mr. Tingle's collection in Pittsville, Maryland, as a very small, dense mass of foliage; Mr. Mitsch describes it as "semi-dwarf, irregular, upright. Ends of branches somewhat twisted showing silvery reverse." In Donald Kellam's garden it has grown to a height of two feet in seven years.

The one in my garden came from Kingsville, Maryland, described as "a very graceful hemlock with crowded branches forming a pyramidal head." It was a small, low shrub with horizontal branches, but I supposed it would grow in grace and make a screen where a screen was needed. But now, after twenty-five years, the trunk is only four inches high and no bigger than a man's wrist, and the spreading branches lie on the ground or grow upward for a few inches and then grow out at right angles for as much as eight feet; the branchlets turn upward, and the tips of the tallest are about three feet from the ground. The glossy, dark green needles are narrow and short—only an inch long—and as fragrant as balsam. It grows in deep shade with a carpet of *Vinca minor* beneath it.

[Of the fourteen species of hemlock, our native Canadian, *T. canadensis,* is the most important for rock garden selections. It is a highly variable species that is apt to produce witches'-brooms, resulting in the development of many useful dwarfs. They are of relatively easy culture, tolerating shade and dry conditions as well as almost any dwarf conifer. However, hemlocks that are watered frequently and sited in full sun with late-day shade give the best results. As a rule of thumb, the more dwarf the cultivar, the less tolerant it is to cultural extremes.

T. c. 'Minuta' is the smallest selection I have grown and the best for very small gardens. It grows less than one-half inch per year and ultimately forms a congested, irregular-shaped mound. 'Jervis' is an upright selection that is similarly slow and dense; it may also be found listed as 'Nearing.'

'Coles Prostrate,' or 'Coles,' is the most useful dwarf Canadian hemlock available. It is a completely procumbent cultivar that reflects the surfaces it carpets. It is most handsomely used above rocks or near a ledge where it creates a leafy cascade. It also develops a wonderful framework of smooth gray older branches and does well in any regime of light short of dense shade. High-grafted specimens that can be trained in a variety of ways are available.

There exist a host of small shrubby selections of this species with subtle differences in foliage and growth characteristics. Most eventually grow too large for the smallest rock gardens but are slow enough to give structure and be useful for many years. 'Jacqueline Verkade,' one of the best, forms a compact, narrow globe with leaves that radiate around the stem. 'Stewarts Pygmaea,' also listed as 'Stewarts Gem' or 'Stewarts,' is another globe-shaped selection with prominent cinnamon-colored branch tips. It is perfectly round and grows to be about the size of a basketball in eight to ten years.

If golden-colored conifers suit your fancy, the brightly yellow-tinted 'Everitt Golden' is the best. The color is pleasant but not overpowering and is contrasted nicely by a dark green interior. To color well it requires a site with at least a few hours of full sun. It will not burn in North Carolina if dry conditions are not too severe.

Other splendid cultivars include the dwarf uprights 'Hussii,' 'Lewisii,' and 'Geneva.' 'Bennett' is a popular variety that grows wider than high and has graceful, pendulous branchlets. It may be sold as 'Minima' and 'Bennett's Minima.' Sargent's weeping hemlock, *T. c.* 'Pendula,' is often popularized as a dwarf conifer, but it spreads many yards wide and several feet high in a relatively short time.

Selections of *T. mertensiana*, the mountain hemlock, are increasingly available. I have kept 'Argentea,' a stiff, upright, silvery dwarf, for several years. PJ]

Vaccinium

Two small native blueberries are useful but not enough used. This is probably because there is some difficulty in getting them established, except in the gardens near the savannahs and wet pinelands where they grow naturally from North Carolina to Florida.

V. crassifolium I have found, however, in gardens in Charlotte and Asheville, which leads me to believe that the problem is one of culture rather than climate. Once we make up our minds to learn to grow these charming native plants, the beauty of our gardens will be enhanced. I think the main points in the cultivation of *V. crassifolium* are acid soil with a mulch of decayed leaves and frequent moisture. If the soil is not already acid enough, sprinkle the ground around it with aluminum sulfate. It is a flat, vinelike shrub that makes a light evergreen carpet. The stems are reddish, and the small oval leaves are dark and shining. The flowers are variously described as rosy red and pink, but I have never seen the plant in bloom. The small berries are black.

V. myrsinites is somewhat taller, to about two feet. William Bean, who has much more to say about our native plants in *Trees and Shrubs Hardy in the British Isles* than most American writers, says that there are two forms, one upright and one spreading.

I have no luck with the mountain cranberry, which is one of the shrubs that grows well enough as long as the nights are cool but dries up suddenly and completely as soon as the real heat descends.

It is a pretty little bush and prettily named—*V. vitis-idaea* (vine of Mount Ida) because the Cretans made wine from the red berries.

[North Carolina State University has introduced two beautiful ornamental selections: *V. crassifolium* 'Wells Delight' and *V. sempervirens* 'Bloodstone.' Both of these southern natives are vigorously carpeting evergreen ground covers that are suitable for exposed, dry sites in large rock gardens, or, with pruning, in smaller gardens. Of the two, 'Wells Delight' has the more ornamental foliage, establishes more readily, and seems to have better disease resistance. The small, highly glossed leaves of this cultivar have a reddish-purple hue, accentuated by winter cold if grown in full sun. The larger, more coarsely textured foliage of 'Bloodstone' also takes on winter color, especially the young stems, which are brilliant cherry red.

V. macrocarpon, the native cranberry, is another prostrate vaccinium rarely thought of as a rock garden shrub. The selection 'Hamilton' is a marvelous compact mat with fleshy burgundy-colored leaves. It creeps tamely along, rooting as it grows. Cranberries are commercially cultivated in peaty bogs with controlled flooding, so although this selection does not require boggy conditions, it is not a plant that tolerates southern drought. 'Hamilton' is surprisingly heat-enduring, however, and I get excellent results by adding decayed bark or peat to a planting site that is slow to dry, or by planting where water can be conveniently supplied. PJ]

Viburnum

One evergreen viburnum is low enough to be called a saxatile plant, for it does not ordinarily become more than two feet tall, and at the rate at which it grows here, it will need a long while to reach that. *V. davidii* is a Chinese shrub with white flowers, handsome bright blue berries (if both sexes are present), and striking foliage. The leaves are five inches or more in length, oval, and deeply veined, becoming wine-colored in winter. Henry Hohman says that this species is not hardy north of Virginia.

Walter B. Mayer and I had five plants between us here in Charlotte, of which three still exist. They have survived three winters and two murky summers, but none have yet bloomed. I made the mistake of putting the first one in full sun, but I learned later that this species needs some shade.

[Much to my dismay, *V. davidii* is borderline cold tender in piedmont North Carolina, but it should do well in warmer parts of the South. It forms a compact, low mound under two feet and is rather wide spreading. The flowers are not particularly showy, but the pearl-sized turquoise fruits are. Several plants are often necessary to ensure good fruit set.

V. carlesii 'Compactum' would certainly be my choice if there was space in my garden for only one viburnum. This selection has several attributes that make it an outstanding garden shrub. It is compact of habit, has handsome disease-resistant foliage, is easily grown, and, best of all, carries pink-tinged white flowers that possess a heaven-sent fragrance. 'Compactum' grows most densely in full sun and stretches out as shade increases. It is easily kept small by pruning begun at an early age but is recommended only for the largest rock gardens. PJ]

Appendixes ✣

1. Plant Requirements ❁

This chart is intended only as a suggestion for appropriate sites for the plants mentioned in this book. Different locations will often prove just as satisfactory in other parts of the country. Apparently contradictory recommendations are sometimes given because of the varied requirements of different species within a genus.

Plant name	Sun	Shade	Semishade	Moisture	Drainage
NONWOODY PLANTS					
Achillea	yes				yes
Acorus			yes	yes	
Adonis			yes		
Aethionema	yes				yes
Ajuga			yes		
Alchemilla			yes	yes	
Alyssoides	yes				yes
Alyssum	yes				yes
Anemone	yes	yes	yes		yes
Anemonella		yes	yes		
Anthemis	yes				yes
Anthericum	yes			yes[a]	
Aquilegia	yes		yes		
Arabis	yes				yes
Arenaria	yes		yes		yes
Arisaema		yes			
Armeria	yes				yes
Arrhenatherum	yes		yes		
Artemisia	yes				yes
Arum		yes			

Plant name	Sun	Shade	Semishade	Moisture	Drainage
Aruncus		yes			
Asarum		yes			
Astilbe		yes		yes	
Aubrieta			yes		yes
Aurinia	yes				yes
Begonia		yes		yes	
Bellis	yes		yes		
Bletilla	yes		yes	yes	
Brachycome	yes				
Brimeura		yes	yes		
Brodiaea	yes		yes	yes	
Bulbocodium			yes		
Calanthe		yes			yes
Callirhoe	yes				yes
Campanula	yes	yes	yes		yes
Carex		yes	yes		
Cerastium	yes		yes		
Chionodoxa		yes			yes
Chrysogonum	yes	yes	yes		
Claytonia	yes		yes		
Collinsea		yes	yes		
Cooperia	yes				
Corydalis		yes	yes	yes	
Crocus	yes		yes		yes
Cuthbertia	yes				yes
Cyclamen		yes	yes		yes
Delosperma	yes				yes
Delphinium	yes	yes	yes		
Dentaria		yes			
Deschampsia	yes		yes		
Dianthus	yes				yes
Diascia	yes				yes
Dicentra		yes	yes	yes	yes
Draba	yes				yes
Dracocephalum	yes		yes	yes	
Dyssodia	yes				yes
Epimedium		yes			
Eranthis			yes		yes
Erigeron	yes		yes	yes	yes
Erinus			yes		yes
Euphorbia	yes				yes
Festuca	yes				yes
Filipendula		yes			yes

Plant name	Sun	Shade	Semishade	Moisture	Drainage
Galanthus	yes		yes		yes
Gentiana	yes		yes		yes
Geranium	yes		yes		yes
Geum	yes				yes
Goodyera			yes		
Gypsophila	yes				yes
Habranthus	yes		yes		
Hakonechloa			yes		yes
Hedyotis			yes		
Helleborus		yes	yes		
Hemerocallis	yes		yes		
Hepatica		yes			
Hermodactylus	yes				
Heuchera	yes	yes	yes		yes
× Heucherella			yes	yes	
Hippeastrum	yes				
Hosta		yes	yes	yes	
Hyacinthella			yes		yes
Hypoxis		yes			yes
Iberis	yes				yes
Imperata	yes				
Ionopsidium	yes		yes		
Iris	yes		yes	yes	yes
Kniphofia	yes			yes	
Koeleria	yes				
Lamiastrum		yes			
Lamium	yes		yes		
Lapeirousia	yes				
Lavandula	yes				yes
Leucojum	yes				yes
Lewisia	yes		yes		yes
Lilium	yes		yes		yes
Limnanthes	yes		yes	yes	
Lobularia	yes				
Luzula		yes	yes		
Lychnis	yes				yes
Lycoris	yes		yes		
Lysimachia	yes		yes		
Mazus		yes	yes		
Mertensia		yes	yes		
Milium		yes	yes		
Miscanthus	yes				
Mitella		yes	yes		

Plant name	Sun	Shade	Semishade	Moisture	Drainage
Muscari			yes		
Myosotis		yes	yes	yes	
Narcissus	yes		yes		yes
Nemophila	yes				yes
Nerine	yes				yes
Nierembergia	yes				yes
Oenothera	yes				
Omphalodes		yes	yes		yes
Ophiopogon	yes		yes		yes
Origanum	yes				yes
Orostachys	yes				yes
Paeonia	yes		yes		
Penstemon	yes		yes		
Petrorhagia	yes				yes
Phlox	yes	yes	yes		yes
Phyteuma		yes	yes		
Platycodon	yes				
Polemonium		yes	yes		
Polygonatum		yes			
Portulaca	yes				yes
Potentilla	yes		yes		
Primula		yes	yes	yes	yes
Prunella		yes		yes	
Pulmonaria		yes		yes	yes
Pulsatilla	yes				yes
Puschkinia			yes		
Ranunculus	yes		yes		
Rosemarinus	yes				yes
Salvia	yes				
Sanguinea		yes	yes		
Santolina	yes				yes
Saponaria	yes				yes
Satureja	yes				yes
Saxifraga		yes			yes
Scabiosa	yes				
Scilla	yes	yes			yes
Sedum	yes	yes	yes	yes	yes
Semiaquilegia		yes	yes		
Sempervivum			yes		yes
Setcreasea	yes				
Silene	yes	yes	yes		
Sisyrinchium	yes		yes		
Smilacina		yes			

Plant name	Sun	Shade	Semishade	Moisture	Drainage
Solidago	yes		yes		
Spigelia			yes	yes	
Stellaria		yes			
Stylophorum			yes		
Tagetes	yes				
Tellima		yes		yes	
Teucrium	yes		yes		
Thalictrum		yes	yes		
Thymus	yes				yes
Tiarella		yes	yes		
Torenia		yes	yes	yes	
Tradescantia	yes				yes
Tricyrtis		yes	yes		
Trillium		yes			
Tulbaghia	yes			yes	yes
Tulipa	yes		yes		yes
Uvularia		yes	yes		
Vancouveria		yes		yes	yes
Verbena	yes				yes
Veronica	yes		yes	yes	yes
Viola		yes	yes		
Zephyranthes	yes	yes	yes	yes	
WOODY PLANTS					
Abies			yes	yes	yes
Acer	yes	yes	yes		yes
Arctostaphylos			yes		yes
Berberis	yes		yes		yes
Buxus			yes		
Calluna			yes		yes
Cedrus	yes		yes		
Cephalotaxus	yes		yes		
Chaenomeles	yes		yes		yes
Chamaecyparis	yes		yes	yes	
Chamaedaphne			yes	yes	
Cistus	yes				yes
Convolvulus	yes				yes
Cotoneaster	yes				yes
Cryptomeria	yes		yes	yes	
Daphne	yes		yes		yes
Deutzia	yes				yes
Enkianthus			yes	yes	yes
Epigaea		yes	yes		yes

Plant name	Sun	Shade	Semishade	Moisture	Drainage
Erica			yes		yes
Escallonia	yes		yes		
Forsythia	yes		yes		
Fothergilla	yes		yes	yes	yes
Gardenia		yes			
Gaultheria		yes			
Genista	yes				yes
Hedera		yes			
Helianthemum	yes				yes
Hypericum	yes				yes
Ilex	yes	yes	yes		yes
Jasminum	yes		yes		
Juniperus	yes		yes		
Leiophyllum	yes				yes
Leucothoë			yes		
Lithodora			yes		yes
Lonicera		yes	yes		
Mahonia		yes	yes		yes
Muehlenbeckia	yes				
Paxistima			yes	yes	yes
Picea	yes		yes		
Pieris			yes		
Pinus	yes		yes		
Polygala			yes		yes
Rhododendron	yes		yes	yes	yes
Rosa	yes		yes		yes
Ruscus		yes	yes		
Sarcococca		yes	yes		
Serissa	yes	yes	yes		
Skimmia		yes			
Spiraea	yes		yes		yes
Taxus			yes		
Thuja	yes		yes		
Thujopsis			yes		
Tsuga	yes	yes	yes		yes
Vaccinium			yes		
Viburnum	yes	yes	yes		

[a]at blooming time

2. Sources for Seeds and Plants ✤

Seed Exchanges

There are a number of fine horticultural societies with excellent seed exchanges. This is the best way to obtain plants that are not popular enough for a commercial seed house to produce. Each group is only as good as its members, so it is important to be prepared to give your best seeds so that you can receive someone else's. Never send seeds of plants whose identity you aren't sure of, and never trust completely the identity of the plants which result from sowing the seeds you obtain. The bulletins of such societies are filled with excellent articles and information not available anywhere else.

Alpine Garden Society: Lye End Link, St. John's, Woking, Surrey, GU21 1SW, England
American Rock Garden Society: 15 Fairmead Rd., Darien, CT 06820
Cyclamen Society: 9 Tudor Dr., Otford, Sevenoaks, Kent TN17 4LB, England
Hardy Plant Society (East): 539 Woodland Ave., Media, PA 19063
Hardy Plant Society (West): 33530 SE Bluff Rd., Boring, OR 97009
North American Lily Society: PO Box 476, Waukee, IA 50263
Northwest Horticultural Society: c/o Center for Urban Horticulture, University of Washington, GF 15, Seattle, WA 98195
Primula Society: 6730 West Mercer Way, Mercer Island, WA 98040
Scottish Rock Garden Club: 21 Merchiston Park, Edinburgh, EH10 4PW, Scotland, U.K.

There are also several excellent commercial sources of unusual plants. The following are highly recommended:

Jim and Jenny Archibald, 'Bryn Collen,' Ffostrasol, Llandysul, Dyfed, SA44 5SB, Wales, U.K.

J. L. Hudson, Seedsman, PO Box 1058, Redwood City, CA 94064
Klaus Jelitto, PO Box 560127, D-2000 Hamburg 56, W. Germany
Prairie Nursery, PO Box 365, Westfield, WI 53964

Nurseries

Appalachian Wildflower Nursery, Rt. 1, Box 275A, Reedsville, PA 17084
B & D Lilies, 330 P St., Easton, PA 18042
The Bovees Nursery, 1737 SW Coronade, Portland, OR 97219
Camellia Forest Nursery, 125 Carolina Forest Rd., Chapel Hill, NC 27516
Canyon Creek Nursery, 3527 Dry Creek Rd., Oroville, CA 95965
Carroll Gardens, 444 East Main St., Westminster, MD 21157
Coenosium Gardens, 6640 S. Lone Elder Rd., Aurora, OR 97002
Crownsville Nursery, 1241 General Highway, Crownsville, MD 21032
Cummins Garden, 22 Robertsville Rd., Marlboro, NJ 07746
Daffodil Mart, Rt. 3, Box 208R, Gloucester, VA 23061
Daystar, Rt. 2, Box 250, Litchfield, ME 04350
Dilatush Nursery, 780 Rt. 130, Robbinsville, NJ 08691
Eco Gardens, PO Box 1227, Decatur, GA 30031
Forestfarm, 990 Tetherow Rd., Williams, OR 97544
Foxborough Nursery, 3611 Miller Rd., Street, MD 21154
Glass House Works, Church St., Box 97, Stewart, OH 45778
Russell Graham, 4030 Eagle Crest Rd. NW, Salem, OR 97304
Greer Gardens, 1280 Goodpasture Island Rd., Eugene, OR 97401
Holbrook Farm and Nursery, Rt. 2, Box 223B, Fletcher, NC 28732
Janet and Michael Kristick, 155 Mockingbird Rd., Wellsville, PA 17365
Lamb Nurseries, E. 101 Sharp Ave., Spokane, WA 99202
Logee's Greenhouse, 55 North St., Danielson, CT 06239
John D. Lyon, Inc., 143 Alewife Brook Parkway, Cambridge, MA 02140
Merry Gardens, Camden, ME 04843
Montrose Nursery, PO Box 957, Hillsborough, NC 27278
Nature's Garden, Rt. 1, Box 488, Beaverton, OR 97007
Niche Gardens, 1111 Dawson Rd., Chapel Hill, NC 27516
Nichols Garden Nursery, 1190 North Pacific Hwy., Albany, OR 97321
Prairie Nursery, PO Box 365, Westfield, WI 53964
Primrose Path, RD 1, Box 78, Scottdale, PA 15683
Rocknoll Nursery, 9210 U.S. 50, Hillsboro, OH 45133
Sandy Mush Herb Nursery, Rt. 2, Surret Cove Rd., Leicester, NC 28748
Siskiyou Rare Plant Nursery, 2825 Cummings Rd., Medford, OR 97501
Ellie and Joel Spingarn, PO Box 782, Georgetown, CT 06829

Sunlight Gardens, Rt. 1, Box 600, Andersonville, TN 37705
Andre Viette Farm and Nursery, Rt. 1, Box 16, Fishersville, VA 22939
Washington Evergreen Nursery, PO Box 388, Leicester, NC 28748
We-Du Nurseries, Route 5, Box 724, Marion, NC 28752
Woodlanders, 1128 Colleton Ave., Aiken, SC 29801

Bibliography ❁

The American Horticultural Magazine: Daffodil Handbook. Washington, D. C.: American Horticultural Society, January 1966.

Bean, William J. *Trees and Shrubs Hardy in the British Isles.* 5 vols., 8th ed. London: John Murray, 1980–88.

Bowles, E. A. *A Handbook of Crocus and Colchicum for Gardeners.* London, 1924. Reprint. Portland, Ore.: Timber Press, 1985.

———. *A Handbook of Narcissus.* London, 1924. Reprint. Portland, Ore.: Timber Press, 1985.

Brown, Deni. *Aroids: Plants of the Arum Family.* Portland, Ore.: Timber Press, 1988.

Charlesworth, Geoffrey B. *The Opinionated Gardener: Random Offshoots from an Alpine Garden.* Boston: David R. Godine, 1988.

Dirr, Michael A. *Manual of Woody Landscape Plants: Their Identification, Ornamental Characteristics, Culture, Propagation, and Uses.* Champaign, Ill.: Stipes, 1983.

Dormon, Caroline. *Natives Preferred: Native Trees and Flowers for Every Location.* Baton Rouge, La.: Claitor's Book Store, 1965.

Elias, Thomas S. *The Complete Trees of North America: Field Guide and Natural History.* New York: Van Nostrand Reinhold, 1980. Reprint. New York: Gramercy, 1987.

Everett, Thomas H. *The New York Botanical Garden Illustrated Encyclopedia of Horticulture.* 10 vols. New York: Garland, 1980.

Federson, G. K. *A Synoptic Guide to the Genus Primula.* Lawrence, Kans.: K. S. Allen Press, 1986.

Flint, Harrison L. *Landscape Plants for Eastern North America: Exclusive of Florida and the Immediate Gulf Coast.* New York: John Wiley and Sons, 1983.

Foster, H. Lincoln. *Rock Gardening: A Guide to Growing Alpines and Other Wild-flowers in the American Garden*. Boston: Houghton Mifflin, 1968. Reprint. Portland, Ore.: Timber Press, 1982.

Galle, Fred C. *Azaleas*. Birmingham, Ala.: Oxmoor House, 1974. Reprint. Portland, Ore.: Timber Press, 1985.

Grey-Wilson, Christopher. *The Genus Cyclamen*. London: Christopher Helm; Portland, Ore.: Timber Press, 1988.

Griffith, Anna N. *Collins Guide to Alpines & Rock Garden Plants*. London: Chancellor Press, 1985.

Harper, Pamela, and Frederick McGourty. *Perennials: How to Select, Grow & Enjoy*. Tucson, Ariz.: HP Books, 1985.

Harrison, Charles Richmond. *Ornamental Conifers*. New York: Hafner Press, 1975. Reprint. Portland, Ore.: Timber Press, 1983.

Hillier, Harold G. *Hillier's Manual of Trees and Shrubs*. London: David and Charles, 1972. 5th ed., New York: Van Nostrand Reinhold, 1981.

Hortus Third: A Concise Dictionary of Plants Cultivated in the United States and Canada. Rev. and exp. by the staff of the Liberty Hyde Bailey Hortarium. New York: Macmillan, 1976.

Isaacson, Richard T., comp. *Andersen Horticultural Library's Source List of Plants and Seeds*. Chanhassen, Minn.: Andersen Horticultural Library, 1987.

Jekyll, Gertrude, and Sir Lawrence Weaver. *Gardens for Small Country Houses*. London: Country Life, 1912. Reprint. Ithaca, N.Y.: Antique Collectors' Club, 1981.

Justice, William S., and C. Ritchie Bell. *Wild Flowers of North Carolina*. Chapel Hill: University of North Carolina Press, 1968.

Kolaga, Walter A. *All About Rock Gardens and Plants*. Garden City, N.Y.: Doubleday, 1966.

Krussman, Gerd. *Manual of Cultivated Broad-leaved Trees and Shrubs*. Vols. 1–4. Beaverton, Ore.: Timber Press, 1984.

——— . *Manual of Cultivated Conifers*. Beaverton, Ore.: Timber Press, 1985.

Lawrence, Elizabeth. *A Southern Garden: A Handbook for the Middle South*. Chapel Hill: University of North Carolina Press, 1942. Reprint, 1967. Paperback, 1983.

——— . *Gardening for Love: The Market Bulletins*. Ed. Allen Lacy. Durham, N.C.: Duke University Press, 1987. Paperback, 1988.

——— . *Gardens in Winter*. New York: Harper and Brothers, 1961. Reprint. Baton Rouge, La.: Claitor's, 1977.

——— . *The Little Bulbs: A Tale of Two Gardens*. New York: Criterion Books, 1957. Reprint. Durham, N.C.: Duke University Press, 1986.

Mathew, Brian. "A Review of the Genus Tricyrtis," *Plantsman* 6, pt. 4 (March 1985): 193–224.

————. *The Crocus: A Revision of the Genus Crocus (Iridaceae)*. London: B. T. Batsford, 1982. Reprint. Portland, Ore.: Timber Press, 1983.

————. *The Iris*. New York: Universe Books, 1981.

————. *The Smaller Bulbs*. London: B. T. Batsford, 1987.

Maxwell, Sir Herbert Eustace. *Memories of the Months, Sixth Series*. London: Edward Arnold, 1919.

Ouden, P. den. *Manual of Cultivated Conifers Hardy in the Cold- and Warm-Temperate Zone*. The Hague: M. Nijhoff, 1965. 3d ed., 1982.

Parkinson, John. *Paradisi in sole paradisus terrestris: Or a Garden of All Sorts of Pleasant Flowers*. London: Lownes and Young, 1629. Reprint. Norwood, N.J.: W. J. Johnson, 1975.

Phillips, Harry R. *Growing and Propagating Wild Flowers*. Ed. C. Ritchie Bell and Ken Moore. Chapel Hill: University of North Carolina Press, 1985.

Polunin, Oleg, and Anthony Huxley. *Flowers of the Mediterranean*. Boston: Houghton Mifflin; Cambridge, Mass.: Riverside Press, 1966.

Radford, Albert E., Harry E. Ahles, and C. Ritchie Bell. *Manual of the Vascular Flora of the Carolinas*. Chapel Hill: University of North Carolina Press, 1968.

Rehder, Alfred. *Manual of Cultivated Trees and Shrubs*. New York: Macmillan, 1940. 2d ed., Portland, Ore.: Dioscorides Press, 1986.

Rhode, Eleanour Sinclair. *The Scented Garden*. London: Medici Society, 1931. Reprint. Detroit: Singing Tree Press, 1974.

Rickett, Harold William. *Wild Flowers of the United States: The Southeastern States*. 2 vols. New York: McGraw-Hill, 1967.

Rix, Martyn, and Roger Phillips. *The Bulb Book: A Photographic Guide to Over 800 Hardy Bulbs*. Ed. Brian Mathew. London: Pan Books, 1981.

Rowntree, Lester. *Hardy Californians*. New York: Macmillan, 1936. Reprint. Salt Lake City: Peregrine Smith, 1980.

The Royal Horticultural Society. *Dictionary of Gardening: A Practical and Scientific Encyclopedia of Horticulture*. 4 vols. and suppl. Ed. Fred J. Chittenden. Oxford: Clarendon Press, 1981.

Schacht, Wilhelm. *Rock Gardens*. Ed. Jim Archibald. New York: Universe Books, 1981, 1987.

Synge, Patrick. *The Garden in Winter*. London: Lindsay Drummond, 1948.

Thomas, Graham Stuart. *Perennial Garden Plants: Or the Modern Florilegium*. London: J. M. Dent and Sons, 1976. 2d ed., London: Dent, 1982.

Vertress, J. D. *Japanese Maples: Momiji and Kaede*. Forest Grove, Ore.: Timber Press, 1978. 2d rev. ed., 1988.

Welch, H. J. *Dwarf Conifers: A Complete Guide*. London: Faber, 1966.

————. *Manual of Dwarf Conifers*. Little Compton, U.K.: Theophrastis, 1979.

Wilder, Louise Beebe. *Adventures with Hardy Bulbs*. New York: Macmillan, 1936.

————. *Pleasures and Problems of a Rock Garden*. Garden City, N.Y.: Garden City Publishing Company, 1937.

————. *The Fragrant Path: A Book about Sweet-scented Flowers and Leaves*. New York: Macmillan, 1932. Reprinted as *The Fragrant Garden*. New York: Dover, 1974.

Yeo, Peter F. *Hardy Geraniums*. London: Croom Helm; Portland, Ore.: Timber Press, 1985.

Index

communis (common juniper), 169:
  'Berkshire,' 'Compressa,' 'Repanda'
horizontalis, 169
procumbens, 168: 'Nana'
squamata, 168, 169: 'Prostrata,' 168;
  'Blue Carpet,' 'Blue Star,' 169
Kniphofia (torch lily, Tritoma), 81
  pfitzeri (red-hot poker), 81: 'Towers of
  Gold'
  rufa, 81
Koeleria, 81
  glauca, 81

Lady's mantle, 29
Lamiastrum, 81
  galeobdolen, 81: 'Herman's Pride'
Lamium, 82
  maculatum, 82: 'Aureum,' 'Beacon
  Silver,' 'White Nancy'
Lapeirousia, 82
  laxa, 82
Larkspur, 56–57
Lavandula (candytuft, lavender), 82–83
  angustifolia, 83: 'Alba,' 'Nana,' 'Twickel
  Purple'
  latifolia, 82–83
  stoechas, 83
Lavender, 82–83
Lavender cotton, 111
Leather leaf, 155
Leiophyllum, 169–70
  buxifolium (box sandmyrtle), 169–70
Leucojum, 83
  autumnale, 83
  roseum, 83
Leucothöe, 170
  catesbaei, 170
  fontanesiana, 170
  keiskei, 170
Lewisia, 83–84
  cotyledon, 84
  nevadensis, 83–84
Lilium, 84
  pumilum (turk's-cap lily), 84
Lily: Atamasco, 143; fairy, 143; Guernsey,
  85; knight's star, 72; mondo grass,
  96; oxblood, 72; plantain, 72–73;
  rain, 143; toad, 130–31; torch, 81;
  turk's-cap, 84; zephyr, 143

Limnanthes, 84, 92
  douglasii (meadow foam, marsh flower),
  84, 92: *nivea,* 92
Lithodora, 170
  diffusa, 170: 'Grace Ward'
Live-forever, 116
Lobularia, 84
  maritima, 84: 'Carpet of Snow,' 'Violet
  Queen'
Lonicera, 171
  nitida, 171
  pileata (privet honeysuckle), 171
Lords-and-ladies, 39
Lotus, 93
  formosissimus, 93
Lungwort, 107–8
Luzula (woodrush), 84
  nivea (snowy woodrush), 84: 'Nana'
  sylvatica (greater woodrush), 84:
  'Marginata'
Lychnis, 85
  alpina, 85
Lycoris, 85
  radiata (Guernsey lily), 85
Lysimachia (moneywort), 85
  japonica, 85: *minutissima*
  nummularia (creeping jennie), 85:
  'Aurea'

Magnolia, 150
  heptapeta (yulan), 150
Mahonia (barberry), 171
  nervosa, 171
  repens, 171
Maidenhair vine, 172
Mallow, poppy, 44
Maple, 146–47: Japanese, 146–47
Marigold, 123
Marjoram, 96–97: knotted, 97; pot, 97;
  sweet, 96–97. See also *Origanum*
Marsh flower, 84
Mayflower, 161
Mazus, 86
  miquelli, 86: *albiflorus*
  reptans, 86
Meadow foam, 84
Mertensia, 86
  maritima, 86
  virginica, 86

The Authors

Elizabeth Lawrence is the author of *A Southern Garden*, *The Little Bulbs*, *Gardens in Winter*, *Gardening for Love*, and *Through the Garden Gate*.

Nancy Goodwin is a cyclamen specialist who owns and operates Montrose Nursery in Hillsborough, North Carolina.

Allen Lacy is a garden columnist for the *New York Times*. He is the author of *Home Ground*, *Farther Afield*, and *The Garden in Autumn* and the editor of *The American Gardener: A Sampler* and *Gardening for Love*.

Paul Jones is a horticulturalist at The Sarah P. Duke Gardens in Durham, North Carolina.

Library of Congress Cataloging-in-Publication Data
Lawrence, Elizabeth, 1904–1985.
A rock garden in the South / Elizabeth Lawrence ;
edited by Nancy Goodwin with Allen Lacy.
Includes bibliographical references.
ISBN 0-8223-0986-6
1. Rock gardens—Southern States.   I. Goodwin,
Nancy (Nancy Sanders)   II. Lacy, Allen, 1935–
III. Title.
SB459.L38   1990
635.9′672′0975—dc20   89-49426CIP